Lucy Hone and Denise Quinlan, two of education field, have written this critical book for all educators (or any person working in a school). This is not only a book you can refer to regularly but one that will engage you whenever you pick it up. This book will tap into your unique learning style by providing strategies, processes, tools, metaphors, case examples, scientific findings, video links, powerful stories, and practical anecdotes from leaders in the field.

– **Ryan M. Niemiec, PsyD,** education director of the VIA Institute on Character and author of *Character Strengths Interventions, Mindfulness and Character Strengths, The Strengths-Based Workbook for Stress Relief,* and co-author of *The Power of Character Strengths*

This is a beautifully written, comprehensive and compelling book. The authors are a rich source of knowledge that comes from both their own extensive, international practice and also from a wide evidence base. They respectfully acknowledge many other authorities in the field and include these throughout. The book makes extensive information fully accessible for the practitioner, with illustrative examples, case-studies and links to podcasts embedded in the text. It is especially good to see issues such as cultural responsiveness and the voice of the student given their rightful place. I would imagine everyone working in this field would want a copy of this excellent book – and will be referring to its wisdom over and over again.

– **Dr Sue Roffey,** Honorary Associate Professor at Exeter and Western Sydney Universities, Director of Growing Great Schools Worldwide, and the author of many books relating to wellbeing in education including *Changing Behaviour in Schools*

A fantastic book for anyone interested in positive education, whether you are at the beginning of your journey or an experienced practitioner. This book is unique in its breadth and depth in outlining and reviewing the diverse frameworks, research and practices that underpin positive education across the world. An outstanding strength of the book is the authors' skills in harnessing and collating the voices and insights of many different researchers and practitioners. The end product is a highly practical book that provides the most comprehensive overview to date of positive education. A great 'guide book' in implementing positive education initiatives that I confidently recommend to all educators.

– **Dr Toni Noble,** Adjunct Professor at the Institute for Positive Psychology and Education Australian Catholic University and co-author of the Bounce Back programme

In *The Educators' Guide to Whole-school Wellbeing,* Drs Hone & Quinlan have skilfully integrated all the essential pieces and processes of living, teaching, and embedding wellbeing and resilience in a holistic and harmonious whole. This whole is comprehensive, inclusive, nuanced, illuminated with well researched insights, case studies, reflective questions and relevant resources. In a pile of books on positive education, this guide will pave your way in creating a school climate imbued with compassion, empathy appreciation and meaning.

– **Dr Tayyab Rashid,** licensed clinical psychologist
University of Toronto Scarborough and co-author of Positive
Psychotherapy with Prof Martin Seligman

It is important school leaders, teachers and educators in general take time to pause and reflect on how best to implement a wellbeing programme that is not only effective, but contextual, doable and understood by the whole community. While pausing, make sure you have by your side a copy of *The Educators' Guide to Whole-school Wellbeing.* If you do, you will learn much about why wellbeing needs to be placed at the heart of education. You will consider the numerous examples of applied wellbeing initiatives from around the world, which will, I am sure, inspire you to reflect on your current wellbeing programmes and seek change or modification or a complete overhaul. At a time when our youth are often in turmoil and schools are being called upon more and more to educate beyond the subject this book will offer wise counsel to all who read it.

– **Charlie Scudamore,** Vice Principal,
Geelong Grammar School

The Educators' Guide to Whole-school Wellbeing

The Educators' Guide to Whole-school Wellbeing addresses challenges faced by schools wanting to improve wellbeing. While many schools globally now understand the need to promote and protect student wellbeing, they often find themselves stuck – not knowing where to start, what to prioritise, or how to implement whole-school change. This book fills that gap.

This book provides companionship through rich stories from schools around the world that have created wellbeing practices that work for their schools. It guides educators through processes that help create individualised, contextualised school wellbeing plans. With chapters addressing 'why wellbeing?', 'what is "whole school?"', change dynamics, measurement, staff wellbeing, coaching, cultural responsiveness, and how to build buy-in, it is the first of its kind. Balancing research and practice for each topic with expert practitioner and researcher insights, this book gives schools access to best-practice guidance from around the world in a user-friendly format, designed for busy educators.

What sets the authors apart from the many school wellbeing practitioners globally is their substantial experience working alongside diverse school groups. While many have experience in one school, few work across a multitude of very different schools and clusters, giving these practising academics a unique appreciation for effective, cross-context processes.

Denise M. Quinlan was 'present at the birth of Positive Education', training Australian and UK educators with the University of Pennsylvania team. Published academic researcher and creator of a validated student strengths programme, she lectures globally on wellbeing and hosts Bringing Wellbeing to Life, a popular podcast on wellbeing topics.

Lucy C. Hone is a published academic researcher, International Positive Education Network Global Rep, a best-selling author and contributor to *Psychology Today*. Trained by thought-leaders in the field at the University of Pennsylvania, she works with a diverse range of schools helping them understand and build wellbeing and resilience.

The Educators' Guide to Whole-school Wellbeing

A Practical Guide to Getting Started, Best-practice Process and Effective Implementation

*Denise M. Quinlan
and Lucy C. Hone*

Routledge
Taylor & Francis Group

LONDON AND NEW YORK

First published 2020
by Routledge
2 Park Square, Milton Park, Abingdon, Oxon OX14 4RN

and by Routledge
52 Vanderbilt Avenue, New York, NY 10017

Routledge is an imprint of the Taylor & Francis Group, an informa business

© 2020 Denise M. Quinlan and Lucy C. Hone

The right of Denise M. Quinlan and Lucy C. Hone to be identified as authors of this work has been asserted by them in accordance with sections 77 and 78 of the Copyright, Designs and Patents Act 1988.

All rights reserved. No part of this book may be reprinted or reproduced or utilised in any form or by any electronic, mechanical, or other means, now known or hereafter invented, including photocopying and recording, or in any information storage or retrieval system, without permission in writing from the publishers.

Trademark notice: Product or corporate names may be trademarks or registered trademarks, and are used only for identification and explanation without intent to infringe.

British Library Cataloguing-in-Publication Data
A catalogue record for this book is available from the British Library

Library of Congress Cataloging-in-Publication Data
A catalog record has been requested for this book

ISBN: 978-0-367-23605-2 (Paperback)

Typeset in Galliard
by Apex CoVantage, LLC

Visit the eResources: www.routledge.com/9780367236052

To the many educators across the globe working hard to promote and protect young people's wellbeing in schools.

DQ: To Nigel, Oisín and Clora, and family dinners.

LH: To my family, friends and colleagues for the support that made this book possible.

Contents

Figures, tables, boxes, expert insights and case studies

Figures

Tables

Boxes

Expert researcher/practitioner insights

Case studies

Foreword

Some of the most influential educational ideas have come from New Zealand. For example, what we know about effective school leadership and how teachers are the most significant in-school factor influencing student outcomes comes from New Zealand researchers. I am delighted to add Dr Denise Quinlan and Dr Lucy Hone's *The Educators' Guide to Whole-school Wellbeing: A Practical Guide to Getting Started, Best-practice Process and Effective Implementation* to that list. It has been over a decade since Martin Seligman, Randy Ernst, Jane Gillham, Karen Reivich and Mark Linkins published their ground-breaking article 'Positive education: Positive psychology and classroom interventions' in the *Oxford Review of Education* in 2009. Since then, research in the field of wellbeing and positive education has grown. Some applications have been high on enthusiasm, low on science and fallen flat. Others appear to have taken hold in schools' policy, process and professional practice – and these find their way into this book. What has been missing in the field is a book that interrogates the research-into-practice and practice-into-research nexus. *The Educators' Guide to Whole-school Wellbeing* is such a book. It will be handy for many educators. As school leaders are becoming increasingly aware of the importance of wellbeing, Dr Quinlan and Dr Hone's book combines three key elements: scientifically informed approaches, evidence-based strategies and practical wisdom from interviews and case studies for wellbeing education. Reading this book, I was struck by how Dr Quinlan and Dr Hone have synthesised key learning gleaned after collaborating with in excess of 80 schools in Aotearoa/New Zealand – for that alone, this book is significant. It is from this unique perspective that this publication draws its point of difference. Dr Quinlan and Dr Hone integrate reflections and case studies from university thought leaders at the forefront of the field and school leaders reflecting on the application of research in the early-year, junior primary and secondary schooling. Significantly, this book emphasises the importance of culture and context for wellbeing education, a topic much overlooked in the past ten years. Critically, this book investigates practical examples of the application of wellbeing within ethnically and linguistically diverse (ELD) communities, underrepresented insights from special needs parents and strategies to include the LGBTQI+ community. I would expect nothing less from two trailblazers from the New Zealand and international wellbeing education scene. Dr Quinlan and Dr Hone have published in peer-reviewed journals, authored book chapters and are frequently invited to deliver keynote speeches on the topics of wellbeing and resilience in education at conferences in Australia, the USA and Europe. Significantly, Dr Quinlan and Dr Hone are founding members of NZAPP, and Dr Hone is the NZ global representative of the International Positive Education Network (IPEN). This is a book many of us will return to again and again.

Associate Professor Mathew A. White PhD
The University of Adelaide
President, Education Division, International
Positive Psychology Association
Wednesday, 16 October 2019 – Adelaide

Reference

Seligman, M. E. P., Ernst, R. M., Gillham, J., Reivich, K., & Linkins, M. (2009). Positive education: Positive psychology and classroom interventions. *Oxford Review of Education, 35*(3), 293–311.

Preface

Our purpose in writing this workbook for you and your school

Schools are on the front line of wellbeing efforts in many countries as communities attempt to deal with the growing crisis of mental health worldwide. There is a growing understanding that what is required is more than a Band-Aid approach to fixing problems, but rather an ability to create schools that are communities supporting the growth and development of young people who can be resilient, contributing citizens over their lifetimes.

For this to happen we have to consider the school as an institution and a living community and explore how we can engineer the kind of climate in which our children can flourish. There is a growing body of evidence suggesting this is possible: schools can develop whole-school wellbeing through explicit teaching of wellbeing and by adopting policies, processes and practices that engender belonging, inclusion, purpose and mental agility – all factors that contribute to resilience and wellbeing. Educators' long history of developing and applying best-practice pedagogy to a range of topics also provides us with much hope that this is possible.

Developing whole-school wellbeing requires a long-term commitment to professional development and, for most schools, significant culture change. What has quickly become apparent from our conversations with schools around the world is that there is no quick fix and no 'one size fits all' approach to wellbeing promotion. Schools are grappling with the challenge of upskilling in wellbeing knowledge and then applying and adapting this knowledge to their particular context. This practical guide is informed by the work we do in a diverse range of schools and responds to the very real concerns of educators. It is designed to support wellbeing change leaders step by step, through different stages of change, in the hope of creating lasting, measurable and meaningful impact in your school community.

The schools having most success in making this change have typically committed to staff professional development in wellbeing, adopted evidence-based frameworks to guide their actions, and, critically, the teachers and staff responsible for implementing whole-school wellbeing are drawing on familiar pedagogical and reflective practice to design the best approaches for their school.

Our aim in writing this book is to provide schools with:

- The research evidence and practices that support wellbeing;
- Advice on frameworks and wellbeing models to guide the journey and evaluate impact and progress;
- Learning from other schools and practitioners; and
- Tools and processes to guide the ongoing decision-making that comes with implementing long-term wellbeing change in a school.

Acknowledgements

It took a village to write this book – more accurately, a community of people, across the globe, dedicated to improving wellbeing in education. It has been our privilege to work alongside many of you and to learn from all of you. Thank you for the work you are doing to improve the lives of educators and our children. We are grateful to the following people for their very direct contributions to this book:

Laura Allison; Mike Anderson; at Appli: Paula Robinson and Nichole Walker; Pete Beswick and staff and students at Shirley Boys' High School; Urie Bronfenbrenner, Tom Brunzell, Adele Carran, Camilo Castellon, Jillian Coppley Darwish, Scott Cowie, James Davis, Brenda Dobia, Clare Erasmus, the Education Review Office (NZ), Chris Eyre, Sherri Fisher; at Geelong Grammar School/IPE: Charlie Scudamore, David Bott, Georgie Cameron, Justin Robinson, Rhiannon McGee; Mark Gooden, Wiremu Gray, Grow Waitaha and all the Canterbury schools who contributed to the Grow Waitaha research; Rebecca Wilson and the staff at Haeata Campus; Chris Jansen, Greg Jansen, Peggy Kern, Muhammad Khalifa, Janina Konia and her colleagues at Mātauraka Mahaanui; Sylvia Kwok, Clive Leach, Dan Loton, Sonya and Angus Macfarlane; at Maroondah Project: Edwina Ricci, Adam Cooper and Mel Jeffery (both Maroondah City Council); Rich Matla, Faye McCallum, Helen McGrath, Grant McKibbin, Toni Noble, Jacolyn Norrish; the Positive Education Programme researchers: Teuntje Elfrink, Jochem Goldberg, Karlein Schreurs, Ernst Bohlmeijer, Aleisha Clarke; at Palmerston North East Kāhui Ako: Carissa Davies, Wayne Jenkins, Jaco Broodryk, and all the Wellbeing Leads; Sonya Papps, Jude Pentecost, Deborah Price, Tayyab Rashid; at Raroa School: Christine Brown and Stephen Eames; Nathan Riki, Sue Roffey; at Rolleston College: Rachel Skelton, Sophie Ralph, Kelly Tippett and Sarah Forward; Ben Rosenfield, Reuben Rusk, Gill Rutherford, Gilda Scarfe, Ara Simmons; at St Peter's School, Adelaide: David Kolpak and Meg Reid; at St Peter's Cambridge: Julie Small, Jess Patrick and Micheal Brown; Helen Street; at Sumner School: Anna Granger and Georgia McRae; Linda Tame; at Teaching with the Heart and Mind: Shiri Lavy, Ofra Mayseles, Roza Leikin, Michal Zion and Zemira Mevarech; at the Battle Against Boredom in schools: Nadia Holmgren, Mette Marie Ledertoug, Nanna Paarup and Louise Tidmand; Paul Tupou-Vea, Christian van Nieuwerbergh, Leanne Whitfield, Gabrielle Wall, Lea Waters, John Weeks, Mathew White, Garry Williams, Melinda Wilson and Shaen Yeo.

Writing this book meant time away from work, during which time Debs Abraham, Adrienne Buckingham and Sally Murray kept the show on the road and looked after us. We are very grateful to them and all the team at the New Zealand Institute of Wellbeing & Resilience.

Introduction

Introduction

Schools face a raft of challenges such as: Where do we start? Do we need a curriculum? When might we need one? Which is the best curriculum for our particular needs? Shall we buy one or create our own? Who's going to run this programme? Where in the timetable will we fit it; what will we let go? Which is the best wellbeing model for our school? Why do we need a model? How will we fit in the required professional learning on top of everything else we are already supposed to do? What could it replace? How will we know if what we are doing is working? What strategies help get naysayers on board? How do we make sure wellbeing is not just another fad? How do we engage our parent community? What do students think, and what are the best ways to get them involved in an authentic way that's actually meaningful? These are just some of the questions we hear from educators week after week and were the genesis for this book, which responds to the growing global interest in taking an evidence-based, whole-school approach to wellbeing promotion.

Among the many reasons for this focus on wellbeing is the evidence indicating rising levels of mental distress among young people. According to the World Health Organization, more than 300 million people globally suffer from depression, while mental illness is predicted to be the greatest cause of disability by 2030, meaning many of today's school entrants will likely be affected by the time they graduate from school.[1]

Countries across the globe are witnessing a decline in youth mental health. More than one in four Australians aged 16 to 24 experience a mental disorder in any given year, with almost half of all cases emerging by the age of 14 and suicide now the leading cause of death among 15- to 24-year-olds.[2] Over 14% of Australian school students report experiencing a mental disorder in the past 12 months.[3]

A British study comparing two nationally representative cohorts of adolescents 20 years apart demonstrated the rising prevalence of emotional problems among students.[4] Similar findings have been observed across all developed world nations, making youth mental health a growing concern for policy makers, educators, parents and young people. World leaders at the 2015 UNESCO World Education Forum named health and fulfillment part of their vision for 2030 education.[5] In some countries, chronic non-attendance caused by mental health problems is also a pressing issue.[6] An additional concern comes from the fact that mental distress now appears to be common, even among students bearing none of the risk factors traditionally linked to mental illness, causing one US principal to share his concerns about the worrying increase in 'fragile thoroughbreds'.[7]

On top of the individual, social and developmental costs of this level of mental distress comes the economic impact: mental illness is estimated to account for between 3% and 16% of total health expenditure across many countries (Organisation for Economic Co-operation and Development, OECD, 2011), from loss of labour supply, high rates of unemployment, high incidence of illness, absence from work and study and decreased productivity.

Those working with young people and witnessing mental distress in their classrooms first hand do not require much convincing of the need to build students' capacity for wellbeing and resilience. Given that 120 million new first-time learners attended school in the last ten years,[8] that youth spend on average 30 hours a week in school and school is the only universal institution in our young people's lives, schools represent a key opportunity to equip young people with the ways of thinking and acting that science suggests promote healthy functioning and protect against mental illness.

As a result, multiple efforts have aimed to promote resilience and protect wellbeing among young people over the last decade, with preliminary studies signalling their potential to be effective.[9][10][11] Early forays in this field include the Strath Haven Positive Psychology curriculum[12] and Penn Resilience Program,[13] both of which came out of the University of Pennsylvania.

The idea of promoting resilience and protecting wellbeing within schools is additionally motivated by rising awareness of high levels of mental distress and burnout among educators and senior leadership in schools. International reports indicating the profession's inability to attract new teachers – and the large numbers leaving in search of alternative employment – present further cause for concern. For example, it is currently estimated that half the people in Britain trained as teachers do not teach, while 40% of newly qualified teachers in the UK do not make it to five years in the job[14]. In New Zealand, the current teacher shortage is driven by declining retention rates, an ageing workforce and the lowest number of students enrolled in teacher training in ten years.[15]

There is some good news, however. The widespread interest in wellbeing in schools is also motivated by two positive reasons. The two 'pull factors' are a) the large amount of robust research indicating the desirable outcomes associated with higher levels of personal wellbeing (these include better physical health/longevity, relationships, academic, career and societal benefits) and b) preliminary research findings indicating that aspects of wellbeing and resilience can be taught and learned. These lines of evidence suggest promoting wellbeing to be a worthwhile endeavour and, in the right circumstances at least, doing so has been shown to be effective.[16][17][18]

The reasons outlined here have gone a long way toward persuading researchers, practitioners, policy makers and global education stakeholders of the wisdom of making wellbeing promotion an additional operational goal of the modern education system.[19][20] We concur with other wellbeing researchers, believing that wellbeing promotion must go beyond individual responsibility and be considered through the lens of the whole school sytem. As researchers Faye McCallum and Deborah Price put it, 'educator and learner wellbeing is an individual, collective and community responsibility',[21] a sentiment shared a decade earlier by Chris Peterson, one of the founding researchers in wellbeing science. Calling for wellbeing research to go beyond individual application and develop 'enabling institutions',[22] Peterson was one of the first psychologists to encourage schools to go beyond the pursuit of academic excellence alone. Many schools are now taking up this challenge, as illustrated by a 2018 study indicating school belonging and mental health promotion featured in the vision and mission statements of over half the Australian schools investigated.[23]

However, while many schools now agree on the rationale and merit of promoting wellbeing, they are struggling to understand what's involved in taking a whole-school approach. Confusingly for educators, there are as many ways to develop educational establishments as 'enabling institutions' as there are ways to promote individual wellbeing. The abundance of literature on the topic makes it challenging for schools to know where to start, what might work for their particular context and culture, and how to identify priorities and evaluate impact.

Our aim is to help you and your team 'navigate wellbeing change' – which is the phrase we use to refer to the complex challenge of co-designing, implementing and reviewing, reiterating and re-modelling school-wide wellbeing policies, processes and practices. We want to help you understand foundational wellbeing concepts and implementation processes so you and your staff can apply wellbeing in your own lives, as well as throughout your schools and wider communities.

Box 1.1: A brief history and explanation of positive psychology and positive education

Positive psychology: Positive psychology (PP) focuses on understanding and building optimal functioning in individuals, organisations and communities (Seligman & Csikszentmihalyi, 2000), essentially focusing on what's right, instead of psychology's traditional preoccupation with fixing what's wrong. As a dedicated field of scientific inquiry, it gets its name from an article written by Professor Martin Seligman when he (as incoming president of the American Psychological Association (APA)), co-authored a special millennial issue of the *American Psychologist* scientific journal. Calling for a redirection of psychological research away from its 'almost exclusive attention to pathology' and 'preoccupation only with repairing the worst things in life', Seligman and Csikszentmihayli urged their field to move toward a more balanced discipline also investigating 'the positive features that make life worth living'.[24]

Positive psychology's roots can, however, be traced back long before Seligman, to the historical philosophical debates of Aristotle and Plato and then, more recently in 1897, when William James published his considerations of the ingredients of optimal human functioning. While Seligman gets credit for naming the field, Abraham Maslow was the first to use the term 'positive psychology' back in the 1950s,[25] and several of Seligman's academic predecessors had been investigating aspects of human flourishing as far back as the 1950s.

The discernible groundswell among scientists that investigating what's right – in individuals, teams, families, relationships, communities and organisations – is equally as important as researching what's wrong (psychological pathology) is new though. The redirection of psychological inquiry taking a strengths, as well as a deficit, approach is demonstrated by the substantial research published on the topic over the past two decades (for more details on the field's size, reach, impact and breadth, see Rusk and Waters's much-cited article from 2013).[26] Over the past two decades, positive psychology researchers have sought to understand and build wellbeing, resilience, strengths and related positive qualities, with interventions implemented online, in schools, in workplaces, in communities and beyond, testing their effectiveness to help people feel good, be productive and potentially inoculate them from mental illness.[27]

Positive education: In 2009, writing in the *Oxford Review of Education*, Seligman posed a question, asking readers to describe, in two words or less, what they most wanted for their children. 'If you are like the hundreds of parents I've asked, you responded, "Happiness", "Confidence", "Contentment", "Balance", "Good Stuff", "Kindness", "Health", "Satisfaction", and the like. In short, you most want well-being for your children'. Yet what do schools teach? Achievement, conformity, discipline, literacy and mathematics. Emphasising the distinct lack of overlap between these two lists, Seligman concluded: 'The schooling of children has, for more than a century, been about accomplishment, the boulevard into the world of adult work. . . . imagine if schools could, without compromising either, teach both the skills of well-being and the skills of achievement. Imagine *Positive Education*'.[28] Over the decade since, the term *positive education* has been adopted in several countries to describe the process of applying scientifically validated theories and interventions from wellbeing science to educational contexts, designed to have an impact on student and staff wellbeing.[29] [30]

The language of wellbeing in education in this book

Positive psychology refers to the branch of psychology focused on building on strengths and enhancing wellbeing. Positive education refers to the process and practice of implementing positive psychology and other wellbeing interventions, pedagogies and practices into schools in partnership with educators. We understand that some of us bristle at the label 'positive education' ('Are you saying everything we've been doing is negative?') and for that reason we tend not to use the term in schools unless they do. In this book we refer to the science of wellbeing to include findings from positive psychology, education and other fields such as positive youth development and social and emotional learning (SEL). We prefer to use terms like *whole-school wellbeing*, *wellbeing in education*, and *the science of wellbeing* to include practices and learning that come from a range of disciplines. Where a contributor has referred to a practice as *positive education* or *PosEd*, that terminology has not been changed.

Box 1.2: Busting PosEd myths (Charlie Scudamore, Geelong Grammar School)[31]

We believe positive education is NOT . . .

- About being happy all the time, and certainly not about avoiding negative emotions;
- About ensuring a child is free from failure and adversity; and
- A a one-size-fits-all approach and not just another program for schools to introduce.

We believe positive education . . .

- Unites a community through promoting a common language of wellbeing;
- Nurtures healthy and cohesive learning environments; and
- Equips people with tools to meet challenging times and situations.

Myths and misunderstandings about positive education:

- So what is 'negative' education?
- It's about making students happy.
- It's only looking 'on the bright side'.
- It's all about having fun!
- It's about ignoring weaknesses.
- It's what non-academic schools do.
- It's wellbeing for rich kids.

What the research says

A growing body of literature suggests wellbeing education programmes can have a positive impact on the way many students 'know and understand themselves, their peers, and their families'.[32] Studies have also demonstrated that students with higher levels of wellbeing perform better academically, reporting higher levels of self-control and lower procrastination than students who are either moderately mentally healthy or languishing[33] and that students with the highest wellbeing levels at the start of the year showed the strongest academic performance at the end of the school year.[34] A meta-analysis of 213 school-based programmes involving over 270,000 students from kindergarten to high school showed that students developing social and emotional skills and adopting healthy behaviours reported improved academic perfor-mance in overall grades and standardised maths and reading scores.[35] Simi-larly, Alejandro Adler's study involving hundreds of thousands of students in Bhutan, Mexico and Peru also suggests wellbeing can be taught to stu-dents, and increased wellbeing scores relate to improvements in academic achievements.[36]

Assessments conducted at St Peter's College, Adelaide, a flagship school for PosEd, over the period 2011 to 2016 also demonstrated desirable pro-gramme effects: students understood the signficance of wellbeing and resilience for themselves and their friends, with over 90% of junior school students reporting some understanding of that importance and agreeing that positive education helped them to be better students and to have better relationships with family and friends.[37] Lower-performing students perceived greater benefits from the school's programme than higher-performing stu-dents. St Peter's research also indicates that, since introducing a school-wide student merit system in 2011, there's been a steady decline in the number of behaviours and concerns reported by school staff. It seems taking a whole-school approach to promoting wellbeing is having positive outcomes.

Like others in the field, however, we are aware of the limitations of both positive psychology and positive education. Theories and empirical findings from wellbeing science can do much to guide us in our actions, but the practice of promoting wellbeing is out-pacing the science. Like many of our colleagues, we are concerned that the field's rapid growth may lead to hype regarding the field's potential and over-inflated expectations, disillusionment and perhaps even unintentional harm: 'PP interventions are beneficial for some people, some of the time, in some places, and in some ways, but are far from panaceas'.[38] We therefore urge schools to tread with caution and eval-uate impact at every opportunity – using both qualitative and quantitative measures and assessments beyond subjective self-reports. To this end, we are part of the newly created Ethical Guidelines for Positive Psychology, in a bid to safeguard the field's academic rigour, promote best practices and hopefully ensure that wellbeing 'becomes a core part of education as a whole, and not simply a short-lived fad'.[39]

The book's format

The book is set out in the following way. Each chapter deals with a different aspect of taking a whole-school approach to wellbeing promotion, reflecting our understanding that building wellbeing across a complex organisation is never a linear process. It is, in fact, complex, puzzling and, at times, taxing! Schools will all have individual histories when picking up this book and will be at different stages of the journey, driven by a variety of goals and motivations.

Accordingly, there are chapters addressing the multitude of aspects of school life in which wellbeing can be considered.

Each chapter is laid out as follows:

- Brief introduction to the topic;
- The research – provides evidence and describes what the studies so far tell us. Instead of being an exhaustive literature review, we have selected findings we have found most relevant for schools;
- Putting it into practice – our advice based on the best of what we are seeing in the field and hearing from colleagues in conversation and at conferences. Because of the rapid uptake of wellbeing initiatives in schools globally, not all the practices covered here are yet thoroughly research-based. The reality is that each school is different, meaning that even when the science is robust, it cannot be reliably regarded as generalisable to your particular context until you have tested it yourself. We have done our best to only include practices and case studies that are research informed and follow what is currently regarded as best practice. We have sourced our examples of good practice from all corners of the world, with the generous help of our respected international colleagues. We urge readers not to be put off reading case studies, boxes and practical wisdom from beyond their own shores: as we all know, so much can be gained from collaboration and open-minded curiosity. The examples featured here have been selected for their broad appeal, creativity and good sense;
- Case studies – stories from, or about, different schools (and/or practitioners working with schools) about specific areas of practice;
- Boxes – summaries of particular topics (often considered from multiple schools' perspectives);
- Expert insights – provided by researchers and practitioners with useful experience to share;
- Self-reflection questions – above all, we want this to be your workbook, a place to build up your own school's vision, strategy and practice around wellbeing, so we've dedicated space for personal/team reflections and insights
- Watch, read and listen – additional resources aimed at sharing either examples or insights to spark, challenge or deepen your thinking; and
- References – we are academics at heart, so of course we always want you to have ready access to the supporting evidence;

This is not a systematic review of the latest literature, nor is it a prescriptive 'how-to' guide. Rather it is a companion workbook setting out the approaches we (and respected colleagues) have seen support wellbeing change in a diverse range of education communities. This is an adventure you are embarking with your school – fortunately, one that does not have to happen entirely in the dark. There are tools and practices to illuminate the journey and learning to be gained from the experiences of your peers and the many practitioners and researchers who have so generously shared their insights in this book. The best news – many educators describe their wellbeing work within their schools as the most inspiring and invigorating work they have done in their careers. For some, it has been a reminder of why they came into teaching. As well as contributing to their school's wellbeing, this process has provided a deepened sense of meaning to their work, reconnecting them to their purpose, which in turn has contributed to their and others' wellbeing.

Reflection questions

- Why do you want to promote wellbeing in your school?
- What do you consider the purpose of education?
- What key factors are driving your own interest in wellbeing?
- What do you think is most likely to motivate your staff, students and wider school community to take a proactive systemic approach to wellbeing?
- What other resources can you draw upon?
- What will be the principal aims of your wellbeing programme?
- What do you hope to gain?
- Who will benefit?
- Are your expectations realistic?
- What sort of time frame are you expecting this to take?

Notes

1 White, M. A., & Kern, M. L. (2018). Positive education: Learning and teaching for wellbeing and academic mastery. *International Journal of Wellbeing, 8*(1).

2 Robertson, S., Blanchard, M., Coughlan, F., & Robertson, A. (2013). *How did we score? Engaging young people in the development of a national report card on mental health and suicide prevention.* Melbourne, Australia: Young and Well CRC and Batyr Australia Limited.

3 Lawrence, D., Johnson, S., Hafekost, J., Boterhoven De Haan, K., Sawyer, M., Ainley, J., & Zubrick, S. R. (2015). *The mental health of children and adolescents: Report on the second Australian child and adolescent survey of mental health and Wellbeing.* Canberra: Department of Health.

4   Collishaw, S., Maughan, B., Natarajan, L., & Pickles, A. (2010). Trends in adolescent emotional problems in England: A comparison of two national cohorts twenty years apart. *Journal of Child Psychology and Psychiatry, 51*(8), 885–894.

5   UNESCO. (2015). *Incheon declaration: Education 2030: Towards inclusive and equitable quality education and lifelong learning for all.* Retrieved from www.uis.unesco.org/Education/Documents/

6   Yamamoto, T., Matsumoto, Y., & Bernard, M. E. (2017). Effects of the cognitive-behavioral you can do it! Education program on the resilience of Japanese elementary school students: A preliminary investigation. *International Journal of Educational Research, 86,* 50–58.

7   Randolph, D. (2009). *Lecture to the masters of positive psychology class.* Philadelphia, PA: University of Pennsylvania.

8   World Bank statistics. Cited by Steve Leventhal at WCPP, opening plenary address, World Congress of Positive Psychology, July 18, 2019. Melbourne, Australia.

9   Pluess, M., Boniwell, I., Hefferon, K., & Tunariu, A. (2017). Preliminary evaluation of a school-based resilience-promoting intervention in a high-risk population: Application of an exploratory two-cohort treatment/control design. *PLoS One, 12*(5), e0177191. https://doi.org/10.1371/journal.pone.0177191

10 Brunwasser, S. M., Gillham, J. E., & Kim, E. S. (2009). A meta-analytic review of the Penn resiliency program's effect on depressive symptoms. *Journal of Consulting and Clinical Psychology, 77*(6), 1042.

11 Durlak, J. A., Weissberg, R. P., Dymnicki, A. B., Taylor, R. D., & Schellinger, K. B. (2011). The impact of enhancing students' social and emotional learning: A meta-analysis of school-based universal interventions. *Child Development, 82*(1), 405–432.

12 Seligman, M., Ernst, R., Gillham, J., Reivich, K., & Linkins, M. (2009). Positive education: Positive psychology and classroom interventions. *Oxford Review of Education, 35*(3), 293–311.

13 Brunwasser, S. M., Gillham, J. E., & Kim, E. S. (2009). A meta-analytic review of the Penn resiliency program's effects on depressive symptoms. *Journal of Consulting and Clinical Psychology, 77,* 1042–1054.

14 Eyre, C. (2016). *The elephant in the staffroom: How to reduce stress and improve teacher wellbeing.* UK: Routledge.

15   Post Primary Teachers' Association. (2016). *Theory of secondary teacher demand and supply*. Retrieved from www.ppta.org.nz/dmsdocument/180

16   Adler, A. (2016). Teaching well-being increases academic performance: Evidence from Bhutan, Mexico, and Peru. *Scholarly Commons Journal*, 1572.

17   Durlak, J. A., Weissberg, R. P., Dymnicki, A. B., Taylor, R. D., & Schellinger, K. B. (2011). The impact of enhancing students' social and emotional learning: A meta-analysis of school-based universal interventions. *Child Development, 82*(1), 405–432.

18   Waters, L. (2011). A review of school based positive psychology interventions. *Australian Educational and Developmental Psychologist, 28*(2).

19   White, M. A. (2016). Why won't it stick? Positive psychology and positive education. *Psychology of Well-Being, 6*(1), 2. doi:10.1186/s13612-016-0039-1

20   White, M. A., & Waters, L. E. (2015). A case study of 'The Good School:' Examples of the use of Peterson's strengths-based approach with students. *The Journal of Positive Psychology, 10*(1), 69–76.

21   McCallum, F., & Price, D. (Eds.). (2015). *Nurturing wellbeing development in education: From little things, big things grow* (p. 128). Routledge.

22   Peterson, C. (2006). *A primer in positive psychology*. Oxford University Press.

23   Allen, K. A., Kern, M. L., Vella-Brodrick, D., & Waters, L. (2018). Understanding the priorities of Australian secondary schools through an analysis of their mission and vision statements. *Educational Administration Quarterly, 54*(2), 249–274.

24   Seligman, M. E. P., & Csikszentmihalyi, M. (2000). Positive psychology: An introduction. *American Psychologist, 55*(1), 5–14.

25   Maslow, A. H. (1954). *Motivation and personality*. New York: Harper.

26   Rusk, R. D., & Waters, L. E. (2013). Tracing the size, reach, impact, and breadth of positive psychology. *The Journal of Positive Psychology, 8*, 207–221.

27   Kern, M. L., Williams, P., Spong, C., Colla, R., Sharma, K., Downie, A., . . . Oades, L. G. (2019). Systems informed positive psychology. *The Journal of Positive Psychology*. doi:10.1080/17439760.2019.1639799

28 Seligman, M. E. P., Ernst, R. M., Gillham, J., Reivich, K., & Linkins, M. (2009). Positive education: Positive psychology and classroom interventions. *Oxford Review of Education*, *35*(3), 293–311. doi:10.1080/03054980902934563

29 Oades, L. G., Robinson, P., & Green, S. (2011). Positive education: Creating flourishing students, staff and schools. *InPsych: The Bulletin of the Australian Psychological Society Ltd*, *33*(2), 16.

30 White, M. A. (2016). Why won't it stick? Positive psychology and positive education. *Psychology of Well-being*, *6*(1), 2.

31 Scudamore, C. (2019, April 8). *10 lessons learned in 10 years of positive education (what went wrong)*. Conference paper presented at the Positive Education NZ Conference, Christchurch, NZ.

32 White, M. A., & Kern, M. L. (2018). Positive education: Learning and teaching for wellbeing and academic mastery. *International Journal of Wellbeing*, *8*(1).

33 Howell, A. J. (2009). Flourishing: Achievement-related correlates of students' well-being. *Journal of Positive Psychology*, *4*, 1–13.

34 Suldo, S. M., Thalji, A., & Ferron, J. (2011). Longitudinal academic outcomes predicted by early adolescents' subjective well-being, psychopathology, and mental health status yielded from a dual factor model. *Journal of Positive Psychology*, *6*, 17–30.

35 Durlak, J. A., Weissberg, R. P., Dymnicki, A. B., Taylor, R. D., & Schellinger, K. B. (2011). The impact of enhancing students' social and emotional learning: A meta-analysis of school-based universal interventions. *Child Development*, *82*(1), 405–432.

36 Adler, A. (2017). Positive education: Educating for academic success and for a fulfilling life. *Papeles Del Psicólogo*, *38*(1), 50–57.

37 White, M. A., & Kern, M. L. (2018). Positive education: Learning and teaching for wellbeing and academic mastery. *International Journal of Wellbeing*, *8*(1).

38 Kern, M. L., Williams, P., Spong, C., Colla, R., Sharma, K., Downie, A., . . . Oades, L. G. (2019). Systems informed positive psychology. *The Journal of Positive Psychology*. doi:10.1080/17439760.2019.1639799

39 Slemp, G. R., Chin, T. C., Kern, M. L., Siokou, C., Loton, D., Oades, L. G., . . . Waters, L. (2017). Positive education in Australia: Practice, measurement, and future directions. In *Social and emotional learning in Australia and the Asia-Pacific* (pp. 101–122). Singapore: Springer.

Watch

Four videos showing Dr Lucy Hone, co-founder of The NZ Institute of Wellbeing & Resilience, explaining what wellbeing is, why it matters and what we mean by taking a whole-school approach to wellbeing. Retrieved from https://vimeo.com/326727310

Grit: The power of passion and perseverance (Angela Lee Duckworth). Retrieved from www.youtube.com/watch?v=H14bBuluwB8

What is Positive Education (Geelong Grammar School). Retrieved from https://vimeo.com/99798574

What is Positive Education? (International Positive Education Network). Retrieved from www.youtube.com/watch?v=i92eh8sx45w

Read

Allen, K. A., Kern, M. L., Vella-Brodrick, D., & Waters, L. (2018). Understanding the priorities of Australian secondary schools through an analysis of their mission and vision statements. *Educational Administration Quarterly, 54*(2), 249–274.

Norrish, J. M., Williams, P., O'Connor, M., & Robinson, J. (2013). An applied framework for positive education. *International Journal of Wellbeing, 3*(2), 147–161. doi:10.5502/ijw.v3i2.2

Seligman, M. E. P., & Adler, A. (2019). *Positive education in global happiness and Wellbeing policy report (2019)*. In J. F. Helliwell, R. Layard, & J. Sachs (Eds.), *Global Happiness and Wellbeing Policy Report: 2019*. Global Council for Wellbeing and Happiness. Retrieved from https://www.researchgate.net/publication/331936613_Positive_Education_Seligman_M_E_P_Adler_A_2019_Positive_Education_In_J_F_Helliwell_R_Layard_J_Sachs_Eds_Global_Happiness_and_Wellbeing_Policy_Report_2019_Pp_52_-_71_Global_Council_for_Wellbeing_and_Ha

Seligman, M. E. P., Ernst, R. M., Gillham, J., Reivich, K., & Linkins, M. (2009). Positive education: Positive psychology and classroom interventions. *Oxford Review of Education, 35*(3), 293–311. doi:10.1080/03054980902934563

Slemp, G. R., Chin, T. C., Kern, M. L., Siokou, C., Loton, D., Oades, L. G., . . . Waters, L. (2017). Positive education in Australia: Practice, measurement, and future directions. In *Social and emotional learning in Australia and the Asia-Pacific*. Singapore: Springer (Particularly the questions on page 109). Retrieved from https://scholar.google.com/scholar?hl=en&as_sdt=0%2C5&q=Positive+Education+in+Australia%3A+Practice%2C+Measurement%2C+and+Future+Directions&btnG=

Listen

NZIWR podcasts are available from https://nziwr.co.nz/category/podcast/

NZIWR Podcast: Dr Sue Roffey (The heart of a school)

NZIWR Podcast: Dr Lucy Hone and Dr Denise Quinlan (Building whole-school wellbeing)

What do we mean by whole-school?

Introduction

Whole-school wellbeing change requires attention to every level of the school's operation for students and staff: from enrolment and induction through reporting, reviews, curricula, disciplinary processes, awards systems, timetabling, assessment and many more. In short, wellbeing can be 'taught' (via explicit teachings and lessons) *and* 'caught' (built implicitly throughout all aspects of the school experience, the physical environment and structures as well as overarching culture). 'The greatest benefit will arise from the combination of caught and taught approaches. . . . Successful positive education programmes blend evidence-based learning and teaching, whole school strategy, and evaluation, and consider pedagogy, philosophical assumptions, and the school's culture', write leading researchers White and Kern.[1] Enabling wellbeing across the entire school system is a complex challenge which, like any large-scale change management, takes time. Most schools say that you should expect a full cohort change or longer before wellbeing practices can be considered to be embedded.[2]

The ecology of whole-school wellbeing: A complex web of wellbeing factors

> '*Positive education is relevant to all aspects of education, from interactions between individual teachers and students to classroom interventions to school building level policies to public policy*'.[3]

A large range of influences operating at different levels affect school wellbeing (see Figure 2.1). While school-level factors such as location may be

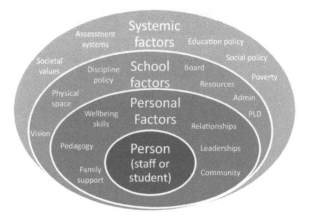

Figure 2.1 A whole-school view of wellbeing influences

Source: Quinlan and Hone, 2019

outside school leadership control, other factors such as discipline policy and assessment schedules, while complex, are in fact under the control of the school. Factors affecting individual wellbeing can be outside the school's control (e.g. illness of family members) while other factors, such as provision of wellbeing professional development and access to wellbeing coaching or wellbeing planning, fall within the school's control.

Kern and colleagues in defining the field of *Systems-Informed Positive Psychology*[4] emphasise the importance of viewing the whole school system in our efforts to build wellbeing. This whole-systems approach to wellbeing acknowledges the messy reality that the elements within a system can interact and change each other in often unpredictable ways. For schools, this may seem like a late recognition by psychology of the reality of work in schools.

Who is included in 'whole-school'?

Whole-school wellbeing includes all those who have a stake in what the school is and does – those who care and are affected by the decisions the school makes:

- Students;
- Teachers;
- Senior leadership team;
- Support staff;
- Board of trustees or board of governors;
- Parents and families of students and staff;
- The wider local community that serves the school and is served by it; and

- Local iwi in Aotearoa/New Zealand (indigenous people on whose land the school may be and whose children may attend the school).

Wellbeing is for all: inclusion and belonging

Belonging and inclusion are essential for wellbeing[5] and, in a school setting, also predict engagement and motivation for learning.[6] Some groups within our school communities have specific characteristics that have not always been adequately addressed. Failure to fully include these groups in school wellbeing efforts would be a 'double whammy', ignoring wellbeing plus other needs. These groups include students and staff:

- With disability or for whom learning support may be helpful;
- From minority ethnic and religious groups;
- Who are trauma affected;
- Who experience deprivation and economic hardship;
- With mental illness; and
- Who identify as gender diverse, including as LGBTQI.

What the research says

Recognition of the importance of addressing the whole school in wellbeing interventions has been growing for almost two decades. Researchers have shown the benefits of utilising all the levers for change within a school system and highlighted the inadequacies of interventions focused solely on a deficit model of fixing mental health problems.[7] Weare and Nind's systematic review of mental health promotion in schools shows that the characteristics of more effective programmes included teaching skills; focusing on positive mental health; balancing universal and targeted approaches; starting early with the youngest children and continuing with older ones; and operating for a lengthy period of time and embedding work within a multi-modal/whole-school approach. This whole-school approach included such features as changes to the curriculum, including teaching skills and linking with academic learning, improving school ethos, teacher education, liaison with parents, parenting education, community involvement and coordinated work with outside agencies.[8]

'Multi-year, whole school approaches are likely to have even greater impact than curriculum or classroom-only approaches'.[9] We also know that the quality of implementation of social-emotional learning programmes has a substantial impact on academic effect: a recent Flinders University study found that the difference for students in 'high-implementing' and 'low-implementing schools' equated to a difference in academic performance of up to six months schooling.[10]

Evaluation of whole-school wellbeing initiatives

Geelong Grammar School (GGS) pioneered a whole-school wellbeing approach in 2008. That journey included a commitment by staff to learning and teaching the skills of wellbeing, developing a school model of wellbeing, embedding wellbeing practices throughout the school, and taking time from the core subjects of mathematics and science to create space for the teaching of wellbeing. The school's journey is documented in Jacolyn Norrish's book, which provides rich detail on how the school has implemented positive education.[11] GGS has continued to evaluate and develop its whole-school approach, maintaining a focus on staff training in the principles amd practices of positive education, and ensuring that practices are explicitly and implicitly taught at the school. Evaluation results have indicated that GGS's year 9 outdoor-focused residential programme is an important contributor to student wellbeing.[12]

As part of learning and developing, the school has published an updated implementation process proposed as four cyclical interconnecting processes: Learn it, Live it, Teach it, and Embed it.[13] They propose that each of these four processes represent unique opportunities to build whole-school wellbeing and that failure to address any one of these will reduce the overall impact of a wellbeing initiative.[14] Failure to enable staff to learn about wellbeing can result in lack of knowledge and a reluctance to teach about wellbeing. Failure to encourage and support staff to live wellbeing leaves the school and its staff open to claims of hypocrisy from students and resistance to learning from staff who are not themselves adopting wellbeing practices. Failure to teach wellbeing results in a missed opportunity to prioritise wellbeing for students and can result in misunderstanding of some key constructs. Failure to embed wellbeing in school policy and practices can result in independent or isolated efforts in which staff and students more easily feel ineffective or lonely.

Another school that has embraced whole-school wellbeing and commited to research and evaluation of its wellbeing journey is St Peter's College in Adelaide, Australia.[15][16] Following 18 months of planning and staff training in wellbeing, the school undertook a number of initiatives in 2012 to implement and embed character strengths in the English curriculum, school sport, student leadership and counselling. A curriculum for the explicit teaching of wellbeing skills was also introduced to all students. Sport was chosen following a review that indicated some coaching remained deficit focused, 'with coaches focusing on correcting the weaknesses and errors of the student athletes rather than building up strengths and optimism'.[17] This focus on wellbeing has been 'gradually incorporated throughout the school's ecosystem with the school emphasising the importance of leadership and vision on wellbeing, staff training, evidence based wellbeing programmes, and implicit teaching of wellbeing in sports, leadership and co-curricular activities'.[18] St Peter's has reported that at-risk students (for lower academic, behaviour and psychosocial outcomes) have benefited most from the wellbeing focus and that senior students perceive wellbeing and resilience as less significant and positive education as less useful to them than do junior students.[19]

Both GGS and St Peter's have emphasised the importance of assessment and feedback from a range of sources in order to inform pastoral care, future programme development and ongoing adjustment to the programmes delivered. This reminds us that whole-school wellbeing is an emergent discipline and one that requires schools to remain in the 'sandpit' of trial and experimentation on an ongoing basis.

A 2014 study that compared an intermediate school in Israel implementing a one-year whole-school wellbeing programme with a control school, found reductions in depression and anxiety and increases in self-efficacy and optimism two years later.[20] While there is widespread understanding that whole-school wellbeing is a long-term undertaking, nonetheless, these early positive results were encouraging.

The Values Education Project in Australia demonstrated the value of a whole-school approach in a longitudinal study involving 166 schools and 70,000 students, which showed 'better results, deeper commitment and improved sustainability when compared to similar programmes not using a whole school approach'. Even though whole-school involvement was resource intensive, 'there were deeper commitments to the program, better results, and better sustainability using a whole-school approach, compared to similar programs that didn't'.[21]

Box 2.1: Whole-school wellbeing: Parents and teachers as wellbeing assessors

A pilot study of whole-school wellbeing in primary schools in the Netherlands that aimed to improve student wellbeing and school climate began with teachers' identifying their teaching values and developing a set of 'life rules' for the school.[22] Teachers were also trained in observational assessment of student wellbeing and engagement and provided with a range of intervention support strategies. Parents also received training to support their child's wellbeing at home. The programme had a positive impact on both teachers and students, with teachers feeling 'refreshed' for teaching and students reporting higher wellbeing and health-related quality of life.

Learning from other whole-school approaches: School-wide positive behaviour support

Valuable lessons are available to schools and teachers from other whole-school approaches. For example, participants from schools that had worked within a school-wide positive behaviour support (SWPBS) approach for five years identified these factors as important in implementation success:

- School readiness (investment and commitment);
- Student empowerment (opportunities to upskill and participate);
- Community input (contextually appropriate values, language and practices);
- Professional learning (adequate time and support); and
- Evidence-based decision-making (data/feedback informed).[23]

These findings are consistent with the approach we advocate and reinforce the processes we share in this book.

Context and implementation matter in whole-school wellbeing

Positive psychology has been criticised for failing to appreciate the importance of context when applying scientific findings and theories to real-world practice, particularly in schools,[24][25][26] and research on positive education has now begun to address the importance of context. (See Helen Street on this topic in Chapters 4 and 16.) The field of implementation science also provides tools to examine real-world programme effectiveness.[27] As an example, the implementation quality of KidsMatter primary school programmes affected academic achievement, with the difference between high- and low-implementation quality schools equivalent to six months schooling by year 7.[28] The importance of teachers as a contextual factor in wellbeing research was demonstrated in research conducted by Denise M. Quinlan that showed students' benefits from a strengths programme depended on the extent to which their classroom teacher practised strengths spotting.[29]

Expert researcher and educator insight 2.1: *Dr Gill Rutherford. Whole-school wellbeing means everyone – including students with disability*

Many students with disabilities experience discrimination when trying to access education in many countries, and even when students gain funding support and a place at school, their right to education may be compromised. These students are less likely to access the affective and emotional benefits of attending school, more likely to be bullied, less likely to get access to the best teaching a school has to offer, more likely to be in the care of a teacher aide and likely to have more limited opportunities to make friends.

Article 24 of the United Nations Convention on the Rights of Persons with Disabilities recognises the right of persons with disabilities to an inclusive education system at all levels and lifelong learning that supports 'the full development of human potential and sense of dignity and self-worth'.[30] Senior Lecturer in Inclusive Education and Disability Studies at the University of Otago's College of Education, Dr Gill Rutherford, encourages schools to consider the following:

- Get to know and develop a positive relationship with each child, focusing on their strengths, interests, capacities and rights – just as we do with all students.
- While certain labels may be useful in accessing funding and possible supports, we do not need to highlight the disability every time we mention the student (e.g. saying 'Joe has cerebral palsy' tells us nothing about who Joe is as a human being). Instead, provide constructive information about Joe that will inform our teaching and work with him (e.g. 'Joe uses a communication device as his main form of communication and finds it easier to write using an iPad'). Cerebral palsy (like other forms of human differences) affects each person uniquely.
- The most frequent plea from students is 'treat us like normal kids, get to know us and ask us what we want or need'.
- Remember that every student in the school has a right to have a say in matters that affect them.
- Access resources like the *Index for Inclusion*,[31] a whole school development tool that provides guidelines regarding key values, inclusive school cultures, policies and practices.
- Utilise inclusive pedagogies and frameworks like Universal Design for Learning that support inclusive education (See Chapter 9 – The sandpit phase).
- Be aware of the 'ableist bias' that exists in most societies and gets in the way of people with disability even being included in discussions about wellbeing.

Box 2.2: An evidence-based national initiative: Be You

Be You is a national initiative from Australia supporting educators to promote and protect positive mental health in children and young people.[32] It uses a whole-school approach, with five domains:

- Family partnerships;
- Early support;
- Responding together (to critical incidents);
- Learning resilience; and
- Mentally healthy communities.

Each domain contains professional learning modules to help educators and school leaders understand more about wellbeing and the processes that support it.

The Be You initiative emerged from over a decade's work comparing, implementing and evaluating programmes to promote social and emotional learning.[33] This work highlights the role of education in improving mental health outcomes and calls for a 'mental fitness and wellbeing' agenda in schools that is co-designed with local communities and recognises that some children experience significant risk factors, which should be considered as part of a school-based response. Be You calls for mental health and wellbeing education to become part of teacher and early childhood worker training and ongoing professional development.[34]

Box 2.3: Restorative practice: An evidence-based whole-school wellbeing initiative

Restorative practices are another whole-school wellbeing approach with a strong practice and evidence base. Restorative practices are a relational approach which values respectful relationships between people. Conflict is viewed as something that breaks relationships and causes harm which has to be addressed.[35] When we understand the importance of relationships for wellbeing, then adopting a restorative approach seems like a sensible choice.

Jansen and Matla emphasise that restorative practice is done *with* rather than done *to*. Their Social Discipline Window (Figure 2.2) contrasts the high-support and high-structure environment of restorative practice with the low-support and high-structure environment of the punitive approach.

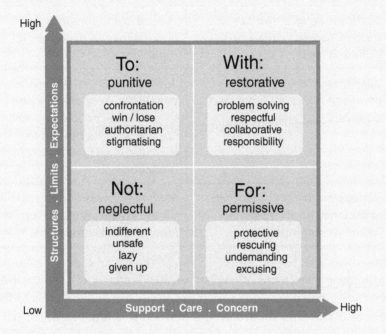

Figure 2.2 Jansen and Matla's Social Discipline Window

They clearly set out the differences between punitive and restorative responses:[36]

Punitive response	Restorative response
• What law/rule was broken? • Who was to blame? • What punishment is needed?	• Who was affected? • What are their needs? • Who is obligated to put things right?

(continued)

Punitive response	Restorative response
Response focuses on . . . establishing blame (whose fault is it?) and delivering punishment and pain.	*Response focuses on . . .* identifying the need created by harm and making things right.
Justice is sought through . . . making people prove who is right and wrong.	*Justice is sought through . . .* understanding, dialogue and reparation.
Justice is achieved when . . . someone is proven guilty and punished.	*Justice is achieved when . . .* people take responsibility for their actions, people's needs are met and the healing of individuals and relationships is encouraged.
Limits possibilities . . . for full acceptance back into family, school or community.	*Maximises possibilities . . .* for full acceptance back into family/school/community.

Restorative practitioners emphasise that working effectively with restorative practice is not just about using the big conferences for serious events. It's about having a restorative culture in which relational conversations are the norm and all teachers (and students) feel equipped to have restorative conversations with others in the school community. This is a long-term culture change and one that requires time and commitment.[37]

The impact of restorative practices in education now has evidence from Europe, the USA, Australia and New Zealand.[38] This research highlighted the importance of teacher commitment to the principles of restorative practice and the potential to reduce conflict and disciplinary issues, including expulsions. Other evaluation of restorative practice points to the significant changes in school climate that have been achieved and the extent to which staff and students feel safe and understood.[39]

Putting it into practice

Schools and researchers around the world are implementing whole-school wellbeing in a variety of ways and exploring how best to assess and report on their progress. We have collected case studies from around the world illustrating the range of approaches.

> 'We view this whole process as spiral and interconnected, in that teachers' learning affects the school organizational climate which affects teacher and student competency development'. (Teaching with the Heart and Mind)

Case study 2.1:   Teaching with the heart and mind: An integrative whole-school model

Led by Ofra Mayseless, Shiri Lavy, Roza Leikin, Michal Zion and Zemira Mevarech of Israel, this project's goal is to provide an evidence-based model for fostering deep learning of 21st century competencies in schools, which can be scaled up and transferred to schools.

'Deep learning, or learning for transfer, is related to the capacity to apply knowledge and competencies learned in one context to other contexts. Crucial for children living in today's rapidly changing world, it is expected to become increasingly important as the pace of change increases. 21st century competencies can be categorised under three main domains: 1) cognitive competencies (e.g. creativity, critical thinking, analysis); 2) intrapersonal competencies (e.g. perseverance, integrity, self-regulation, curiosity); and 3) interpersonal competencies (e.g. teamwork, leadership, interpersonal skills).[40] The 24 character strengths (Peterson and Seligman, 2004) correspond with many of these competencies[41] and were also consistently associated with wellbeing.[42][43]

Project Framework/Guiding Principles

The main characteristics of the project are:

1   Targeting **the whole school** while acknowledging the crucial effects of school leadership and climate on developing sustainability of deep learning processes;

2   Targeting **the teacher**, while acknowledging the effects of personal competencies and motivations on instruction; and

3   Examining and refining the intervention with quantitative and qualitative research in numerous different schools to enable development of **an effective model** of intervention for scaling up.

We view this whole process as spiral and interconnected, in that teachers' learning affects the school organisational climate, which affects teacher and student competency development.

Project Components

Targeting the teachers: "Teaching with your heart and mind" helps teachers develop their own 21st century competencies. Teachers "teach who they are", and the "inner landscape of a teacher's life" is a pivotal facet of the teacher's teaching and the learning process of students[44] (Palmer, 1998, pp. 1–3). Teachers learn, practice and reflect upon core concepts, theories and exercises to develop their socio-emotional competencies as part of a two-year professional development programme. Teachers initially focus on their experiences and wellbeing and then practice using new ways to incorporate their learning into their teaching practices.

Targeting the organisation: School leadership is often considered the most important factor in change processes.[45] Some of the most crucial competencies of principals who lead effective change processes are similar to the socio-emotional competencies mentioned earlier. School leadership's ownership of change is a predictor of its sustainability,[46][47] nurturing change by creating a supportive organisational climate and structures. As part of the programme, an organisational consultant works with the principal and school leadership team (25–30 hours a year for two years) applying the programme's ideas to the school's routines, structures, and organizational habits'.

Case study 2.2:   St Peter's School Adelaide, Australia: A whole-school commitment

Head of Wellbeing and Acting Head of St Peter's Junior School David Kolpak emphasises the importance whole-school wellbeing beginning with staff wellbeing.

St Peter's school spent time discussing and defining what wellbeing meant to the community. Beginning with a focus on character strengths enabled the development of a shared language around wellbeing and the positive qualities of each person in the school. One of the principal benefits for the school has been the development of social and emotional competency among its students. Students at this all-boys school became more willing and able to articulate emotional experiences and struggles, with a broader vocabulary for doing so. David's advice from St Peter's to other schools starting down this path:

- *Start with the staff first. Where schools work with students first they have missed an important opportunity for staff to understand wellbeing and apply it in their own lives.*
- *Define wellbeing for your school – it will be different from school to school. You need to have that benchmark to be able to evaluate progress against it.*
- *Develop a shared language that is understood and used regularly across the school in all departments and classrooms.*

Box 2.4: Letter from a special-needs mum

Dear Schools,

Inclusion in a school can be felt the moment you enter the grounds. It can also be smelt, tasted, heard and is clearly visible. As a parent of a special-needs child, all my senses pick up moments of inclusion but sadly, more often than not, the reality is a lack of integration between my daughter's satellite class and the rest of the school. It is the invisibility of our special children, the indirect looks they get

(continued)

from the other children, hearing their classroom being used as a 'put down' and not having our children's learning celebrated in a public way with the rest of the school community.

Inclusion is not a new concept. It is an attitude, a way of being. It's simply the ability to see an individual as another human being. It's understanding that each individual has unique strengths to bring to our world, regardless of the challenges they may face.

My dream is that one day there will be no difference in the way my daughter is seen by other students. I will know that this has happened when I see other pupils greet her by her name, instead of giving her sideways glances or whispers about her behind cupped hands. One day I hope to drop into school on an unscheduled visit to witness her engaged in a game with students during break time. I dream that each individual child will be valued for who they are and seen beyond their label or diagnosis. My hope for the future is that parents with special-needs children won't have to fundraise for teacher aide hours, just so their child can attend school. My wish is for every child to have the curriculum adapted to their needs so that they may feel what it is to succeed and learn.

Last week I witnessed inclusion happening in its purest and most beautiful form. I had tears in my eyes watching the school cross country. Each child from my daughter's satellite class had a buddy to run with them. The youngest boy in the class had the hugest smile on his face when running up the hill with his buddy beside him. It was no surprise that the buddy also had a huge smile on his face. He'd been given a position of responsibility, an opportunity to demonstrate his leadership skills. And maybe he felt that little bit better about himself because he knew that running for him was a breeze compared to the little guy he was helping get up that hill.

What's really important to know and understand about inclusion of children with special needs and increasing children's wellbeing in a school is that they go hand in hand. The example of the buddy and special-needs pupil in the school cross country demonstrates how everyone wins when we collaborate and connect with one another. It is these simple changes within the school environment that create inclusive schools. Sometimes it's really tough as a classroom teacher to have to integrate a child with high needs into an already full and busy class of students. However, the lessons around diversity that all students will learn through their interactions will best help prepare your students for the future world of work and to build inclusive communities. The attitudes that you convey to your students have far-reaching consequences. You are making our society a better place for us all to live in. By modelling inclusion and honouring diversity, you are creating a much-improved society of the future and improving the wellbeing of our nation.

Thank you.

A Special-Needs Mum

Case study 2.3:   Hong Kong primary schools: A whole-school approach yields benefits

Dr. Sylvia Kwok, Associate Professor in the Department of Social and Behavioural Sciences at City University of Hong Kong led a team of researchers, school leaders and teachers to conduct this whole-school wellbeing intervention in a Hong Kong primary school.

'Integrating experiential learning theory (ELT)[48] and the applied model of positive education in Geelong Grammar School,[49] we developed a six-level implementation process described as "learn it", "live it", "reflect it", "conceptualize it", "apply it" and "embed it" in the school setting (Figure 2.3). This six-level process guided positive education delivery. It was not just a pedagogy, but a way of life within the school and daily lives.

"Learn it" refers to regular learning opportunities to understand the science of wellbeing provided to primary students, teachers, and parents. "Live it" encourages participants to enact evidence-based wellbeing practices in their unique ways both in schools and their own lives. "Reflect it" and "conceptualize it" means that individuals are assisted to "reflect" on what they have learned and experienced so as to "conceptualize" their experiences with a deeper understanding of the concepts and principles. "Apply it" means designing and conducting positive education programs or activities in schools and communities. Finally, "Embed it" advocates building long-term, school-wide policies and a positive culture which support and nurture wellbeing within individuals, schools, and the community.

Our project included four components: (1) curriculum and activities for students, (2) professional development for teachers, (3) education for parents and (4) school support. Positive education concepts were incorporated in teacher and student evaluation, school management, year plans, formal and informal curricula, teaching language and school environment, so as to build up a positive culture in the schools. Students reported significant increases in positive emotions, improvement in teacher-student relationships, enhancement of parent-child relationships and improvement in study engagement and purpose'.

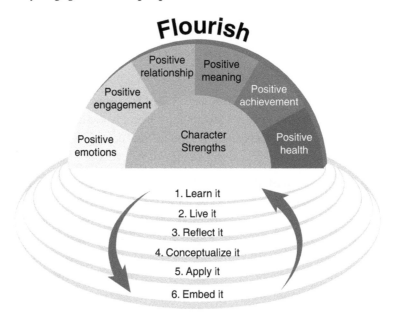

Figure 2.3 Theoretical model of the whole-school approach

Case study 2.4:   Taipei European School: Engaging parents, students and staff in whole-school wellbeing

When Taipei European School (TES) embarked on its whole-school wellbeing journey, the leadership communicated very clearly to staff that this was a journey rather than a short-term programme, and this long-term culture change would take several years to achieve and was not a flash in the pan. TES committed to a three-year whole-school approach to wellbeing focused on staff in its first year, students in the second year and the parent community in the third year.

The first year was about staff learning about the science of wellbeing. Staff did a lot of reading and debating and planning the next two years. A key part of the approach adopted at TES was the introduction of a coaching model that equipped staff to have solution-focused conversations with each other. Providing this ongoing and constructive peer support proved important for the school's progress in implementing wellbeing.

Wellbeing sceptics were encouraged to challenge and check the evidence. Because it was 'all about learning' and not 'preaching to', most teachers quickly came on board and could see the need for wellbeing support for both staff and students.

The advice from TES to other schools starting down this path:

- *Take the time to do it right, be patient and accept that you will be in the sandpit for a long time, if not forever.*
- *Take the time to do the learning yourself as a leader – go to conferences and attend professional development on wellbeing.*
- *Take the learning to staff before students. Staff cannot take wellbeing learning to students if they haven't experienced it themselves.*
- *Treat the staff learning stage as an exploration. Be open to wellbeing discussion and debate, and don't expect everyone's buy-in immediately.*

Reflection questions

- Is student wellbeing a specific goal in your strategic plan, and how is it resourced?
- Is staff wellbeing a specific goal in your strategic plan, and how is it resourced?
- What's one step that will make your school more inclusive for students with disability?
- What first steps can you take to align wellbeing with your school's governance, strategy and vision?

- Who will/could support your vision (within the school)?
- Who will/could support your vision (beyond the school gates)?
- How can you draw on a systems perspective to create a whole-school strategy?
- Are there practices and processes in your school that might undermine wellbeing? What might they be?

Notes

1   White, M. A., & Kern, M. L. (2018). Positive education: Learning and teaching for wellbeing and academic mastery. *International Journal of Wellbeing, 8*(1).

2   Ten Year of Positive Education: What we got wrong. Keynote presentation at the Positive Education New Zealand Conference, April 8–9, 2019, Christ's College, Christchurch, NZ.

3   Gomez-Baya, D., & Gillham, J. E. (2018). Positive education: Promoting well-being at school. Chapter 34 in Muñiz, V. J. A., & Pulido, C. M. (Eds.). (2018). *The Routledge handbook of positive communication: Contributions of an emerging community of research on communication for happiness and social change.* Retrieved from https://ebookcentral. proquest.com

4   Kern, M. L., Williams, P., Spong, C., Colla, R., Sharma, K., Downie, A., . . . Oades, L. G. (2019). Systems informed positive psychology. *The Journal of Positive Psychology.* doi: 10.1080/17439760.2019.1639799

5   Baumeister, R. F., & Leary, M. R. (1995). The need to belong: Desire for interpersonal attachments as a fundamental human motivation. *Psychological Bulletin, 117*, 497–529.

6   Furrer, C., & Skinner, E. (2003). Sense of relatedness as a factor in children's academic engagement and performance. *Journal of Educational Psychology, 95*(1), 148.

7   Weare, K., & Markham, W. (2005). What do we know about promoting mental health through schools? *Promotion & Education, 12*(3–4), 118–122.

8   Weare, K., & Nind, M. (2011, December). Mental health promotion and problem prevention in schools: What does the evidence say? *Health Promotion International, 26*(Suppl 1), i29–i69. https://doi. org/10.1093/heapro/dar075

9   Gomez-Baya, D., & Gillham, J. E. (2018). Positive education: Promoting well-being at School. Chapter 34. In J. A. M. Velázquez & C. M. Pulido (Eds.), *The Routledge handbook of positive communication: Contributions to an emerging community of research on communication for happiness and social change* (p. 10). Routledge, 2018. ProQuest Ebook Central http://ebookcentral.proquest Created from aut on 2019–08–22 15:35:43.

10 Dix, K. L., Slee, P. T., Lawson, M. J., & Keeves, J. P. (2012). Implementation quality of whole-school mental health promotion and students' academic performance. *Child and Adolescent Mental Health, 17*(1), 45–51.

11 Norrish, J. M., & Seligman, M. E. (2015). *Positive education: The Geelong grammar school journey.* Oxford Positive Psychology Series.

12 O'Connor, M., & Cameron, G. (2017). The Geelong grammar positive psychology experience. In *Social and emotional learning in Australia and the Asia-Pacific* (pp. 353–370). Singapore: Springer.

13 Hoare, E., Bott, D., & Robinson, J. (2017). Learn it, live it, teach it, embed it: Implementing a whole school approach to foster positive mental health and wellbeing through positive education. *International Journal of Wellbeing, 7*(3).

14 Hoare, E., Bott, D., & Robinson, J. (2017). Learn it, live it, teach it, embed it: Implementing a whole school approach to foster positive mental health and wellbeing through positive education. *International Journal of Wellbeing, 7*(3).

15 White, M. A., & Waters, L. E. (2015). A case study of 'The Good School': Examples of the use of Peterson's strengths-based approach with students. *The Journal of Positive Psychology, 10*(1), 69–76.

16 Kern, M. L., Adler, A., Waters, L. E., & White, M. A. (2015). Measuring whole-school well-being in students and staff. In *Evidence-based approaches in positive education* (pp. 65–91). Dordrecht: Springer.

17 White, M. A., & Waters, L. E. (2015). A case study of 'The Good School': Examples of the use of Peterson's strengths-based approach with students. *The Journal of Positive Psychology, 10*(1), 69–76.

18 White, M. A., & Kern, M. L. (2018). Positive education: Learning *and* teaching for wellbeing and academic mastery. *International Journal of Wellbeing, 8*(1), 1–17. doi:10.5502/ijw.v8i1.588

19   Kern, M. L., Adler, A., Waters, L. E., & White, M. A. (2015). Measuring whole-school well-being in students and staff. In *Evidence-based approaches in positive education* (pp. 65–91). Dordrecht: Springer.

20   Shoshani, A., & Steinmetz, S. (2014). Positive psychology at school: A school-based intervention to promote adolescents' mental health and well-being. *Journal of Happiness Studies, 15*(6), 1289–1311.

21   Lovat, T., Clement, N., Dally, K., & Toomey, R. (2011). The impact of values education on school ambience and academic diligence. *International Journal of Educational Research, 50*, 166–170. doi:10.1016/j.ijer.2011.07.008

22   Elfrink, T. R., Goldberg, J. M., Schreurs, K. M., Bohlmeijer, E. T., & Clarke, A. M. (2017). Positive educative programme: A whole school approach to supporting children's well-being and creating a positive school climate: A pilot study. *Health Education, 117*(2), 215–230.

23   Savage, C., Lewis, J., & Colless, N. (2011). Essentials for implementation: Six years of school wide positive behaviour support in New Zealand. *New Zealand Journal of Psychology, 40*(1), 29–37.

24   Ciarrochi, J., Atkins, P. W. B., Hayes, L. L., Sahdra, B. K., & Parker, P. (2016). Contextual positive psychology: Policy recommendations for implementing positive psychology into schools. *Frontiers in Psychology, 7*, 1561. doi:10.3389/fpsyg.2016.01561

25   Hoffman, D. M. (2009). Reflecting on social emotional learning: A critical perspective on trends in the United States. *Review of Educational Research, 79*(2), 533–556. https://doi.org/10.3102/0034654308325184

26   Street, H. (2017). Measures of success: Exploring the importance of context in the delivery of well-being and social and emotional learning programmes in Australian primary and secondary schools. In E. Frydenberg, A. Martin, & R. Collie (Eds.), *Social and emotional learning in Australia and the Asia-Pacific*. Singapore: Springer.

27   Kelly, B. (2012). Implementation science for psychology in education. In B. Kelly & D. F. Perkins (Eds.), *Handbook of implementation science for psychology in education* (pp. 3–12). New York: Cambridge University Press.

28   Dix, K. L., Slee, P. T., Lawson, M. J., & Keeves, J. P. (2012). Implementation quality of whole-school mental health promotion and students' academic performance. *Child and Adolescent Mental Health, 17*(1), 45–51.

29 Quinlan, D., Vella-Brodrick, D. A., Gray, A., & Swain, N. (2018). Teachers matter: Student outcomes following a strengths intervention are mediated by teacher strengths spotting. *Journal of Happiness Studies*, 1–17.

30 The United Nations Convention on the Rights of Persons with Disabilities and its Optional Protocol (A/RES/61/106) (2006). Retrieved August 26, 2019 from www.un.org/development/desa/disabilities/convention-on-the-rights-of-persons-with-disabilities/convention-on-the-rights-of-persons-with-disabilities-2.html

31 Booth, T., & Ainscow, M. (2016). *Index for inclusion: Developing learning and participation in schools*. Centre for Studies on Inclusive Education (CSIE).

32 Be You Evidence Summary. (2019). Retrieved August 19, from https://beyou.edu.au/about-be-you/evidence-base

33 Slee, P. T., Lawson, M. J., Russell, A., Askell-Williams, H., Dix, K. L., Owens, L., . . . Spears, B. (2009). *KidsMatter primary evaluation final report*. Centre for Analysis of Educational Futures, Flinders University of South Australia, 1–120.

34 Be You Evidence Summary. (2019). Retrieved August 19, from https://beyou.edu.au/about-be-you/evidence-base, p. 4.

35 Macfarlane, A., Jansen, G., Daley, J., Thorsborne, M., Berryman, M., Matla, R., . . . Dharan, V. (2011). *Responsive Pedagogy*. New Zealand Council for Educational Research. PO Box 3237, Wellington 6140 New Zealand.

36 Macfarlane, A., Jansen, G., Daley, J., Thorsborne, M., Berryman, M., Matla, R., . . . Dharan, V. (2011). *Responsive Pedagogy*. New Zealand Council for Educational Research. PO Box 3237, Wellington 6140 New Zealand.

37 Thorsborne, M., & Blood, P. (2013). *Implementing restorative practice in schools: A practical guide to transforming school communities*. Jessica Kingsley Publishers.

38 Anfara Jr, V. A., Evans, K. R., & Lester, J. N. (2013). Restorative justice in education: What we know so far. *Middle School Journal*, *44*(5), 57–63.

39 Cameron, L., & Thorsborne, M. (2001). Restorative justice and school discipline: Mutually exclusive. *Restorative Justice and Civil Society*, *180*, 194.

40   Pellegrino, J. W., & Hilton, M. L. (2012). *Education for life and work: Developing transferable knowledge and skills in the 21st Century* (p. 257). Washington, DC. Retrieved from http download Nap Educ. Cgi.

41   Lavy, S. A. (2019). Review of character strengths interventions in twenty-first-century schools: Their importance and how they can be fostered. *Applied Research in Quality of Life*, 1–24. doi.org/10.1007/s11482-018-9700-6

42   Gillham, J., Adams-Deutsch, Z., Werner, J., Reivich, K., Coulter-Heindl, V., Linkins, M., . . . Contero, A. (2011). Character strengths predict subjective well-being during adolescence. *The Journal of Positive Psychology*, 6(1), 31–44.

43   Lavy, S., & Littman-Ovadia, H. (2011). All you need is love? Strengths mediate the negative associations between attachment orientations and life satisfaction. *Personality and Individual Differences*, 50(7), 1050–1055.

44   Palmer, P. J. (2017). *The courage to teach: Exploring the inner landscape of a teacher's life* (pp. 1–3). John Wiley & Sons.

45   Fullan, M. (2002). The change. *Educational Leadership*, 59(8), 16–20.

46   Coburn, C. E. (2003). Rethinking scale: Moving beyond numbers to deep and lasting change. *Educational Researcher*, 32(6), 3–12.

47   McLaughlin, M. W., & Mitra, D. (2001). Theory-based change and change-based theory: Going deeper, going broader. *Journal of Educational Change*, 2(4), 301–323.

48   Kolb, D. A., Boyatzis, R. E., & Mainemelis, C. (2001). Experiential learning theory: Previous research and new directions. *Perspectives on Thinking, Learning, and Cognitive Styles*, 1(8), 227–247.

49   Norrish, J. M., Williams, P., O'Connor, M., & Robinson, J. (2013). An applied framework for positive education. *International Journal of Wellbeing*, 3(2).

Watch

Dianne Vella-Brodrick's Dean's Lecture imploring educators to make well-being education more of a TREAT than a treatment plan. Treat stands for tangible, relevant, evidence-based, alluring and transformational. Retrieved from www.youtube.com/watch?v=u0J8rwCZpus&feature=

Dr Lucy Hone talking about taking a whole-school system approach to whole-school wellbeing. Retrieved from https://vimeo.com/326726914

Read

Erasmus, C. (2019). *The mental health & wellbeing handbook for schools: Transforming mental health support on a budget.* Jessica Kingsley Publishers.

Hoare, E., Bott, D., & Robinson, J. (2017). Learn it, live it, teach it, embed it: Implementing a whole school approach to foster positive mental health and wellbeing through positive education. *International Journal of Wellbeing, 7*(3).

Norrish, J. M., & Seligman, M. E. (2015). *Positive education: The Geelong grammar school journey.* Oxford Positive Psychology Series.

Norrish, J. M., Williams, P., O'Connor, M., & Robinson, J. (2013). An applied framework for positive education. *International Journal of Wellbeing, 3*(2), 147–161.

Weare, K., & Nind, M. (2011, December). Mental health promotion and problem prevention in schools: What does the evidence say? *Health Promotion International, 26*(Suppl 1), i29–i69. https://doi.org/10.1093/heapro/dar075

https://www.jacquigibsonwriter.co/stories-content/shaun-markham-a-reluctant-stand-out

Listen

NZIWR podcasts are available from https://nziwr.co.nz/category/podcast/

NZIWR podcast: Clive Leach (whole-school wellbeing).

NZIWR podcast: Sonya Papps (Taipei European School).

NZIWR podcast: David Kolpak (St Peter's School).

NZIWR podcast: Greg Jansen (restorative practice).

Whole-school wellbeing is taught

The explicit curriculum

Introduction

For schools wanting to build capacity and understanding of the dynamic processes enabling and inhibiting wellbeing and resilience, there comes a time when wellbeing literacy must be explicitly taught. Wellbeing literacy is 'the vocabulary, knowledge, and skills that may be intentionally used to maintain or improve the wellbeing of oneself or others'.[1] The taught curriculum involves intentional, explicit delivery of wellbeing literacy in dedicated class time, requiring deliberate planning, scope and sequencing. A large number of wellbeing curricula are now available to schools around the world. The best of them are scientifically validated or clearly apply the scientific evidence base to support the teaching of wellbeing in a practical and developmentally appropriate manner.[2][3][4] The challenge for schools is selecting programmes that are relevant to the school context and aligned with the school's values.

Putting it into practice

Where a school intends to teach wellbeing, it is important there is sufficient timetabling for explicit teaching of wellbeing. Geelong Grammar School committed in 2010 to provide regular curriculum time to wellbeing teaching, and the class time for wellbeing was willingly given by the school's mathematics and science departments.[5]

A review of wellbeing interventions reported that the bulk were run in classrooms (83%), followed by after-school programmes (10%), school sports teams (4%), whole-school initiatives (2%) and other (1%).[6] There is some evidence already to suggest that interventions have the greatest impact on students when they are delivered by teachers,[78] but this may also depend on the particular nature of the intervention. Perhaps interventions that tap the pathways of coping and relationships have a greater effectiveness in the classroom due to the stronger bond with one's teacher, but it could be that strengths interventions and goal interventions do equally well in other context, such as sport teams, after-school programmes, student-buddy programmes and peer coaching.

The ways in which wellbeing is explicitly taught vary widely from school to school and include:

- A focus on specific topics sometimes purchased from specialist providers (e.g. mindfulness or character education programmes);
- Separate sequenced wellbeing curricula for different year levels (focused on topics that are developmentally appropriate for different age groups);
- Diverse delivery options (delivering timetabled wellbeing lessons, in tutor groups, in house groups or as part of service learning or ethics/ religious studies); and
- As part of the health and physical education curriculum (personal and social health education in the UK).

A large number of wellbeing programmes are now available to schools, many of which are based on sound scientific theory and evidence. On page 41 we've added a box with the validated or evidence-based programmes we are aware of. This is not an exhaustive list but a good place to start. These programmes can target specific age groups or specific skill set or competencies (e.g. social and emotional learning, resilience competencies, adolescent relationships and consent). Some involve an off-the-shelf book, others training and online support and resources, and vary accordingly in expense.

For schools wishing to develop their own tailor-made programme, it is critical to note this requires the same level of comprehensive research and planning usually reserved for teaching more traditional academic subjects. Developing your school's own dedicated wellbeing programme requires substantial investment in time and resources.

Given the time required to create in-house curricula, many schools prefer to focus their wellbeing efforts on changes in school practice and processes and opt to invest less time and more budget purchasing evidence-based curricula for their school.

The Be You initiative reminds us that more effective interventions start young and follow through schooling, are one part of a multi-modal whole-school commitment to wellbeing, and are characterised by:[9]

- Explicit teaching of mental health or social and emotional learning skills and competencies;

- A focus on positive mental health, not problems; and
- A balance of approaches for all students, and targeted approaches for those groups experiencing particular challenges.

Bywater and Sharples's review[10] of UK-available social and emotional learning programmes provides useful information to help educators to become critical consumers of wellbeing programmes. Questions to ask of any programme provider include:

- Is the programme based on scientific evidence, and is that specifically referenced?
- Is the programme universal or targeted?
- If targeted, has the programme been designed specifically for your target age group?
- What are the protective/risk factors that are addressed and how?
- What specific outcomes has this programme produced, and how are these outcomes demonstrated?
- What is the length of the programme (for students, teachers and parents)?
- How will your school manage these important aspects of programme implementation: fidelity (sticking to the programme), dosage (giving enough teaching time to it) and quality of delivery (taught by teachers who know and understand the programme)?[11]
- What has it cost schools to implement the programme in terms of investment, teacher training, relief times and resources?
- What types of reviews have been conducted (including process reviews and randomised control trials)?

As yet, there is no single best-practice way to teach wellbeing. What schools are doing is finding the approach that works best for them, given the available time and budget; the topics and issues that are most pressing or relevant; the teachers who are most willing and best equipped to deliver this teaching; and the availability of curricula that are appropriate for the school community. Our experience of working with scores of schools over the past decade has shown that these three guidelines can ease the process of introducing and embedding wellbeing teaching in your school:

- Don't rush into explicit teaching of wellbeing. Give staff delivering the programme sufficient time to feel confident with the material;
- Provide a selection of content to broaden appeal for students; and
- If your school is creating its own unique curriculum, encouarage input from staff *and* students in this process.

Box 3.1: Evidence-based wellbeing curriculum resources

When your school is ready to explicitly teach wellbeing, use these links to explore the range of programmes and resources that are available. We have selected this list on the grounds that they are all evidence-based or have been validated directly through research.

Berry Street Education Model
https://learning.berrystreet.org.au/focus-areas/
berry-street-education-model

Be You
https://beyou.edu.au/get-started

Bounce Back
www.bounceback-program.com/

Circle Solutions
https://growinggreatschoolsworldwide.com/csn/
circle_solutions_training/

DotB Mindfulness in Schools Programme
https://mindfulnessinschools.org/teach-dot-b/

Growing Strong Minds
www.growingstrongminds.com/

Headspace
www.headspace.com/work

Mental health education and *hauora*: teaching interpersonal skills, resilience, and wellbeing
www.nzcer.org.nz/nzcerpress/mental-health-education

Mind Up programme
https://mindup.org/

Mindfulness Education's Pause, Breathe, Smile programme
https://mindfulnesseducation.nz/pause-breathe-smile/

Penn Resilience Program
https://ppc.sas.upenn.edu/services/penn-resilience-training

(continued)

Positive Detective
https://positivedetective.com

Personal Well-being Lessons for Secondary Schools
Boniwell, I., & Ryan L. (2012), Open University Press, Berkshire,
UK
www.amazon.com/Personal-Well-Being-Lessons-Secondary-
Schools/dp/0335246168

Positive Education Enhanced Curriculum (PEEC)
https://positiveeducation.myshopify.com/pages/about-our-peec-
curriculum

Reaching In, Reaching Out programme (RIRO)
www.reachinginreachingout.com/

Smiling Mind
www.smilingmind.com.au/education

Strengthen Your School
https://nziwr.co.nz/

Strengths Gym
www.pprc.gg/products/

Strengths-Based Resilience Program
https://www.strengthsbasedresilience.com/

Thriving Learning Communities (The Mayerson Academy)
https://mayersonacademy.com/

The Happy Classroom Programme
http://educaposit.blogspot.com/

The High School Positive Psychology Curriculum (The Strath
Haven Positive Psychology curriculum)
https://www.authentichappiness.sas.upenn.edu/learn/educator
resilience

The VIA Character Strengths Survey
www.viacharacter.org

Visible Wellbeing™
www.visiblewellbeing.org/

YouCanDoIt!
www.youcandoiteducation.com.au/

Youth Connect
https://youthconnect.com.au

Case-study 3.1:   St Peter's School Adelaide, Australia: Teaching
                     wellbeing curricula

When wellbeing was introduced to the junior school at
St Peter's College, David Kolpak's role changed from being
the Deputy Head with resposibility for discipline to also being
the Junior Head of Wellbeing. This change alone enabled
connection and relationships to be developed more easily as
he was seen in a different light. The Head of Wellbeing was
also appointed as 'wellbeing driver', which meant supporting,
overseeing and helping teach the wellbeing classes that were
scheduled at the same time for each year group class. A deft
combination of carrot and stick, depending on the teacher's
perspective, this timetabling of wellbeing was important in
supporting skill development across the teacher group. The
Head of Wellbeing was able to teach a class, freeing up a less
confident class teacher to go and observe a colleague teaching the same topic to their class. Coupled with adequate staff
meeting time dedicated to discussion of wellbeing teaching,
reflection and sharing best practice, ideas for improvement and
things that didn't work, St Peter's was able to develop professional skills and confidence in teaching wellbeing across the
teaching staff.

'St Peter's supported a responsive pedagogy, where teachers who
were observing a colleague's class were encouraged to 'look at
the students and be guided by how they're responding – are they
enjoying the class? Are they engaged?'. Two strategies gave teachers a greater sense of autonomy and minimised the sense that they
were having to implement a new kind of teaching:

- Teachers were reminded that they know their students and they had the right to adapt and innovate with the wellbeing material to make it work for their classes.
- Rather than thinking of wellbeing as a whole new area to focus on, St Peter's reminded teachers where they were already asking similar questions, and that what was required was 'some tweaking'. For example, teachers were used to asking students to write about themselves and what they had done over the holidays. Now they focused on where they had been at their best over that time and what they were like at their best. In this way, wellbeing teaching was described as a lens through which each subject could be taught'.

Case study 3.2:   Taipei European School: Crash and core in teaching wellbeing

Sonja Papps, Head of the British Secondary and High School Section of the Taipei European School has played a key part in introducing and embedding wellbeing in the school over the past four years.

'Wellbeing was introduced to students at the end of the first year (which was dedicated to staff learning). Strategies used to introduce wellbeing to students included:

- "Crash Days" where the school "crashes the timetable" and takes over learning for a special focus day. On a "Crash Day" students received training in the PERMA wellbeing model, the Five Ways to Wellbeing model, coaching, and character strengths. As well as keynotes, students have opportunities to attend a series of wellbeing workshops.
- Different year levels focus on different aspect of wellbeing with earlier years focused on character, and topics such as mental toughness introduced to senior students.
- The School operates Core time for 80 minutes per week in the timetable where social and emotional learning is taught. Each year level has Core at the same time, with these sessions sometimes taught to the full cohort, in their individual class groups,

or based on specific need. The Core team can work together
and support and learn from each other.

- The Wellbeing teaching is led by the Deans of each year level
who have received most wellbeing professional development.
The Dean supports the planning and preparation that goes into
all Core teaching.

- Students complete an online wellbeing and mental toughness
assessment in September and April. Those assessments are
debriefed in one-on-one meetings with a member of the senior
leadership team or a member of the pastoral care team. Individual intervention plans may be developed, and parents may be
included if there are significant issues. These assessments can
also be used to inform plans for a whole cohort of students that
have a particular wellbeing need'.

Case study 3.3:   Making a START at St Peter's Cambridge, New
Zealand

Jess Patrick, Wellbeing Curriculum writer, deputy principal shares
their journey:

'According to Zig Ziglar, "You don't have to be great to **start**,
but you have to **start** to be great". Our wellbeing journey
started with a desire to be brave. Brave to implement a shift in
our thinking, to carve out precious time and resources, and to
pioneer a wraparound approach to a problem all schools face
– 'How can we help the wellbeing of each and every student
who walks through our gates?' Outlined below are five guidelines that have helped us make a **START**:

S = Select a model unique to your context. We have an overarching wellbeing theme each term (e.g. connect, care and lead)
that's broken down and translated into weekly wellbeing actions.
We implement initiatives to outwork the themes in hands on and
memorable ways. Care, for example, was 'Gratitude'. This theme
saw students writing letters to community members, planting
rocks with hopeful messages around the school and reminding
students to be thankful. For the Lead theme Year 13's worked

alongside Year 9's on an aspect of wellbeing. Weekly actions and foci are discussed in "Learning Groups". We communicate our wellbeing initiatives via newsletter, social media and offer community presentations to keep everyone informed and have School TV as another accessible platform.

T = Themes allow us to build a positive environment. That means walking the talk and make wellbeing a habit so we can build a school-wide wellbeing culture.

The wellbeing curriculum content must be contextualised and reflect what students are experiencing. Our content is informed by our wellbeing consultants (counsellors and the wellbeing director), the deans and the Wellbeing Lead Team. Wellbeing prefects and ambassadors are also consulted, and Learning Group Coaches (responsible for implementing our wellbeing curriculum) are constantly asked to reflect on what works during their time with students. Challenges arise with the reflective and personal nature of the content, so ongoing training and professional learning for all staff is essential.

A = Activities work so much better when Learning Group Coaches have familiarised themselves with the content beforehand. Each Learning Group Coach is given pre-written lessons to teach during their time with students, twice a week for 20 minutes. Staff need to prepare to "run" this lesson, with freedom to put their own twist on content. The wellbeing lesson writer, therefore, needs to be well researched and responsive to feedback and have a thick skin! It's essential to embrace feedback from the Learning Group Coaches and know that there will be content that "does not land" with everyone. Brene Brown has great advice for wellbeing writers: "Show up, face fear, and move forward' and 'Seek excellence, not perfection'.

R = Relationships and resources. Surround yourself with wellbeing champions and draw on character strengths. Like any ambitious endeavour, community is everything. The NZ Institute of Wellbeing & Resilience's partnership with St Peter's Cambridge has been of great value to us, continually updating and supporting us through our wellbeing journey.

T = Trust in yourselves. As educators, there comes a time when we must step up, lead and play better. It's not enough to just hope that our students are healthy inside and out; we need to be actively targeting and teaching ways to enhance their wellbeing. A wellbeing curriculum allows students the opportunity to acquire genuine tools and skills for their *kete* (basket) to navigate life. We have a responsibility to help them to be the best versions of themselves, to feel good and function well'.

Case-study 3.4:   Meeting local expectations: Teaching Wellbeing in Valdivia, Chile

Camilo Castellon leads a regional municipality-funded wellbeing project in Valdivia, in the south of Chile, where he works with a group of 42 vulnerable public schools. After initially attempting to teach the schools about character strengths, Camilo encountered challenges: he described schools as being 'like a train running, they are very busy places where it's not easy to get foot in the door'. When he began working with busy teachers, he realised they wanted to continue their traditional way of teaching, which was strongly curriculum based. For a new subject to be acceptable in Chile, teachers would need a curriculum with books and materials they could use.

Camilo's wellbeing curriculum research led him to curricula on gratitude, kindness and mindfulness from the USA. He uses the Greater Good Science Center at Berkeley's Gratitude Curricula: Thanks! A Strengths-Based Gratitude Curriculum for Tweens and Teens,[12] and Nurturing Gratitude From the Inside Out: 30 Activities for Grades K-8.[13] For social and emotional learning, Camilo has turned to the SEE (Social, Emotional and Ethical) Learning Programme from Emory University's Center for Healthy Minds.[14] This is a full curriculum on social, emotional and ethical education, which adds to SEL attention training, compassion and ethical training, systems thinking, and resilience and trauma-informed practice.

Reflection questions

- Where can you get some initial staff PLD training in wellbeing?
- How will you create time and funding for staff PLD in wellbeing?
- How will staff be encouraged to enage with, practice and implement their wellbeing learning in their own lives before they begin to teach wellbeing?
- Where and how is wellbeing currently taught in your school?
- How many people are explicitly and actively involved in teaching that relates directly to wellbeing?
- How will you decide whether to buy a curriculum or develop your own?
- If you decide to purchase resources, how will you decide what wellbeing needs are most important for your school?
- Will you select a general wellbeing curriculum or one that addresses specific wellbeing issues (e.g. belonging and inclusion, relationships and respect, resilience, or emotional and behavioural self-regulation), which can include a range of mindfulness approaches?

Notes

1   Oades, L. G., Slade, M., & Jarden, A. (2017). Wellbeing and recovery. *Wellbeing, Recovery and Mental Health*, 324–332.

2   Brunwasser, S. M., Gillham, J. E., & Kim, E. S. (2009). A meta-analytic review of the Penn resiliency program's effect on depressive symptoms. *Journal of Consulting and Clinical Psychology, 77*(6), 1042.

3   Durlak, J. A., Weissberg, R. P., Dymnicki, A. B., Taylor, R. D., & Schellinger, K. B. (2011). The impact of enhancing students' social and emotional learning: A meta-analysis of school-based universal interventions. *Child Development, 82*(1), 405–432.

4   McGrath, H., & Noble, T. (2018). *Bounce back! A positive education approach to wellbeing, resilience and social-emotional learning. Lower primary, F-Year 2; Middle primary, years 3–4; Upper primary, years 5–6* (3rd ed.). Melbourne, Australia: Pearson Education.

5   Norrish, J. M., & Seligman, M. E. (2015). *Positive education: The Geelong grammar school journey* (p. 22). Oxford Positive Psychology Series.

6   Waters, L., & Loton, D. (2019). *International Journal of Applied Positive Psychology*. Retrieved from https://doi.org/10.1007/s41042-019-00017-4

7   Waters, L., Barsky, A., Ridd, A., & Allen, K. (2015). Contemplative education: A systematic, evidence-based review of the effect of meditation interventions in schools. *Educational Psychology Review*, *27*(1), 103–134.

8   Chodkiewicz, A. R., & Boyle, C. (2017). Positive psychology school-based interventions: A reflection on current success and future directions. *Review of Education*, *5*(1), 60–86.

9   Be You Evidence Summary. Retrieved August 5, 2019, from https://beyou.edu.au/about-be-you/evidence-base, p. 14.

10 Bywater, T., & Sharples, J. (2012). Effective evidence-based interventions for emotional well-being: Lessons for policy and practice. *Research Papers in Education*, *27*(4), 389–408. doi:10.1080/02671522.2012.690242

11 Slee, P. T., Lawson, M. J., Russell, A., Askell-Williams, H., Dix, K. L., Owens, L., . . . Spears, B. (2009). *KidsMatter early childhood evaluation report*. Adelaide, SA: Shannon Research Press.

12 Greater Good Science Center. (2019). *Thanks! A strengths-based gratitude curriculum for tweens and teens*. Retrieved August 26, 2019, from https://ggsc.berkeley.edu/images/uploads/GGSC_Gratitude_Curriculum_MS_HS.pdf

13 Greater Good Science Center. (2019). *Nurturing gratitude from the inside out: 30 activities for grades K-8*. Retrieved August 26, 2019, from https://ggsc.berkeley.edu/images/uploads/GGSC_Gratitude_Curriculum_Elem.pdf

14 The Center for Healthy Minds. (2019). *The social, emotional and ethical learning programme*. Retrieved August 26, 2019, from https://seelearning.emory.edu/

Watch

What is Resilience? How to Thrive (3min 10sec). Retrieved from https://www.youtube.com/watch?v=T2AAJa1zIHo

Read

Erasmus, C. (2019). *The mental health & wellbeing handbook for schools: Transforming mental health support on a budget*. Jessica Kingsley Publishers.

Fitzpatrick, K., Wells, K., Tasker, G., Webber, M., & Riedel, R. (2018). *Mental health education and Hauora: Teaching interpersonal skills, resilience, and wellbeing*. Wellington, NZ: NZCER Press.

Norrish, J. M., & Seligman, M. E. (2015). *Positive education: The Geelong grammar school journey*. Oxford Positive Psychology Series.

Seligman, M. E. P., Ernst, R. M., Gillham, J., Reivich, K., & Linkins, M. (2009). Positive education: Positive psychology and classroom interventions. *Oxford Review of Education, 35*(3), 293–311. doi:10.1080/03054980902934563

White, M. A., & Kern, M. L. (2018). Positive education: Learning and teaching for wellbeing and academic mastery. *International Journal of Wellbeing, 8*(1).

Listen

NZIWR podcasts are available from https://nziwr.co.nz/category/podcast/

NZIWR podcast: Sonya Papps (Taipei European School).

NZIWR podcast: David Kolpak (St Peter's School).

NZIWR podcast: Adrienne Buckingham (the MenFit programme for teenage boys).

NZIWR podcast: Toni Noble (creator of Bounce Back).

NZIWR podcast: Grant Rix (creator of the Pause, Breathe, Smile mindfulness programme)

Whole-school wellbeing is caught

The implicit curriculum

Introduction

Despite good intentions, whole-school wellbeing will not be achieved through teaching an explicit wellbeing curriculum to students, adding co-curricular activities and ensuring all teachers receive training in wellbeing principles. Beyond these, it is vital to consider the multitude of moments, places and interactions where wellbeing is either built or suppressed in schools. This is what we mean by the 'caught' curriculum, a reflection of the overall culture, feeling or tone of a school.[1] According to Mathew White, former director of positive education and wellbeing at St Peter's College in Adelaide and currently associate professor at the University of Adelaide, the caught curriculum appears in the language used, staff and student interactions and the school's implicit norms. Essentially, it's 'the way things are done around here'.

Putting it into practice

Schools are complex places; a collection of a multitude of ever-changing elements. A school system is the result of elements (students, teachers, class rules, teaching practices, timetables, room layout, assessment schedules, school policies) interconnecting in an organised way, often with a shared purpose.[2] Traditionally, classrooms and schools have focused on student learning and academic achievement. Shifting the purpose of education beyond academic development to also include enabling and sustaining student wellbeing is a change being robustly discussed within education philosophy.[3][4] This is a change that reaches into every aspect of the school system, requiring the school to think about how it may function as a 'positive institution' supporting wellbeing in staff and students.

Wellbeing can be implemented in every aspect of school leadership and policy. As Laura Allison, leader of the psychology team at Catholic Education Western Australia, explains: 'Teachers can be powerful change agents for wellbeing within their classroom and have a broader influence on wellbeing across the school'.[5] The concluding part of Allison's statement, 'once they understand that flourishing occurs through human systems',[6] reflects the important understanding that wellbeing doesn't just occur within us, but between and among us.[7] Viewing wellbeing as a collective phenomenon can be both empowering and challenging for educators. Wellbeing researcher and practitioner Alex Linley of the UK has long advocated for each leader in an organisation to be a 'climate engineer', engineering the social climate of their group to support wellbeing and achievement. Caroline Marsh has been engineering the social climate at Christ's College, NZ, by encouraging teachers to notice and acknowledge strengths in students' classroom behaviour and effort. The Manifesto Awards she created acknowledge students' strengths and celebrate them in the school magazine. Students are also encouraged to visit the executive principal to have their Manifesto certificates signed after discussing how they used their strengths. For more on how to promote classroom-wide flourishing, see *Expert Researcher Insight: How teachers can create flourishing classrooms* on page 54.

The range of domains and practices that can be implemented across a school is almost limitless. The checklist in Table 4.1 includes many of these possibilities; detailed discussion of all of them is beyond the scope of this book. Instead, we share some frameworks and meta-strategies to guide you in what to focus on and some practical activities for immediate application in your classroom or school.

Table 4.1 Checklist: Where wellbeing is 'caught' (seen, heard, felt, role-modelled) in schools

The following are some aspects of the school system that have a potential influence on how wellbeing is 'caught' in the school. Review this checklist and tick those areas where your school is already implementing wellbeing initiatives or supports in these areas.		
Leadership • Leadership support (including establishment of roles and provision of resources for wellbeing)	Policy and Process • The school's strategic plan and vision (includes how strategic documents are set out and made accessible)	School-wide Practice • Culturally responsive practices • Disciplinary and restorative practices

• Management of the assessment calendar within high schools • Management of the scheduling and workload of individual teachers • School leadership system/ appointments • Staff appraisals/ reviews	• Adopting an over-arching wellbeing framework/model (evidence-based) • Organisation policies • Student policies • Student enrolment process/ forms • Staff onboarding/enrolment practices/ forms • Internal communications	• Autonomy-supportive, relationship-focused, strengths-focused and culturally responsive pedagogies • A shared language of wellbeing (and, more generally, the language used within the community) • Professional learning communities • Pastoral care and student support services
Staff • Staff professional learning and development • Staff coaching • Support staff (embracing wellbeing practices and competencies too) • Educator wellbeing practices (role modelling) • Opportunities for staff to share effective strategies and learnings with colleagues, students and wider community (e.g. through a staff wellbeing-focused book clubs)	**Students** • Student partnership and voice • Student learning conferences • Student coaching • Pastoral care and student support services	**Community** • Parent and community engagement (including student learning conferences) • External communications, (e.g. parent newsletters, school annuals)

(continued)

Table 4.1 (Continued)

Occasions	Teaching/Coaching	Environment
• Staff meetings • Chapel (some special charac-ter schools lead wellbeing and service learning from the school's chaplaincy) • Prize-giving and other award ceremonies • Assemblies • House meetings	• Quality of student-teacher interactions across all contexts • Sports coaching • Staff coaching • Student coaching • Parent coaching • Sports leadership • Extracurricular activities (music, drama etc.) • Tutor group meetings/check-ins	• Availability of a wellbeing resource library • Design and lay-out of the school • Classroom and school environ-ment (e.g. wall decorations and information featured)

Expert researcher insight 4.1: *Laura Allison, Catholic Education Western Australia. How teachers can create flourishing classrooms*

Laura Allison, leader of the psychology team at Catholic Education Western Australia, is focusing her work on helping schools understand wellbeing is a collective, not individual, phenomenon.

'Teachers are often passionate and motivated to do the best for the students in their care. Supporting student wellbeing is fundamental to their quality of life and foundational to their learning. The classroom is an important place for supporting student wellbeing. But how can teachers use that space well?

Flourishing is not about individual intervention (a phenomenon that sits within a student) but arises instead through an interconnected system (between and among every person in that system). Studies show the wellbeing of a student is influenced by the wellbeing of their classmates[8] and group flourishing occurs when a group as a collective, independently and interdependently feels good and functions well.[9]

Wellbeing is contagious

As parts of the systems influence one another, wellbeing is contagious, just like the common cold. We tend to be infected by each
other's happiness and laughter and by each other's pain and suffering. At the more extreme end of the continuum, teachers can become
vicariously traumatised by the trauma of the children in their care.

As the leader in the classroom, a teacher is disproportionately
infectious,[10] as all eyes are literally on them for most of the time.
Well-functioning teachers have the potential to create ripples of positive emotions within their classroom. Stressed teachers can create a
stress contagion in their classroom.[11] This means teachers can have a
greater influence on shaping group flourishing by looking after their
own wellbeing and flourishing themselves. If the teacher is languishing, however, efforts to conceal this and reduce contagion require significant emotional labour causing greater depletion for the teacher.

Cultivating Collective Flourishing

So how can teachers cultivate collective flourishing within their
classrooms? This can be achieved through influencing elements of
the system and targeting collective wellbeing. It asks teachers to look
at the wellbeing of their classroom as an inter-connected collective,
rather than as disparate individual students. For example, taking a
traditional individualised perspective, a teacher may consider if an
individual student has friends or reports feeling lonely. The student
might be encouraged to connect with other students, and an intervention might teach them a range of social skills. Relational skills
are an individual phenomenon of the student. In contrast, taking a
systems approach, the teacher might consider the norms and identity
of the class as a whole, monitor the emotional temperature in the
classroom, and target the ways students interact and connect with
one another. The relational skills are a collective phenomenon, which
each student contributes to, creating a whole that's separate from the
sum of the parts.[12]

Cultivating classroom flourishing arguably will promote more
widespread and faster paced flourishing than what could be
achieved by purely focusing on each individual student. Further, this

does not require a school leader to create such change, as a teacher can modify elements of their own classroom system as they choose. Importantly, in light of wellbeing being contagious, such changes potentially can have a broader impact on the school beyond the class-room, positively infecting the larger school system as a whole'. Laura's five tips for promoting flourishing classrooms:

1   Observe the class as an interconnected system, including your-self as the teacher.

2   Cultivate class identity to foster belonging – e.g. have the class create a 'team name'.

3   Reinforce and promote the collective strengths of the class – what is it that makes them unique as a class?

4   Set class climate expectations – how do students want to feel as a group while in your class?

5   Create class level wellbeing goals – have students work together toward a wellbeing outcome.

Expert researcher insight 4.2: *Dr Helen Street, University of Western Australia. Why context matters*

Contextual Wellbeing is an experience of belonging and positive engagement in life stemming from connection to a healthy social context. The Contextual Wellbeing model presents a systems-based approach to developing a thriving community through the devel-opment of healthy context. This approach supports the develop-ment of wellbeing for all members of an organisation in an organic, meaningful and sustainable way.

We are all pieces of the jigsaw of human existence, looking for our fit, our sense of place and purpose within the bigger picture of our reality. When we experience meaningful connection to a healthy social context, we become centred, calm and resilient. When we find connection, we find ourselves and become well beings.

Figure 4.1 shows the four domains of context defined by the Contextual Wellbeing framework. Note that this separation of

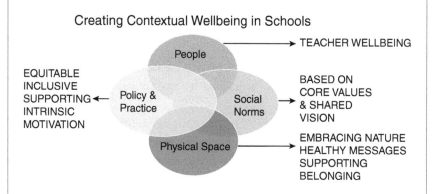

Figure 4.1 The Contextual Wellbeing framework

context into four domains is somewhat artificial – in reality, all aspects of context are interrelated as one. However, the separation can be useful for the purposes of change, development and greater understanding when taking a whole-school approach to building wellbeing. NB: Notes attached to each domain suggest an ideal focus for that domain in terms of creating a healthy context.

Box 4.1: Helping teachers and students win the battle against boredom (TBAB)

Statistics suggest that one in four students' learning is threatened by boredom. Healthy boredom is a signal to explore and find something good to do. Unhealthy or long-term boredom occurs when there is no opportunity to take action to end the boredom. Danish-based Strengths Academy educators and researchers Holmgren, Ledertoug, Paarup and Tidmand share their tips for battling boredom in the classroom (information on their book and podcast is at the end of this chapter):

- Use Seligman's PERMA wellbeing model for developing and designing lesson plans, but also during the lesson.

(continued)

- Check in on the PERMA levels of the class and make adjustments during the lesson by asking:

  - How can you bring more **positive emotion** into your lesson? (Include curiosity, amusement, awe/inspiration and pride, among others.)
  - How can you support student **engagement**?
  - How does your teaching support **relationships**?
  - How can your content be made **meaningful** and relevant to students?
  - How can you help students feel a sense of **accomplishment**?

- Students need to know the *why* of their learning; ask:

  - What is the purpose of going to school?
  - Which aspects of school make most sense to you?
  - Does this discussion put you in a good or bad mood?

- Challenge students to make a creative product (e.g. a poster) to illustrate boredom and another to illustrate engagement. The discussions to decide what goes in the product are likely to be illuminating for any teacher.
- Keep a boredom thermometer in your class for a week and record teacher and student scores on anonymous Post-its. The class can discuss the overall result, what it means and what they would like to do about it.

Case study 4.1:   Rolleston College uses 'Check and Connect' to build connection

Rolleston College teachers Rachel Skelton, Sophie Ralph, Kelly Tippett and Sarah Forward believe everyone benefits from a connection, a champion, a motivator and a *kete* (basket) of wellbeing tools, helping them be *'ready to learn and ready to flourish'*.

'Check and Connect' is an umbrella phrase they created to refer to a suite of activities for the benefit of both staff and learners – enabling a relationship-based approach and designed to act as the fence at the top of the cliff, rather than the ambulance at the bottom. It lives within the curriculum and culture of the school across all areas and is described by them here.

'Using a variety of approaches, from individual to large group, digital to cards and practically applying wellbeing models, character strengths and mindfulness, Check and Connect takes many different forms depending on the size of the group and the context, always ensuring the learner is at the centre'. (See Figure 4.2.)

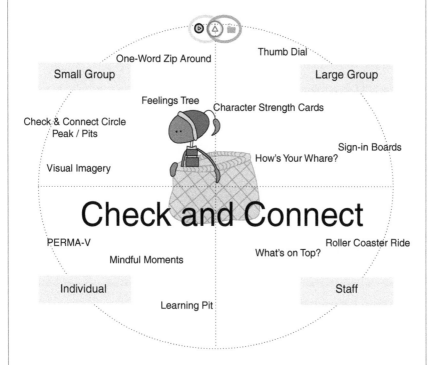

Figure 4.2 Check and Connect options for different group sizes

Some practical Check and Connect Activities we use in all areas of our school include:

- **Peaks and pits:** Decide on the time period for the reflection (e.g. the weekend, the holidays, the week, the term). Learners tell the group what their best part of that time period was (peaks) and what the most challenging part was (pits).
- **Character strength cards:** This activity requires a set of cards with each of the 24 character strengths on them. Lay the cards

out in the centre of the C&C circle. Get the learners to pick a card each. Learners then have to say how they might use this character strength in their week.

- **Values exploration:** Have a values poster available to refer to. Pick one of the values. Ask the learners to describe how they might use it this week, term etc.
- **Critical skills:** Have a copy of the critical skills tree printed for this activity. Learners pick a critical skill and describe how they will use it this week in their learning.
- **Playing cards:** This activity requires a set of playing cards. Hand the cards out at random. Based on the cards, learners need to share one of the following:

  - Hearts: Something they are grateful for;
  - Diamonds: Something special that happened;
  - Spades: Something they learnt about that they want to "go deeper" on; and
  - Clubs: Something they found challenging.

- **Sentence starters:** This activity requires a set of sentence starter cards. Either hand these out randomly or place them in the centre of the circle and allow learners to pick their own. Learners then have to complete the sentence.'

Box 4.2: Vertical form classes/mentor groups: A tool for connection and belonging?

Vertically organised mentor groups place students from different year levels in the same group in order to facilitate learning, role modelling and connection between students across the school. While some schools have adopted this approach with positive results, other schools have moved away to embrace other approaches.

Shirley Boys' High School in Christchurch, NZ, has operated a vertical form class system since the late 1990s. Pete Beswick, assistant dean, explains the benefits and shares insights from students and teachers:

'For teachers, instead of getting one, often streamed, class of year 9s, which could be predominantly well behaved, or predominantly misbehaving, each form teacher gets a range of students, which they form relationships with over the course of 5 years. This is also beneficial for parents, who get to know their teenager's form teacher over the same amount of time, which increases trust and easy communication.

Benefits for the students include being able to forge relationships with fellow students outside their year group, embedding the Māori philosophy of Tuakana Teina (older helping younger, or those with knowledge helping those without) where senior students tell younger about various subjects, study help or mentoring etc. It also allows more freedom for the development of character and relationships as numbers are kept relatively small when compared to teaching classes (our form classes would average 20 students). It's about the ability to form positive relationships, which grows social capital for the students, and the school'.

Comments from students:

'Older students able to motivate younger, get to know them and help the year 9s feel safe. Can offer advice to the younger students'. – James, year 12

'Shows the juniors that the seniors aren't as intimidating as they look, that they are approachable. Can start a chain reaction positive relationship between juniors and seniors'. – Ezra, year 12

'Before high school you don't know what it will be like, but in form time you get discussions with seniors and feel more confident. Make lots of new friends'. – Felix, year 9

'Seeing seniors wearing blazers and badges, they are good role models. You feel more confident talking to seniors because they are in your class'. – Liam, year 9

'You see new students coming in each year and can teach them as they come through. The form teacher has a better understanding of student relationships from year 9 to 13'. – Reuben, year 11

'Seniors can give you more advice, like for exams or homework. Support if you are feeling a bit down. Good way to branch out into different year groups in the school. You can approach them if you are having trouble making friends'. – Connor, year 10

(continued)

Comments from staff:

'Chance for positive role modelling. Student to student account-ability (behaviour/reports etc.). Support for teachers from seniors. Smaller number of reports to write. Course selection easier to com-plete'. – Merryn, 10 years teaching, assistant dean

'I love vertical form classes. The big plus in the early days was the older students helping with the younger, helping with orientation etc. Mixing of the year levels, less likely for the habitual bullying of younger students by older. I've had a couple of instances of senior students in the form class protecting younger ones when trouble is brewing around the grounds. Senior boys would role model the responsibilities of bringing notes etc. and younger students would notice this. Seniors would also become less tolerant of immaturity, juniors would learn the right things to do'. – Steve, 40 years teaching

'Relationships between all the year levels. It gives students a break from their own year levels. Because of the nature of some of our activities, it almost forces them into relationships, and get support from others. Someone close to look up to, not just someone up on stage'. – Anna, 1 year teaching

Box 4.3: Toward an inclusive school environment for LGBQTI students

Adele Carran is a mentor for young people in Auckland. Prior to a corporate career in learning and development, she was a primary and secondary school teacher in NZ and the UK.

'Many of our LGBTQI students are coping with discovering their gender identity and need our support at this crucial life stage. We want to ensure that LGBQTI students' wellbeing is cultivated as they enter a high risk time in their life for their mental health.

The Stonewall organisation in the UK defines gender identity as "a person's internal sense of their own gender, whether male, female or something else".[13] This organisation collaborated with the Cen-tre for Family Research at the University of Cambridge in 2017 to research LGBTQI pupil experiences at school. Over 3,700 lesbian, gay, bi-sexual and transgender students in schools throughout the UK were surveyed on their experiences at school.

The research confirmed the wellbeing of LGBTQI pupils is at risk, through bullying, verbal abuse, social isolation, lack of school support, harassment, self-harm and attempted suicide. Key findings from the study relating to wellbeing and mental health include:

- 40% of students who have been bullied for being LGBTQI have been truant from school because of being bullied;
- 52% of respondents feel the homophobic, biphobic and transphobic bullying has been detrimental to their plans for future education;
- 84% of the pupils have self-harmed;
- 45% of had attempted suicide; and
- Trans young people were at an increased risk of self-harming (23%) and suicide (23%).

Schools can do much to reverse these findings by supporting young people at this critical time in their lives. The Ministry of Education's Te Kete Ipurangi[14] identifies four strategies to make school environments more inclusive, safe and supportive for LGBQTI students:

1   Educate students about sexual diversity through knowledge building of sex, gender and gender diversity inclusion.

2   Create school-wide systems and processes that promote and develop inclusion for all sexes, genders and gender diverse students.

3   Tackle any immediate needs within the school community pertaining to environmental, physical and social needs.

4   Adapt classroom curricula so they are inclusive.

The Victorian State Government in Australia has also created useful resources on simple ways to create safe schools for LGBTQI pupils.[15]

As educators, we are all aware of the importance of students feeling safe before they are able to learn. At secondary school, when students are coping with gender identity at the same time as career decision-making, we need to consider that gender identity needs to take precedence. At this point of transition in their education, when

(continued)

these students are moving from a growth stage to an exploration stage in their career development, they are statistically at risk.

Adapting our schools so they are inclusive to LGBQTI students is about respecting each individual pupil and valuing them for <u>who</u> they are. By supporting LGBQTI students through this challenging time in their lives, we can hope to reduce bullying, social isolation, harassment, self-harm and prevent suicides for these students; and enlighten all of our pupils of the importance of creating a diverse and healthy community'.

Reflection questions

- What areas of the school processes or practices nurture and support your wellbeing?
- What areas of the school processes or practices do you think nurture and support student wellbeing?
- How will you learn more about the effect of existing school practices and processes on wellbeing?
- What small changes to process or practice would most enhance wellbeing?
- Can you list the places where wellbeing is 'caught' in your school?
- How many people are actively involved in supporting school wellbeing?
- What strategies or frameworks do teachers in your school use to monitor student wellbeing and engagement?

The following are some useful questions from Helen Street for schools to ask when considering Contextual Wellbeing. Embedded in an appreciative inquiry approach to change and development, they focus on bringing out the best in a school community and enhancing what works well. Focusing on the positive does not negate issues or barriers, but rather engenders engagement, enthusiasm and a sense of hope within all those involved in the organisation.

- What works well in your school to support students' wellbeing, engagement and motivation?
- Can you describe a time when you felt that the students in your care were engaged in learning/intrinsically motivated and/or happy to be in school/class?
- What about this time made it work well?

- What would need to change at school to mean that experiences like this were the norm?
- What does a thriving school community look like to you?

Notes

1 White, M. A. (2016). Why won't it stick? Positive psychology and positive education. *Psychology of Well-Being, 6*(1), 2.

2 Meadows, D. (2008). *Thinking in systems: A primer* (D. Wright, ed.). Hartford, VT: Chelsea Green Publishing.

3 Kristjánsson, K. (2010). Positive psychology, happiness, and virtue: The troublesome conceptual issues. *Review of General Psychology, 14*(4), 296.

4 Kristjánsson, K. (2012). Positive psychology and positive education: Old wine in new bottles? *Educational Psychologist, 47*(2), 86–105.

5 Allison, L., Waters, L., & Kern, M. L. (in press). *Flourishing classrooms: Applying a systems-informed approach to positive education.*

6 Allison, L., Waters, L., & Kern, M. L. (in press). *Flourishing classrooms: Applying a systems-informed approach to positive education.*

7 King, R. B., & Datu, J. A. (2017, September). Happy classes make happy students: Classmates' well-being predicts individual student well-being. *Journal of School Psychology, 65*(2015), 116–128.

8 King, R. B., & Datu, J. A. (2017, September). Happy classes make happy students: Classmates' well-being predicts individual student well-being. *Journal of School Psychology, 65*(2015), 116–128. https://doi.org/10.1016/j.jsp.2017.07.004

9 Allison, L., Waters, L., & Kern, M. L. (in press). *Flourishing classrooms: Applying a systems-informed approach to positive education.*

10 Barsade, S. G., & Knight, A. P. (2015). Group affect. *The Annual Review of Organizational Psychology and Organization Behavior, 2*, 21–46. https://doi.org/10.1146/annurev-orgpsych-032414-111316

11 Oberle, E., & Schonert-Reichl, K. A. (2016). Stress contagion in the classroom? The link between classroom teacher burnout and morning cortisol in elementary school students. *Social Science and Medicine, 159*, 30–37. https://doi.org/10.1016/j.socscimed.2016.04.031

12 Kern, M. L., Williams, P., Spong, C., Colla, R., Sharma, K., Downie, A., . . . Oades, L. G. (2019). Systems informed positive psychology. *The*

Journal of Positive Psychology. https://doi.org/https://doi.org/10.108
0/17439760.2019.1639799

13   Stonewall Organisation, United Kingdom. (2017). *School report 2017.*
Retrieved from www.stonewall.org.uk/system/files/the_school_report_
2017.pdf

14   Ministry of Education. New Zealand. (n.d.). *Guide to support LGBQ-
TIA+ Students.* Retrieved from www.inclusive.tki.org.nz/guides/
supporting-lgbtiqa-students/

15   Victoria State Government, Education & Training, Australia. (n.d.).
*Safe schools: Guide to make your school safe and inclusive for LGBTI stu-
dents.* Retrieved from www.education.vic.gov.au

Watch

Freedom is Bionic Arms. An inspiring video showing how wellbeing
is built in all aspects of life, retrieved from: www.youtube.com/
watch?v=g2sSLKlDFGM

Youth Advisory Group for the Minister for Education, New Zealand – Keen
Beans. www.youtube.com/watch?v=q9z3gqXtcv0

Read

Daily Good article on one teacher's approach to combat social isolation and
build connection in her young students as a long-term defence against
disaffected teen violence in US schools. Retrieved from www.dailygood.
org/2018/09/26/one-teacher-s-brilliant-response-to-columbine/

Erasmus, C. (2019). *The mental health & wellbeing handbook for schools: Transforming mental health support on a budget.* Jessica Kingsley Publishers.

Holmgren, N., Ledertough, M. M., Paarup, N., & Tidmand, L. (2018). *The
battle against boredom.* Denmark: Strengths Academy. This book offers
a framework or lens for teachers to consider how they can engage students in any area of learning.

Norrish, J. M., & Seligman, M. E. (2015). *Positive education: The Geelong
grammar school journey.* Oxford Positive Psychology Series.

Roffey, S. (2019). *The primary behaviour cookbook.* Routledge.

Roffey, S. (2019). *The secondary behaviour cookbook*. Routledge.

Teachers will pick up these books for the one- to two-page strategies to deal with specific issues they encounter, but they will stay for the long-term guidance on building effective classroom relationships and behaviour management.

Listen

NZIWR podcasts are available from https://nziwr.co.nz/category/podcast/

NZIWR podcast: Sonya Papps (Taipei European School).

NZIWR podcast: David Kolpak (St Peter's School).

NZIWR podcast: Sue Roffey (relationships and behaviour in schools).

NZIWR podcast: Clive Leach (whole-school wellbeing).

Understanding change dynamics

Introduction

Designing, implementing and embedding a whole-school approach to well-being promotion must be considered as a major, long-term change management project. Far from being linear and predictable, change within education can be messy and organic, often feels disorganised, can prompt growth in unexpected areas and even produce unintentional and unanticipated consequences. Early attempts at wellbeing change in schools were frequently stymied by a focus on content (interventions and curriculum) and a lack of attention to process, meaning that change was sometimes superficial and superseded by the next latest thing.

Leading wellbeing promotion is an ongoing process requiring school leaders to work effectively with different stakeholders and through different periods of change. This chapter outlines wisdom regarding the overall process of leading change. Other chapters address particular aspects of change management that will become more important as your school's wellbeing work unfolds. Chapter 6, on building ownership, focuses on practices that build support in the early stages. Chapter 9, on the sandpit phase, identifies the challenges schools face as they start to implement wellbeing and strategies to make success more likely. A number of chapters address working with different groups: Chapter 10 on building an effective wellbeing team, Chapter 13 on working with students and Chapter 14 on engaging parents and the wider community.

What the research says

Bringing about whole-organisation change is tough – taking a whole-school approach to wellbeing directly impacts all stakeholders and can threaten an organisation's underlying values, often causing resistance. In fact, research suggests 74% of private sector and 80% of public sector transformation efforts fail.[1] Those of us working in whole-school wellbeing change can draw on the experience and expertise developed in fields such as Organisational Behaviour,[23] Organisation Development,[45] Positive Organisation Scholarship[67] and Restorative Practice.[8] These disciplines have long recognised the need for a process approach to address the whole system and offer important lessons for change agents in education. As an example of a whole-school change approach, see Thorsborne and Blood's book on the process of implementing restorative practice in a school.[9]

The NZIWR wellbeing change wheel

We created our wellbeing change wheel (see Figure 5.1) as a reminder that the change process is cyclical and ongoing – you can expect to go through several iterations of this process while embedding wellbeing in your school. With a commitment to continuous learning and improvement, this process becomes an integral part of how we work:

Figure 5.1 The NZIWR process of Building Whole-school Wellbeing

Phase 1: Identify the opportunity

All schools are different. What's going on in your school?

- What type of wellbeing change is required?
- What are the unique circumstances in your school?
- What opportunities have opened up, or can you foresee opening up, in the immediate future paving the way for change?
- Why is the change needed? Look from different perspectives:

  - Staff (both teaching and non-teaching);
  - Students;
  - Parents and *whānau*;
  - Board members/governors;
  - Wider community; and
  - Former students.

- What conferences, reading, training or professional learning groups do you (or others) need to attend to grasp what change is needed and what opportunities are out there to help?

Phase 2: Assess readiness

Meeting with a broad array of your school's stakeholders will help assess readiness for change and provide vital insights about strengths, opportunities, threats and the personalities involved, which helps identify potential stumbling blocks or resistance to change.

- Who can see this change is required?
- Who has not seen this coming and will require more explanation and support?
- Is your school's governance, leadership and management aligned with a vision for whole-school wellbeing?
- Who holds the power in your school community?

  - Which individuals and groups?
  - Thinking of each of these in turn, what three concrete steps will help strengthen your relationships with them, paving the way for change?
  - Which of the reasons for taking wellbeing seriously (covered on page 95) are most likely to appeal to them and shift their thinking?

Phase 3: Gather information on the current state of play

Conducting a wellbeing audit and wellbeing inquiry are two actions we encourage schools to take (see Chapter 6, pages 98–102). Conducting an audit and inquiry will identify and value all the things you already do in your school to promote wellbeing. This is a simple and fast way of building ownership among various stakeholders. We also encourage schools to undertake some benchmarking or measurement to clarify their starting point and enable them to track progress (see Chapter 8).

- Who might you involve in a wellbeing audit and wellbeing inquiry from beyond school staff to broaden your perspective of what's going well and gaps requiring your attention?
- What skills and strengths in your school's current wellbeing practices can be built upon or shared more broadly (perhaps spreading the initiatives from one department to another or one area of the school to another)?
- What initial assessments, focus groups and measurements do you need to undertake to identify priorities for change and evaluate the effectiveness of your changes?
- How will you know whether what you are doing is working?

Phase 4: Build ownership

Securing buy-in from your school's different stakeholders is a vital step. Give people time to absorb the reality of the situation and seek their insights about the opportunities to improve. Advance warning helps staff and teachers accept proposed changes.[10] There is no magic recipe to build buy-in, but time, transparency and honest communication all help.

- Which events and meetings do the key wellbeing change leaders really need to attend? Showing your face around school, at relevant meetings and at community evenings helps.
- Who will be good at communicating your vision in a compelling and clear way?
- How can you paint a vivid picture of future reality?
- If communication is not your strength, which of your wellbeing change leaders could take on this role and enjoy doing it well?
- Who are your key influencers? These are the people whose support for wellbeing change will bring others with them over time.

Phase 5: Identify priorities and plan action

Wellbeing change takes time – it's a marathon, not a sprint. It can also be overwhelming for wellbeing change leaders and all staff to have a huge number of wellbeing priorities and actions pushed on them. Identify three priorities important to your community and any actions to give you some quick wins. Making everything equally important is a recipe for overwhelm; in contrast, early quick wins persuade the community you mean business.

- What are your three key priorities?
- How/where will you begin?
- What might be your quick wins?
- Have you got a stepped plan?

Phase 6: Share responsibility – build a team

Organisational change is more likely to be sustained and meaningful when there is broad buy-in and distributed leadership, backed by support from the top. Leading change is hard work, and if one individual is left to carry all the risk, they can become isolated and stifle innovation. Sharing the risk across a broader group brings in a greater range of ideas, shares risk, and encourages innovation. It also reduces the risk of leadership burnout. Similarly, having diverse stakeholders leading change from the outset can reduce resistance and support greater buy-in.[11] Stakeholders will share relevant and useful ideas that leadership are not in a position to know about. Including additional people in leadership positions means the results will likely differ from the preconceived plan,[12] and that's okay. That's what change management is about!

- Who has a passion for this work?
- Who has skills and influence that are important to harness?
- How can you support each other along the way?
- How will you help your staff feel empowered to get involved in the well-being programme and use some of the new skills they're learning?
- How will you empower parents and the wider community to get involved?
- How can you partner with students so they participate fully?

Phase 7: The sandpit: Allowing space for trial and error

The sandpit has four different components we think are important: creating opportunities to share what people are brave enough to try, embracing and learning from failure, celebrating small wins and ensuring stakeholders can provide feedback. It is hard to overstate the importance of this phase. It represents a commitment to learning and an acknowledgement that learning involves the three Fs (failure, frustrations and feedback). The ability to give and receive feedback is an important skill for fostering an environment for growth and learning.[13] For feedback loops to work, an organisation must maintain a culture of continuous improvement, in which all stakeholders feel comfortable sharing – even when their feedback is not positive.[14]

If we are not prepared to enter the 'learning pit' ourselves, then we are denying the reality of learning for our students. Providing ample opportunities for staff to learn and practice wellbeing strategies before being asked to share them with students is something that is frequently overlooked and critical. It is critical for building their self-efficacy.

- How will you let people know in advance you are entering the sandpit phase?
- What support might they need?
- How can you support all community members to embrace mistakes and learning so wellbeing change becomes an opportunity to embed a growth mindset in your school?
- Where, when and how can you provide additional opportunities for all stakeholders to share their experiences? (You will need more than a monthly staff meeting!)
- How will you capture the learning generated from what doesn't work in your wellbeing implementation?
- How will you celebrate the wins?
- How can you provide opportunities for stakeholder feedback?
- What can you do to develop a culture in which people are comfortable sharing feedback?
- How will you learn from each activity you undertake?
- How will you apply that learning so you keep improving?

Phase 8: Monitor (and report on) progress

There are multiple ways to measure progress on wellbeing change projects (see Chapter 8). Schools already collect a huge volume of information, including staff and student absences, student stand downs/suspensions and awards, and some are even starting to offer 'merit' points.

- What information do you already collect on engagement and wellbeing in your school?
- What do you know about the wellbeing of (teaching and support) staff?
- What do you know about the wellbeing of students?
- How do the school policies and practices affect wellbeing for the school community?
- What are your informal/anecdotal sources of information about wellbeing in your school?
- What are the best measurements and opportunities for assessing your school's particular wellbeing priorities?
- How can you gather information most easily and creatively from your school community?

Phase 9: Celebrate success and share broadly

To sustain energy and commitment for change and embed new practices, we need to celebrate our successes – even the small ones. Moir's study of effective leadership in education[15] identified the importance of modelling and genuine recognition. One participant commented on the importance of recognising the efforts and contribution of staff, just as much as students: 'There's a lot of teachers in the school who probably feel that they're not recognised as well as they should be, for things that they do on a daily basis. We're very good at celebrating stuff that the students do – I think there could be more staff members on there'. Taking time to notice, celebrate and share what's going well across the various levels of your school is vital and will provide opportunities for different departments and stakeholders to learn divergent approaches, fast-tracking successful implementation.

Equally effective is harnessing the learning that comes from sharing in communities of practice (COPs), through professional learning groups and at conferences. Clusters of schools in Australia and New Zealand have been working on wellbeing together for some time. As well as sharing professional learning, which is cost effective, some of the benefits they value most are the shared creativity, support and learning. We have seen schools create their own wellbeing COPs and professional learning groups.

- What wellbeing changes have you seen in one department/area that could be most easily rolled out across the *whole* school or a different area?
- What processes will you use to share learning and success between departments?
    - What current opportunities do you have for sharing?
    - What new opportunities do you need to introduce?
    - How will you celebrate and share successes with the whole school?
    - What methods of sharing might make different stakeholders feel proud? (Consider media, conferences, presenting in staff meetings or at COPs, sharing with parents).
- How can you network with other schools to share implementation actions and learning about wellbeing change?
- Which schools and broader groups could you create a COP with?

Phase 10: Reflect, review, reiterate

This involves updating school policies and documentation and considering the barriers and enablers to implementation and embedding. Regular review of policies and documents ensures wellbeing remains prioritised, brings new-comers up to speed with team standards and reminds others of them. Involve diverse staff in agreeing and writing the documents and standards they aspire and agree to meet. As well as building ownership, this will help embed change and ensure wellbeing continues to be prioritised.

Consider barriers and enablers at individual, team and systems levels. For wellbeing change to be successful, it needs to bring all stakeholders and all systems on board. As well as considering the groups of people who may be finding it challenging to participate, we need to consider the systems supporting or discouraging participation.

- How do your school policies reflect your wellbeing goals? For example, how do the school assessment and discipline policies support wellbeing?
- Are your school's wellbeing vision, mission, objectives and measurable goals aligned?
- Do key stakeholders' visions and objectives align?
- Which teams and groups might benefit from creating a mutually agreed team essentials (MATES) agreement?
- Which groups, teams or individuals may find it difficult to participate in school wellbeing discussions?
- How could you or others support these people to participate?
- How will you find out if your systems and processes are discouraging participation by any of your stakeholders?

Putting it into practice

Schools have embraced the concept of whole-school wellbeing change and are getting to grips with how to contextualise and implement long-term change. This is a lot of information to take on board and expertise to develop in a school. Hence, it's all the more valuable to be able to learn from other schools, practitioners, and communities of practice that have been doing this work for some time. With this in mind, the rest of this chapter is dedicated to case studies and insights from practitioners whose change management experience and process we respect.

Short and sharp change-management tips

These are tips that change leaders in education and elsewhere have valued and shared with us. Where possible, we have cited the original source of the material.

The 20–60–20 rule of change management

The 20–60–20 principle says that, when faced with a new challenge, change or opportunity, 20% of the group will react positively to the change and welcome it, 60% of the group will be uncertain (not overly positive or averse) and 20% will be against change and react negatively. Don't get derailed by the 20% naysayers, and don't spend all your time preaching to the 20% already converted; instead, focus your energy on supporting the majority to see the benefits and work to address their concerns.

Every school will have wellbeing cynics. Part of the change process includes embracing these people (listening and responding to their concerns) but not being derailed by them. (For more information, watch: the three-carriage train video.)[16]

Address predictable stages of concern

When facing change, people frequently cycle through predictable stages identified by Zagarmi and Hoekstra.[17] Addressing these will reduce anxiety and friction.

- Information – staff need to know what's going to happen and why it's needed;
- Personal – knowing what it will mean for me;
- Implementation – what will actually happen; when and how will I do it?
- Impact – will the effort be worth it?
- Collaboration – who can I share with to make it work?
- Refinement – what tweaks would improve this?

Get on the balcony: Keep your head above the action

Get on the balcony and off the dance floor. Many wellbeing change leaders find themselves immersed in doing – and trying to do – too much at once. They need to be strategic, with a clear vision of the overall goal; to be flexible on how to get there; and to check in with the school climate to assess support, fatigue or resistance.[18]

Celebrate small gains: Appreciate the progress

Managing the workload, pacing the change, acknowledging setbacks and celebrating/sharing successes along the way are all part of the wellbeing change leader's role. Organisational research shows that the leadership activity most valued by staff is when leaders check in and celebrate small gains with them.[19]

Respect people, their work and their concerns

Address the predictable stages of concern; these can often be addressed from the outset by involving and listening to all stakeholders, respecting existing work and providing genuine opportunities to contribute to the wellbeing vision of the school.[20]

Honour the process and the people

Acknowledge this is an important piece of work and put aside the resources and time to support it properly, particularly resources for professional development for staff leading this work.[21]

Box 5.1: What gets in the way of successful wellbeing change?

- Where the leadership team is in conflict and doesn't agree on the importance of working on wellbeing.
- Where school governance doesn't prioritise wellbeing; wellbeing needs the support of school governance as well as the school leadership.
- Cynicism gets in the way of learning and adopting change. Sometimes the language of wellbeing has been hard for some staff to embrace. This is less significant now as the evidence base has grown. Work hard to find palatable language for your school. Draw attention back to the goal in mind – the importance of protecting young people's mental health – and urge them not to let disagreements about language derail the process. (Also see predictable stages of concern listed earlier.)
- Negative staff members who make it harder for the work to progress. Engagement with resistant staff 'eyeball to eyeball' can result in some interesting turnarounds where a critic becomes a champion for wellbeing change.
- Turnover of good people who have the energy for wellbeing change and may have been leading the wellbeing work; although their departure is a loss, the good news is that they take their learning with them and typically do good wellbeing work in their new schools. Strategically, schools need to ensure that good practice is shared widely, that people are working collaboratively and that there is widespread opportunity to be involved in wellbeing work so a change in staff does not interrupt wellbeing change.

Expert Practitioner Insight 5.1: *Clive Leach. Strategies for successful wellbeing change*

Clive Leach has worked with schools around the world for the past decade to support wellbeing. As well as being an experienced executive coach and facilitator, Clive is a former teacher and youth worker with over two decades' experience in inner-city schools in the UK.

Here are Clive's strategies for successful wellbeing change in schools:

- **Start with buy-in:** from the people who are leading the school. That means engaging with school leaders about their own wellbeing first and to define what wellbeing means for them, their families and their communities.
- **Gain a common understanding of wellbeing:** Have a faculty-wide or whole-school event to discuss what wellbeing means. Help people unpack the multidimensional nature of wellbeing.
- **Find the wellbeing champions:** Harness the energy of the positive deviants (those who are wildly keen to work on wellbeing in the school).
- **Help people understand what it means to flourish:** Share the evidence base that shows we can build wellbeing and explain the benefits of constructs like resilience and mental toughness.
- **Introduce wellbeing models and practices:** Give people practical strategies and interventions that they can use to build their wellbeing. People need an opportunity to try these things out in their own lives.
- **Notice what's working:** Show people how what they are already doing fits within a wellbeing framework.
- **Harness the energy of a school community:** whether from parents, teachers, students or leaders. Make sure the leadership enables the positive deviants to act rather than squashing them.
- **Have strategy, but let people run with a good idea:** There will be good learning from these ideas whether they work or not. Let people go ahead and try out the ideas they are very enthusiastic about.
- **Allow the process to be emergent:** Certain practices and models take on a life of their own. Make use of it and encourage people to implement new practices.

- **Remember that this is about wellbeing:** Of course, we want to alleviate anxiety, depression, suicidal ideation and self-harm, and we need to remember that our big-picture goal is to improve flourishing for all.
- **Take time to reflect during the experimentation phase:** Remember that it's all learning. The key questions as a coach are 'What have you tried? What worked? How would you continue to get more of what worked? What have you learned? What would you do differently?'
- **Remember what we tell the students:** Adopt a growth mind-set and focus on the learning during the trial-and-error stage. Leadership is important – leaders can enable and encourage people to take a risk and try something new.

Box 5.2: Ten tips for leading change (Source: Grow Waitaha, 2017)

These ten tips for leading change emerged out of the work Grow Waitaha did in the Canterbury region in the years after the Christchurch earthquakes. The devestation caused by the quakes presented a significant opportunity for educational renewal in the region, spawning an unprecedented and totally unique cross-sector collaboration under the name of Grow Waitaha. For more about this group's approach to community change, see the case study in Chapter 14 on community. Figure 5.2 shows the group's ten tips for leading change, which combine insights gleaned from interviews with 17 school leaders (mainly principals) and research from change-management literature. They are reproduced here with permission from Ben Rosenfield, Dr Gabrielle Wall and Dr Chris Jansen.[22]

1 **Develop and share the vision for change:** Ensure the 'what', 'how' and, most importantly, 'why' for the change are universally understood.	6 **Prototype and allow space for failures:** Experimentation allows for validation and improvement of new approaches and builds a culture of innovation and ownership.

(continued)

2	**Foster a sense of urgency:** Necessity ignites people to acceptance and action.	7	**Encourage broader collaboration, including interschool:** Collaboration helps stakeholders frame the change initiative in the larger context and allows for innovation while reducing redundancy and reinvention.
3	**Broaden the circle of leadership:** Empowering more individuals reduces the burden on senior leadership and deepens buy-in and accountability across stakeholders.		
4	**Prioritise buy-in throughout the change process:** Ongoing dialogue with stakeholders (students, teachers, parents and community) builds ownership and ensures a wide range of innovative ideas are considered. It also reduces friction during implementation and sets a solid foundation for sustaining the change.	8	**Maintain an active model:** Consciously apply a model of continuous improvement that will keep people invested in the change, discourage complacency and allow for sustained change.
		9	**Measure the change:** Use data and evidence to monitor change outcomes. When data are positive, it will increase buy-in and build momentum, and when negative, it will allow for understanding and improvement.
5	**Be flexible and know your plan will (and should) change:** Rigidity and deterministic planning are inefficient uses of time and impair the effectiveness of leadership.	10	**Entrench changes within culture:** By anchoring values of community, ownership and improvement within school culture, staff become more invested in the success and maintenance of the change.

Figure 5.2 Grow Waitaha's ten tips for leading change

Case study 5.1:   Wellbeing for the 21st Century, Knox Grammar

Over the past decade, Knox Grammar School, a boys' school in Sydney, educating 2,400 day and boarding students from kindergarten to year 12, has based its whole-school approach to wellbeing on positive psychology and organisational change research. Dr Paula Robinson has kindly shared the process.

Knox's positive education journey began in 2009, when the school went through a process of self-reflection and decided its pastoral care programme was not fit for 21st century purposes.[23] After an extensive search of pastoral care models led by then- headmaster John Weeks, positive psychology was selected as an evidence-based framework to underpin a four-year strategic wellbeing plan that would reach all aspects of school life.

In early 2010, Knox began the process of understanding what positive psychology is and how it might benefit students, staff and the wider school community. They engaged Paula Robinson and the Positive Psychology Institute to help them create a culture that:

1   Is underpinned by the Knox values;

2   Is aligned with and supports the Knox mission and vision;

3   Increases/supports student academic performance;

4   Increases student and staff mental fitness (decreases student and staff psychological distress and mental illness);

5   Enhances wellbeing of students, staff and the school community;

6   Assists students, staff and the whole school to live 'the purposeful life';

7   Creates a positive school culture and climate at Knox Grammar, enriching and enabling positive relationships at all levels within the school community (teacher-to-teacher, teacher-to-student, student-to-student, mentor-to-parent);

8   Utilises coaching to create opportunities for solution-focused and strengths-based conversations providing committed and caring feedback for personal and professional growth; and

9   Encourages Knox staff and students to learn, embed and live the principles of positive education.

A 'measurement matrix' was created in conjunction with the University of Wollongong with a research timeline starting in October 2010 (baseline measures) and continuing each year. Knox used appreciative inquiry to decide the key features of its programme, investing in one-on-one appreciative inquiry interviews with all staff. Appreciative inquiry was specifically adopted as a process to commence the process of positive change (with interviews conducted in qualitative and quantitative formats with staff and online data collected from students and parents). Based on the results, strategic implementation of a multi-level programme was created, following four phases:[24]

Phase 1: Initial planning (2010): Positive education program team established and attended professional learning; appreciative inquiry interviews conducted with 70 representative staff to identify wellbeing opportunities and needs; parents and students surveyed.

Phase 2: Implementation using feedback from phase 1 (2011): Professional learning for all staff; mentor as coach programme established; timetable changes to incorporate new mentor system; PosEd induction for new staff; expansion of mental fitness initiatives into boarding and sport.

Phase 3: Setting up formal mentor groups (2012): Timetable changes provided more time for mentoring; different and developmentally appropriate themes designed for mentors across different year groups; formal wellbeing teams established.

Phase 4: Embedding Knox Total Fitness brand across the school (2013): Further 'master class' professional learning provided; Total Fitness rolled out across the school; new staff inducted in Total Fitness.

At the start of 2012, the new mentor as coach programme commenced with over 200 staff trained in the foundations of PosEd and mental fitness. This programme became the major focus over the next two years, designed to improve mentor-student relationships and embed strengths-based and solution-focused language into school policies and practices. The mentor relationship has been central to Knox's positive education journey: Every student has an individual mentor who has received expert training in positive psychology; the mentor helps students identify their strengths and set academic and personal goals; all staff, including sports coaches, receive expert training in positive psychology; positive psychology is implemented into all aspects of school life, for example, in the classroom and in sport, the boarding house, music, drama, debating and cadets. The mentors stay with the same students throughout their schooling at Knox, overseeing the overall wellbeing and mental fitness of each student in their care. This structure allows parents to form meaningful, long-term relationships with their sons' mentors, their key contacts at the school. A team of school psychologists also provide expert support and care to students who have this need.

More recent wellbeing initiatives at Knox include: updating of the design and delivery of the one-day positive education induction programme for new staff; presentations at leading positive psychology conferences worldwide; publication of numerous conference papers, articles and interviews; initiating further links with industry experts, e.g. Professor Michael Bernard; forming a partnership with Macquarie University to assess, design and deliver a PhD on staff wellbeing to inform best-practice recruitment, retention and promotion; the successful design and delivery of the Practising Positive Education Conference; delivering training for the wider education community and, in 2019, the delivery of Appli's new Certificate in Positive Education (see www.appli.edu.au).

Knox also recently formed a Total Fitness Committee (comprising Knox leaders, staff, students, parents, Dr Paula Robinson, community members and a selection of national and international expert advisors). The Total Fitness Committee oversees the strategy, design, delivery and measurement of the Knox Total Fitness model. The committee receive all internal and external requests/ideas relating to positive education and work as a team to reflect and decide what does/does not fit with the overall strategy and objectives. This phase 2 initiative is committed to the following: self-determination, sustainability, an ongoing and rigorous evidence base, best practice, transparency, a collaborative approach, regular communication to all stakeholders, scope and sequence mapping across the whole school community, sharing and partnering with other educational institutions.

Today's Knox Total Fitness Program is a multi-level, strategic approach to creating a positive school climate that supports academic performance, mental fitness and the wellbeing of staff and students. It is delivered through conventional classroom activities, technology platforms, the mentoring programme, coaching and a specially devised online parenting programme. Programme effectiveness is continuously assessed on both subjective and objective measures for students and staff.

Case study 5.2:   How St Peter's College, Adelaide, used appreciative inquiry as an overarching framework to guide wellbeing change

When St. Peter's College, Adelaide, Australia, embarked on its journey of whole-school wellbeing, they wanted to ensure the process they used was collaborative and strengths based. They adopted an appreciative inquiry (AI) approach because it shared these values (see chapter on building ownership for more detail on AI) and conducted an AI summit in 2011 involving all staff.[25] All staff attended the summit and were assigned to groups balanced by gender, department and staff role. The summit followed the four stages recommended in appreciative inquiry, with each of these stages characterised by a question tailored to the school. These were:

- What are we most proud of at St Peter's College? (Discovery)
- What are our greatest strengths? (Discovery)
- What do we deeply care about at St Peter's College? (Discovery/Dream)
- What are our most exciting opportunities at St Peter's College? (Dream)

- What would success look like for boys, staff and parents? (Design)
- How would we know that we were succeeding? (Delivery)

The summit day generated positive emotion amongst staff and a sense of unity and pride in the work the school was undertaking. A post-summit evaluation found staff reflected favourably on the process and, in particular, valued the collaboration process, learning from and appreciating their colleagues, realising the shared values among staff, feeling energised and enthusiastic about the process and the mission and feeling that they now had a clearer vision of the school's strategic plans and direction. In addition, the AI Summit generated eight wellbeing change initiatives. Although four of these initiatives had previously been identified by the senior leadership, they now went ahead with greater ownership and support.

After the success of the AI approach in the development phase with the AI Summit, the school chose to continue to use AI in its implementation and monitoring phases of change.[26] At the start of the implementation phase, the school's senior leadership were trained in the AI approach, and staff were encouraged to use this approach in staff team meetings and in classroom teaching. In addition to the eight initiatives generated at the summit, a further seven 'bottom-up' initiatives were generated from staff during the implementation phase.

Initial wellbeing initiatives:

1　A special interest group on positive psychology;

2　Parent information evenings on wellbeing;

3　Parent-teacher meetings to explicitly discuss student wellbeing;

4　PE department ran a staff wellbeing club;

5　Staff received PD in wellbeing;

6　Staff and students completed a wellbeing survey;

7　Seven explicit wellbeing programmes introduced to the school; and

8　Staff trained in evidence-based techniques to assess and track student wellbeing in the classroom.

In addition to these initiatives, staff identified and implemented a number of other initiatives:

1   Wellbeing concepts (and character strengths in particular) were brought into English literature, religion, and drama;

2   Positive psychology principles were adopted by sports coaches;

3   Senior student leaders were trained in AI;

4   Student leaders led an AI summit for students from other schools;

5   AI questions were included in recruitment and selection processes;

6   AI integrated into the school's change and renewal framework; and

7   The behaviour management policy shifted from a punitive focus ('demerits') to encourage a focus on strengths and positive qualities ('merits').

The school committed to ongoing monitoring of staff and student wellbeing to acknowledge and reflect its importance. Monitoring has also extended to staff being trained to evaluate the effectiveness of their wellbeing teaching for students. The use of the school's behaviour management system to notice good behaviour as well as misbehaviour is also being tracked.

In addition to AI, St Peter's leadership adopted other change leadership approaches including 'top-down planning, trouble-shooting and problem-solving'.[27] The school believes it has made a significant shift in its approach to planning and implementing large-scale change. Among the benefits noted by the leadership are the increased and improved connections throughout the school and a greater focus on the strengths of the school when addressing challenges. The school believes the following factors were central to the success of adopting AI: Senior staff were trained in AI, teams mixed people from across the school at the Summit, a 'quieter' time of the school year was chosen for the Summit, and staff were encouraged to use the AI process broadly, from curriculum design to human resources policy.

Case-study 5.3:   Da Qiao Primary School, Singapore: A range of motivations for wellbeing change

Educator and wellbeing change facilitator Shaen Yeo, shares the story of her work with Da Qiao Primary School.

'Da Qiao Primary School in Singapore began their Positive Education journey for two reasons: First, they wanted to leverage their positive school climate to create a nourishing environment where all students are celebrated and had opportunities to flourish. Second, they had quite a number of concerns surrounding discipline cases that were taking up time and energy.

Inspired by Prof Martin Seligman's work in Geelong Grammar School, they chose PERMA-H as their well-being model; and the Teach, Live, Embed as their approach to implement Positive Education. The PERMA-H framework was first introduced in 2011 to all staff in a year-end training workshop, explaining the rationale for Positive Education. Their vision was to have A Flourishing School with Happy and Confident Learners. This was followed by 8 bite-sized training sessions over the next 6 months, where teachers learned concepts such as resilience, flow and mindfulness in 2012. They strongly believed that teachers were the key. For example, they prepared personalised birthday gifts on teachers' birthdays and matched their duties according to their character strengths. They also organised card games during potluck sessions, as a way to unwind after a busy term. For the students, they shared Good Stories (what students had done well) during morning assembly, and introduced mindfulness in eating during snack break times.

To help drive the efforts of Positive Education in the school, they formed a team of champions. Together this team helped to advocate for Positive Education and clarify doubts along the way. They also looked at how to embed Positive Education into the curriculum, events and school processes. Taking charge of all this was a strong leader who provided support in terms of resources, platforms for teachers to experiment and test out ideas. This enabled teachers to experience well-being themselves so they could teach from personal experience. She also empowered teachers to share their successes at larger platforms e.g. cluster sharing sessions or international conferences. This boosted teachers' confidence and commitment. With some small successes came shifts in students' behaviour and learning attitude, convincing the teachers that focusing on developing well-being skills will also heighten achievement skills. As the efforts took flight, ground up initiatives and ideas on integrating PosEd & flourishing lives started to emerge, gathering momentum.

Of course, they did face challenges along the way. Some teachers had misconceptions about Positive Education – they viewed it as a concoction of programmes instead of a belief and philosophy about what it takes to flourish in school. To address this, the core team held regular conversations to clarify and learn together. Others had initial worries about the Positive Education approach to discipline – that Positive Education is too "soft" and that teachers cannot "punish" students. The School Leaders and Key Personnel had to work very hard to support the ground every step of the way to bring about the shift in mindset on Positive Discipline.

All the hard work paid off. At the end of their 7-year journey in Positive Education, the school saw a significant decrease in discipline cases and an increase in the number of students doing good for others. Their quality of school experience was also above the national average, meaning students found the school experience to be enriching and of high quality. Finally, their school pride was at an all-time high of 91%. To top it off, several of their teachers were awarded the President's Award for Teachers for their emphasis on student-wellbeing'.

Reflection questions

Refer to questions throughout the change process in the research section.

Notes

1   Checinski, M., Dillon, R., Hieronimus, S., & Klier, J. *Putting people at the heart of public-sector transformations.* McKinsey and Company Blog. Retrieved May 20, 2019, from www.mckinsey.com/industries/public-sector/our-insights/putting-people-at-the-heart-of-public-sector-transformations

2   Kotter, J. P. (2012). *Leading change.* Harvard Business Press.

3 Stacey, R. D. (2007). *Strategic management and organisational dynamics: The challenge of complexity to ways of thinking about organisations.* Pearson Education.

4 Whitney, D., & Cooperrider, D. (2011). *Appreciative inquiry: A positive revolution in change.* ReadHowYouWant.com.

5 Holman, P. (2009). *The change handbook: The definitive resource on today's best methods for engaging whole systems.* ReadHowYouWant.com.

6 Cameron, K. S., Dutton, J. E., & Quinn, R. E. (2003). An introduction to positive organizational scholarship. *Positive Organizational Scholarship, 3*(13).

7 Cameron, K. S., & Quinn, R. E. (2011). *Diagnosing and changing organizational culture: Based on the competing values framework.* John Wiley & Sons.

8 Morrison, B., Blood, P., & Thorsborne, M. (2005). Practicing restorative justice in school communities: Addressing the challenge of culture change. *Public Organization Review, 5*(4), 335–357.

9 Thorsborne, M., & Blood, P. (2013). *Implementing restorative practice in schools: A practical guide to transforming school communities.* Jessica Kingsley Publishers.

10 Rosenfield, B., Wall, G., & Jansen, C. (2017). *Leading sustainable change: Wisdom from textbooks and trenches in post-quake Canterbury.* Christchurch, NZ: Grow Waitaha.

11 Kotter, J. P., & Schlesinger, L. A. (2008, July–August). Choosing strategies for change. *Harvard Business Review.*

12 Rosenfield, B., Wall, G., & Jansen, C. (2017). *Leading sustainable change: Wisdom from textbooks and trenches in post-quake Canterbury* (p. 24). Christchurch, NZ: Grow Waitaha.

13 Van Nieuwerburgh, C. (2017). *An introduction to coaching skills: A practical guide* (2nd ed.). London: Sage.

14 Rosenfield, B., Wall, G., & Jansen, C. (2017). *Leading sustainable change: Wisdom from textbooks and trenches in post-quake Canterbury.* Christchurch, NZ: Grow Waitaha.

15 Moir, S. J. (2013). *Teachers' perspectives of 'effective' leadership in schools.* Master's thesis, p. 37.

16 Nashar, R. (2019). *How to lead innovation: The 3 carriage train* [*video*]. Retrieved August 27, 2019, from www.youtube.com/watch?v=HEPinFBcBgU

17   Zigarmi, P., & Hoekstra, J. (2008). *Leadership strategies for making change stick.* The Ken Blanchard Companies. Retrieved December 5, 2019 from www.blanchard.com.tr/media/files/2bf5a258-2f7a-446e-ae5b-dc326df15e7a.pdf

18   Heifetz, R. A., & Linsky, M. (2002). A survival guide for leaders. *Harvard Business Review, 80*(6), 65–74.

19   Amabile, T., & Kramer, S. (2011). *The progress principle: Using small wins to ignite joy, engagement, and creativity at work.* Harvard Business Press.

20   Francis, S. (2019). *Implementing change: Predictable stages of concern.* Retrieved August 27, 2019, from www.happyschool.com.au/wp-content/uploads/Implementing-Change-Predictable-Stages-of-Concern.pdf

21   Anderson, M. (2019). *NZIWR podcast: Building wellbeing using a PsyCap approach.* Retrieved from Apple podcasts, or nziwr.co.nz/podcasts.

22   Rosenfield, B., Wall, G., & Jansen, C. (2017). *Leading sustainable change: Wisdom from textbooks and trenches in post-quake Canterbury.* Christchurch, NZ: Grow Waitaha.

23   Weeks, J. (2018, April 6). *Positive Ed 101.* Keynote address delivered at the Positive Education NZ Confernce. Christchurch, NZ, Friday.

24   Zolezzi, S. (2017). Mental fitness at Knox grammar school. In *Developing leaders for positive organizing: A 21st century repertoire for leading in extraordinary times* (pp. 243–261). Emerald Publishing Limited.

25   Waters, L., White, M., & Murray, S. (2012). Toward the creation of a positive institution. *The International Journal of Appreciative Inquiry, 14*(2), 60–66.

26   Waters, L., & White, M. (2015). Case study of a school wellbeing initiative: Using appreciative inquiry to support positive change. *International Journal of Wellbeing, 5*(1), 19–32. doi:10.5502/ijw.v5i1.2

27   Waters, L., & White, M. (2015). Case study of a school wellbeing initiative: Using appreciative inquiry to support positive change. *International Journal of Wellbeing, 5*(1), 19–32. doi:10.5502/ijw.v5i1.2

Watch

Address resistance by sharing the Three Carriage Train video with those in your wellbeing team. Three carriage train video. Retrieved from www.youtube.com/watch?v=HEPinFBcBgU

The Grow Waitaha Secondary Community of Practice for Wellbeing, Christchurch NZ, 2018–2019. Retrieved from www.youtube.com/watch?v=ZxqrMxSCCBw

Watch Harvard researcher Teresa Amabile's talk on how you can overcome disengagement and use small wins to 'ignite joy and engagement' Retrieved from www.youtube.com/watch?v=XD6N8bsjOEE

Read

Cameron, K. (2012). *Positive leadership: Strategies for extraordinary performance*. San Francisco, CA: Berrett-Koehler Publishers.

Cameron, K. (2013). *Practicing positive leadership: Tools and techniques that create extraordinary results*. San Francisco, CA: Berrett-Koehler Publishers.

Ciarrochi, J., Atkins, P. W., Hayes, L. L., Sahdra, B. K., & Parker, P. (2016). Contextual positive psychology: Policy recommendations for implementing positive psychology into schools. *Frontiers in Psychology, 7*, 1561.

The Grow Waitaha Leading Sustainable Change Guide. Retrieved from www.growwaitaha.co.nz/resources/leadership-of-change/#grow-wait aha-leading-sustainable-change

Kern, M. L., Williams, P., Spong, C., Colla, R., Sharma, K., Downie, A., . . . Oades, L. G. (2019). Systems informed positive psychology. *The Journal of Positive Psychology*, 1–11.

Read how St Peter's, Adelaide, used appreciative inquiry as an overarching change methodology guiding the implementation of positive education across the school: Waters, L., White, M., & Murray, S. (2012). Toward the creation of a positive institution. *The International Journal of Appreciative Inquiry, 14*(2), 60–66. Retrieved from www.research gate.net/profile/Diana_Whitney2/publication/316608503_Appre ciative_Inquiry_Practitioner/links/590774200f7e9bc0d5979498/ Appreciative-Inquiry-Practitioner.pdf#page=60

Thorsborne, M., & Blood, P. (2013). *Implementing restorative practice in schools: A practical guide to transforming school communities*. Philadelphia: Jessica Kingsley Publishers.

Listen

Chris Jansen:NZIWR podcasts are available from https://nziwr.co.nz/category/ podcast/'.

Shaka Senghor Session: Things I learned in Prison. Retrieved from https://podcasts.apple.com/us/podcast/shaka-senghor-session-things-i-learned-in-prison-you/id1264843400?i=1000443498223

Building ownership

Introduction

The benefits of enabling a strong sense of ownership for change should never be underestimated. These include creating a larger circle of support for change, allowing for positive momentum, empowering stakeholders, and creating a larger network of leaders with a unified vision and strategy around the change[1]. The flipside – pushing ahead without buy-in – can be costly in terms of resistance or pushback. Change efforts can wither and die when stakeholders do not provide the support and enthusiasm vital to generate the momentum that keeps change efforts alive. Noticing what you're already doing well is vital for securing staff buy-in and ownership and aligns with a strength-based approach to wellbeing promotion. It is also essential to understand the foundation on which you build and the strengths that can be leveraged for greatest effect.

What the research says

Much of the research in this area from organisational change and educational change leadership is detailed in Chapter 5 on understanding change dynamics. Within education, substantial research has also been done on the factors that enable and support sustainable change in the area of restorative practice.[2] Like wellbeing change, this is an area where schools are making long-term culture change in their communities. Essential strategies and tools for increasing stakeholder buy-in and ownership for any type of major organisational change are discussed next.

Think broadly

No one single person will ever create sustained change. Transformational leadership requires buy-in and ownership from diverse stakeholders representing different opinions and perspectives. AI provides a process for unearthing different and divergent perspectives and developing a shared vision and a roadmap to achieve that new purpose.

Develop the organisation's vision and strategy

Start by outlining the what, how and why of your intended wellbeing change. According to Kotter and Cohen (2002),[3] 'if people buy-into the vision, if you are clear enough about why you are doing what you are doing, and if your rationale is right, most employees will understand even if they are surprised at first'.[4] A recent study on leading sustainable change in education found five key features inherent in describing the vision.[5] They were: 1) embedded within the established mission and values of the schools; 2) focused on the students' futures when describing the rationale for the change (the 'why'); 3) used data to support the proposed change; 4) used language that encouraged stakeholders to see beyond their personal point of view; and 5) The leaders crafted powerful, informal narratives about their vision of the school's future. Research confirms that storytelling is an effective method of gaining support for change. We like our colleague Chris Jansen's recommendation that we 'paint a vivid picture of future reality' to help muster enthusiasm for change.

Learn it, live it, teach it, embed it

Many schools have adopted Geelong Grammar School's approach to developing whole-school wellbeing: learn it, live it, teach it, embed it. Denise first heard this approach articulated by Dr Karen Reivich during the University of Pennsylvania's training of Geelong Grammar School's staff in 2009. It struck a chord with all who trained on the team and with the school, which made it a core part of its philosophy and applied positive psychology model over the next decade. This model is set out in Norrish et al, 2013.[6] We have since heard variations on this theme; for instance, one practitioner adding *listen* to remind those leading change to listen to and engage learners, parents, and other stakeholders. Dr Sylvia Kwok of Hong Kong uses a process of 'learn, live, *reflect, conceptualise,* teach, embed' to remind educators that we need to reflect on the experiences in our schools and respond to what is happening in our environment.[7]

At the heart of this model is the fact that you can't expect staff to have a sense of ownership of something they don't know. Staff need an opportunity to learn about wellbeing before they can be expected to be on board with the school's wellbeing journey.

Express a sense of urgency, but give them time

Creating a sense of urgency is vital: participants of the Grow Waitaha research and practice review indicated that what helped staff and teachers accept change was necessary. 'What [staff] wanted was time. Plenty of lead time [helped] teachers digest and implement the changes over time, rather than be caught out when the time comes', described one participant.[8]

Show, not tell

'Even the most compelling words and facts can fail in convincing individuals to adopt new systems or processes. Second only to providing lead-time, participants found showing stakeholders examples of institutions that have implemented similar changes was the most effective way of gaining buy-in', according to the Grow Waitaha review.

School leaders can also help instil confidence in proposed changes by ensuring they attend relevant meetings, professional development sessions, and community meetings. Always take the opportunity to show your support for these initiatives visibly.

Listen, listen, listen

In contrast to receiving feedback which can have a negative impact on performance, researchers Itzchakov and Kluger found that 'experiencing high quality (attentive, empathic, and non-judgmental) listening can positively shape speakers' emotions and attitudes'.[9] People who were listened to were more able to reflect in a balanced way on the positive and negative aspects of the topic discussed and were less likely to respond defensively. To design or implement change that effectively responds to organisation needs, leaders need to know what those needs are. Listening is a critical tool in any change process.

Putting it into practice

Before you embark upon building school-wide wellbeing, it is vital to ensure all stakeholders understand why promoting wellbeing in schools is important. That includes parents and caregivers, board, students, all staff and other key stakeholders. School boards need to be educated as to why wellbeing matters as an operational goal and hold schools accountable for supporting the wellbeing of all members of the educational community, as well as having the responsibility to support well-designed, evidence-based efforts within the school.[10] All staff need to understand why your school is choosing to take a whole-school approach to building wellbeing. Parents and caregivers and the wider community also need to understand what the school is doing and why. Establishing the 'why' is really vital – we know from psychology that understanding and being personally committed to the 'why' increases the likelihood of change being both successful and sustained.

To do this, we recommend you begin with a full staff professional learning session, dedicated to making the case for whole-school wellbeing. Using outside 'experts' – from your local university or qualified practitioners – can help here. This event also provides you with the opportunity to notice a) who your early adopters (or 'first followers') are and b) listen very carefully to the voice of wellbeing sceptics. Try to listen attentively, not defensively! Understanding the core concerns of your colleagues provides you with vital intelligence that, in the long run, will make the change process easier. Typically, we run these events for multiple schools and encourage them to work together subsequently, in clusters or communities of learning, to build capacity and learn at scale. This also provides all those involved with a community to support them through the change process and share ideas and experiences with.

Making the case for wellbeing in your school – the evidence

Box 6.1 contains a summary of reasons we have heard resonate with schools when initially considering taking a whole-school approach to wellbeing, plus additional research drawn from a range of sources, including Mathew White and Peggy Kern's article in the *International Journal of Wellbeing* (2018)[11] and the International Positive Education Network's State of Education[12] report.

Box 6.1: Making the case for wellbeing – which findings matter most to your school?

- Depression has been on the rise since World War II despite increasing national wealth.
- According to the World Health Organization, mental illness is the greatest cause of disability for young people worldwide.[13]
- One in four young people will have experienced at least one occurrence of severe mental illness by the age of 25.[14]
- Mental illness often recurs, meaning that the earlier a young person experiences mental illness, the greater the risk of repeated incidents, extended disability, poor relationships and physical and mental health problems.[15]
- Almost half of all Australians will experience a mental illness in their lifetime.[16]

(continued)

- Accidents and suicides are the leading causes of death in young people aged 16 to 25 years.
- Almost one in five will experience a major depressive episode before graduating from high school (adapt these statistics to your local country).
- The report to the United Nations on education in the 21st century identified four pillars of education: learning to know, learning to do, learning to be, learning to live together. While 20th century education focused on the first two, it is now clear that the second two are just as important and underpin the effectiveness of the first two.[17]
- Research has shown that character strengths and wellbeing are malleable (qualities that can be developed) and can be improved with good teaching and practice.
- Youth spend on average 30 hours a week in schools.
- Nine out of ten parents in the UK want schools to offer this kind of education.
- Research has shown that character traits like grit can be just as important as IQ in academic performance.
- A focus on wellbeing is not only about how individual students feel but also equipping them to contribute to a flourishing society.
- Wellbeing programmes have been shown to help students understand and regulate their emotions, develop supportive relationships and enhance academic performance.
- Disengaged students are at elevated risk for missing classes, dropping out, academic failure and a variety of antisocial behaviours,[18] while studies have shown that engaging in wellbeing interventions in school can enhance school engagement and retention.
- Depression and anxiety are linked to lower academic performance via reduced concentration, motivation and working memory.[19] [20]
- Longitudinal research has shown that students with the highest levels of wellbeing recorded the best academic performance and lowest school absences one year later.[21]
- Young people experiencing poor mental health between the ages of 16 and 17 are less likely to gain tertiary qualifications by the age of 30 than their non-depressed peers.[22]
- The societal and economic cost and impact of mental illness and suicide are substantial (insert your own country's figures here).

- Where whole-school wellbeing promotion has been practiced over time, assessments suggest that students have benefitted, with at-risk students benefitting the most.[23]
- Flourishing students reported better academic achievements, higher self-control and less procrastination than those who were moderately mentally healthy or languishing.[24]

Wellbeing change in schools has enormous potential to build staff ownership and buy-in when it begins with a focus on staff wellbeing. The evidence for this approach and the endorsement for it comes from those with most experience in the field. Experts like Charlie Scudamore from Geelong Grammar School, Mathew White from the University of Adelaide and leading international wellbeing coach and consultant Clive Leach all agree that focusing on staff wellbeing is an essential first step. It makes sense because:

1   Staff need and appreciate the investment in their wellbeing.

2   Staff wellbeing influences student learning and wellbeing.

2   Equally importantly, staff knowledge of wellbeing is essential to teachers being able to implement relevant and useful strategies in their classrooms.

Expert practitioner insight 6.1: *Clive Leach. What helps convince people to get involved and get started?*

- Help people understand what wellbeing is and the ingredients of flourishing.
- Demonstrate the evidence underpinning the research and practice that shows we can build wellbeing.
- Help people understand the benefits of resilience and mental toughness.
- Give them practical activities they can try.
- Look to see where you've got buy-in (who's keen and trying things out); these are your 'positive deviants'.
- Harness the energy by noticing what's already happening.

- Show there's an evidence base to fill any gaps which will make their wellbeing initiatives more cohesive and strategic.
- Be brave, give things a go and learn from that.

These 'success factors' for whole-school wellbeing change are part of building buy-in:

- **Focus on what you already do well:** What strengths do we have that are contributing to the wellbeing of our community?
- **Be inclusive:** Give all members of the school community an opportunity to say what wellbeing means to them and to be involved in determining how they can build wellbeing.
- **Allow people to follow different wellbeing paths:** Different interventions will work for different people.

Sucessful wellbeing change is contextually relevant and culturally responsive. This work can only be delivered by people who understand wellbeing (having adequate professional learning and development), have lived experience of managing their own wellbeing with stories and insights to share, and have the confidence to create and innovate in the school community.

The New Zealand Institute of Wellbeing and Resilience process for navigating wellbeing change helps school leaders think about the processes they will use to embed wellbeing in their school. Some of the processes and tools used in this process play an important role in building ownership and support for wellbeing change. These include the *wellbeing audit*, the *journey so far*, and the *wellbeing inquiry*.

Buy-in tool #1: The school-wide wellbeing audit

The purpose of the audit is to capture the good work that is already being done within the school. It's about taking time to recognise and celebrate the good work the school is doing. It provides a solid base of knowledge on which to build.

Why conduct a wellbeing audit?

1   Teachers can feel undervalued when 'a wellbeing focus' is introduced if it does not acknowledge all the excellent wellbeing work they have been doing to date. Staff reluctance to become involved is typically higher where there is little or no acknowledgement of existing staff expertise and good practice.

2   An audit of existing practice can help identify areas of strength on which to build and the people who can lead specific interventions. Documenting existing practice builds a bridge between the present and the future and increases optimism and morale. Lastly, if a school doesn't know the good work that is already being done, how can it celebrate that work or ensure it continues in the future?

What does a wellbeing audit include?

Our wellbeing audit enquires into a range of wellbeing outcomes (guided by the wellbeing research literature and by the New Zealand Education Review Office's[25][26][27] indicators for student wellbeing):

- Belonging and connectedness;
- Feeling safe and secure;
- Experiencing success;
- Resilience;
- Being active;
- Student confidence in their own identity;
- Mindfulness;
- Strengths-focused social and emotional learning;
- Restorative practices; and
- Student voice.

Schools can evaluate these wellbeing outcomes across a range of domains such as:

- Classroom or year level;
- Whole-school activity;
- Extracurricular;
- Cocurricular;
- Parent/*whānau*;
- Community; and
- Board of trustees/governors.

Schools are encouraged to adapt the wellbeing audit, adjusting domains and changing the wellbeing indicators to suit their context.

How to conduct a wellbeing audit

The audit is presented as a large spreadsheet that can be completed during staff or syndicate meetings or circulated to different groups to add to it. Conversation with students and the parent community is another important input to the audit. For most schools, doing it within a staff meeting on a shared document allows rapid completion.

Buy-in tool #2: The journey so far

In our wellbeing change work with schools, we encourage groups to map their wellbeing journey. Typically, this leads to reminiscing about important events (both joyful and painful), appreciation of the impact they have had and sharing of different experiences some group members don't know about. For new staff members, this can be an important chance to learn about the school's history and the events that have shaped attitudes and practices in the school.

These maps remind us that we never actually begin with a blank sheet of paper, and it's helpful to acknowledge the past. This process is based around storytelling and drawing. It involves people working in circles with no hierarchy or requirement to perform for the larger group. As such, it is a process that is culturally responsive to indigenous peoples in both Aotearoa/New Zealand and Australia.

Prompts for mapping the wellbeing journey so far:

- What got you started;
- Roadblocks/dead ends;
- Inspiring stories;
- People who drove/influenced events;
- Pain points;
- Off-road moments;
- Warning lights/slow-down signals; and
- Significant connections and contributions.

Buy-in tool #3: Wellbeing inquiry: Finding the positive core of your school

A school-wide wellbeing inquiry is an engaging and strengths-focused process used to gather information. Equally importantly, it can inspire and motivate staff and identify wellbeing champions who will be instrumental in leading and sustaining change.

The process we use is based on the Appreciative Inquiry process[28][29][30] and is conducted in three discussion stages, each one focused on the following questions.

1   Think about a time you've seen our group/school at its best. What did you see? What was best about it? What's the school like at its very best, and what qualities/strengths do you associate with those moments?

2   If you came back in five years and everything was working exactly as you'd like it in our group/school, what would you see, feel, hear [ideal future]?

3   What's one change you'd most like to see happen to move closer to that ideal future? What's one change you as a person can make that would support it?

Working in small groups, people are asked to remember times their school has been at its best, sharing stories and identifying the positive qualities or strengths in those events. Next, groups are asked to imagine that they can wave a magic wand and have everything in their school exactly as they want it. 'What do you see, hear, feel and touch in this school? Describe it as vividly as you can'. Staff share their vision, revealing passions and the priorities staff believe are most important to build wellbeing in their school. As a final stage, each person is asked to identify the one change they would most like to see to bring the school closer to their vision. These priorities for change provide a staff-supported list of actions for change. To remind staff that change is about everyone's actions, we also ask staff to identify one change they *personally* can make to bring the school closer to their ideal vision.

From each AI, schools generate a list of:

•   School strengths;
•   Ideas for the future; and
•   Priorities for action – identified by the group.

Review the strengths: Spend time reflecting on your school's strengths – the place, the staff, the students and the community, i.e. any resources that are supporting the school. What are some of the ways that the school could leverage these strengths to move ahead with wellbeing?
    Review the vision: Is there a clear vision that you want to adopt for the school? Does this picture need to be painted for staff and used to remind them of the journey during the tough stages?
    Review the priorities for action: Are there any that have been consistently identified across all groups? In selecting your three priorities for action, consider:

•   Is there one priority action that will have widespread support?
•   Is there one priority action that can be achieved quickly or with ease?
•   Is there an action that will be an important foundation or piece of groundwork which will make future change easier or more likely to succeed?

Conducting a wellbeing inquiry in your school

Each school conducts its AI sessions in different ways. The primary aim is to acknowledge the strengths of the school and to build buy-in and support for change. In designing your school process; consider:

- Will you bring the whole school together or have department, year level, staff and students meet separately?
- How will you include students and community in your AI?

As part of its commitment to wellbeing, King's College, Auckland, New Zealand, established a wellbeing working group (WWG) of teaching and non-teaching staff and students. The group used an Appreciative Inquiry process to determine the areas they would focus on and to identify the people within the group who wanted to lead those sub-groups.

For more information on how St Peter's College, Adelaide used Appreciate Inquiry to guide the school's wellbeing change process,[31] see Chapter 5 on change dynamics.

Expert practitioner insight 6.2: *Gilda Scarfe. Keystones to successful implementation*

Gilda Scarfe began working with two schools in the UK in 2016 and is now supporting 40 schools across the UK, plus 22 schools in the UAE, Nigeria and Thailand. Here she shares what she's learned about securing buy-in.

'Research shows that successful implementation of new programmes often hinges on teacher buy-in and the process of implementation, making understanding how teachers adopt, adapt, or resist change crucial.

When I started working with Simon Langton Grammar School for Girls and Canterbury High School in 2016, the process began with a workshop showcasing Mental Toughness (MT) and wellbeing research. To be able to create a mentally tough, high performance and positive culture within their classrooms and students, it is important for teachers to be mentally tough themselves. MT is learned through experimentation and observation of the behaviour and emotions of the people closest to them. As key role models for students, it is important to develop MT within teachers.

At the end of the workshop I opened the stage for questions and the staffs' major concerns soon emerged: they had insufficient knowledge of wellbeing or mental health to be able to confidently support their students; their opinion never mattered, programmes were always chosen 'top down'; and they were worried about wellbeing being just another fad.

I decided to make the teachers part of the solution. Collaborating with them to discover what works, what doesn't and what they wanted to achieve, created common ground and things evolved very quickly. Within schools, head teachers, members of SLT, and staff members involved in the implementation of MT were interviewed and trained over a 2-day period. Focus groups with other school staff members captured a broad range of views and perspectives in order to design the most appropriate programme for each school within the time available on the timetable.

Teachers not only need to be upskilled – and understand the importance and impact of the programme – but they needed to see the programme as part their curriculum and them as central part of the solution. They needed support to implement the programme: to facilitate headteachers and teachers' efforts to change their practice, I needed to encourage a culture that balances accountability with experimentation; to provide all stakeholders with adequate time to learn new practices without feeling threatened.

Across both very different schools (one super-selective grammar school and the other an under-performing state school) four keystones to successful implementation of MT in schools emerged:

- **Staff:** Committed individuals are required to champion the approach within their schools, with the support of members of the senior leadership teams;
- **Resources:** Both time and financial resources are required for training, delivery and evaluation of MT which need to be specific to the schools' needs;
- **Journey:** Reflects the fact that outcomes are not immediate, it's a non-linear process with stops and starts; close monitoring and support is vital; and
- **Perceptions:** Highlights the importance of members of the school community sharing an understanding of what MT is and why it is being introduced in each school context'.

Box 6.2: Using books to build buy-in

Palmerston North East Kāhui Ako, a cluster of ten schools in the North Island of New Zealand, committed to focusing on staff wellbeing in their first year of a wellbeing initiative. In addition to professional development for staff, they also instituted a staff book club, meeting each term across all ten schools to work through Elena Aguilar's *Onward*, a text dedicated to supporting teacher wellbeing. Learning and discussion moved ahead across the group, also facilitating discussion around wellbeing and the development of a shared language of wellbeing.

Edwina Ricci, lead on the Maroondah Project (see Chapter 14), uses books in a different way: 'Handing out books is one of my strategies that I have found effective. Shared reading creates a common language. I gifted 27 principals two books to read last Christmas and now we are doing further work with the authors – Helen Street (*Contextual Wellbeing*) and Christian van Nieuwerburgh (*Leading Coaching in Schools*)'.

Case study 6.1: Sumner School: Using AI to reinspire and reignite the wellbeing track

Anna Granger, principal, and Georgia McRae, teacher and wellbeing lead at Sumner school, share how their school used Appreciative Inquiry to reignite the school's commitment to wellbeing.

'In 2016 we took part in a wellbeing and Character Education pilot project led by Dr Lucy Hone. This project gave staff an incredible knowledge base and understanding of the power of Positive Education and Character Strengths. However, we did not adequately embed this learning: when key staff left our school, systems and processes became disjointed as they were not fully understood or owned by current staff.

At the beginning of 2019 a whole staff Appreciative Inquiry (AI) facilitated by Dr Denise Quinlan helped us align our thinking and identify a clear direction for our school for the year ahead. Our key learnings were that we had a great staff culture, a very clear shared vision for the future, which was great (and a relief!), but hugely differing understandings of the language of Character Strengths and wellbeing.

Two main ideas have underpinned all our work and learning this year. The first, to ensure this process was bigger than one leader or team, our pathway needed to be strategic and slow. We needed time to "Learn it" and "Live it" together before we could "Teach it" and then "Embed it". Through our AI process we realised our journey needed to be personalised to our school and our community, and so we gave ourselves full permission to make small steps and take our time to get things right. We regularly talk as a staff about "our next small step" and ensure we have all our people and processes right before we take our next step together.

So what has this process looked like for us?

Learn it and Live it: We took two full terms to develop a shared understanding of wellbeing and Character Strengths. Staff set wellbeing goals and appointed wellbeing buddies which made us hold ourselves accountable for our own wellbeing. We started unpacking Character Strengths and what they looked like within our students. We also decided we wanted to find a wellbeing model individual to us.

Teach it: We then felt ready to take the next small step into the "Teach it" phase. At every assembly we focus on two Character Strengths and our student Wellbeing Leaders share examples of how we can nourish and grow these. We developed a shared language across the school used in class and restorative conversations. We started explicitly teaching wellbeing strategies and Positive Education, with every class putting aside at least one session per week for this.

Embed it: Embedding this mahi (work) is occurring naturally as it becomes part of "how we do things at Sumner", but we continue to take our "next small steps" to ensure that we develop this at our own pace and as a whole staff'.

Case Study 6.2:   Rāroa School: *Really* listening extends to
collaboration and participation

One intermediate school that introduced wellbeing chose to focus on staff wellbeing for almost two years before asking teachers to introduce wellbeing inquiry into their classrooms. During that two years, the school leadership collaborated with staff to develop a model of wellbeing that staff supported and wanted to use in the school. They built the staff wellbeing model around their school vision, which staff created and which had high buy-in. This staff model of wellbeing was used to help staff articulate what wellbeing meant to them and to give them a shared understanding and language of wellbeing.

By engaging in an un-rushed commitment to finding out what staff really wanted, the school leadership demonstrated a willingness to listen. This listening process began all over again when teachers engaged with students to find out what wellbeing meant to them and to understand what a wellbeing model would look like for students. The journey of Rāroa School in choosing a wellbeing model for staff is detailed in Chapter 7 on wellbeing models.

Case study 6.3:   Valdivia, Chile – generating ownership by addressing school priorities

Camilo Castellon, charged with leading wellbeing change in 42 public schools in Valdivia, Chile, began by working with the 22 schools for which wellbeing was a priority. (Beginning with volunteers was an approach successfully used to introduce wellbeing at Knox Grammar, Sydney.) Schools were concerned about poor attendance, which was harming student achievement, so that became Camilo's first project. He showed how wellbeing and connection to school were adversely affected by chronic absence. Sessions were held for parents and staff on the teenage brain and the importance of relationship for learning and wellbeing. Camilo's work encouraged parents to move from a paradigm of punishment/reward to one of encouraging gratitude, growth mindset, and self-regulation and has helped improve school-family relationships and attendance.

Case study 6.4:   St Peter's College, Adelaide: The 'driver'

School leaders are already challenged by having to manage an overcrowded timetable with pressure to focus on numeracy, literacy and passing exams, with the consequence that wellbeing is very often regarded as a fad or a marginalised topic. Similarly, there exists among some educators a tendency to view wellbeing as a marketing tool, employed by schools as the new competitive recruitment edge.

When it comes to ownership and buy-in, small things matter. When St Peter's embarked on a major whole-school wellbeing initiative they found that some staff lacked confidence and were therefore sometimes reluctant to teach the wellbeing class that was scheduled throughout the school at the same time each week. They appointed a senior teacher as the 'driver'. This teacher would visit different classes at the scheduled time and was available for observation, support or to teach the class. In addition, a teacher could be invited to go to a different classroom and observe a colleague teaching a class. This strategy provided teachers with a range of professional-development support. The school delivered the message that wellbeing was a nonnegotiable subject, but it also emphasised that all teachers would be supported and enabled to deliver the wellbeing message.

Case study 6.5:   Taipei European School: Looking after staff
wellbeing and professional development

Among the practices that Taipei European School (TES) found useful in building buy-in and support for wellbeing among staff were:

- Adopting an inquiry approach – the school was honest about the long-term goal of culture change and the different paths that could lead there.
- Professional learning communities – teachers were dissecting the research together in small groups.
- The PERMA Champions Group – this group met over lunch each fortnight with a mission of supporting staff wellbeing. They presented to staff and shared research and ideas.
- All these actions helped build trust in the leadership's commitment to improving staff wellbeing. Leadership also became

clear that wellbeing was not something anyone could do to you – only you could choose to work on your wellbeing.

- Teachers were allocated 80 minutes per week in their schedules to focus on their own wellbeing. There is no need to account for this time, and it can include mindfulness, going to the gym or taking a walk.
- Wednesdays include protected professional reflection time for teachers to reflect on the impact their professional practice is having on their students. On this day, after school co-curricular supervision and meetings have been removed and replaced with time for professional development. Stimulus material on wellbeing is sent out every few weeks, and teachers record their reflections using vlogs, journals or Google Docs.
- The head has two one-to-one meetings with each staff member at the start and the end of the year. Staff are asked to discuss wellbeing and asked questions like 'When are you at your best?' These discussions have revealed the staff commitment to and understanding of wellbeing and application to their own lives.

Reflection questions

- Have you acknowledged all the good work that already exists at your school? How might you conduct a wellbeing audit at your school?
- Have you identified and acknowledged the people responsible for contributing that work?
- Have you sought input from the wider community, whose knowledge of the problems, ideas for their solution and vision for the school are critical to successful change?
- Have you involved a large group of people in leading the change? How easily and well can they connect with the school community and involve others?
- What external factors and internal factors affect wellbeing in your school?
- Who can you collaborate with to build wellbeing in your school?
- How can you identify the priority needs for your school – and be sure that all your community is agreed on these priorities?
- Have you allocated time to listen to people throughout the wellbeing change process?

Notes

1   Rosenfield, B., Wall, G., & Jansen, C. (2017). *Leading sustainable change: Wisdom from textbooks and trenches in post-quake Canterbury.* Christchurch, NZ: Grow Waitaha.

2   Thorsborne, M., & Blood, P. (2013). *Implementing restorative practice in schools: A practical guide to transforming school communities.* Jessica Kingsley Publishers.

3   Kotter, J. P., & Cohen, D. S. (2002). *The heart of change: Real-Life Stories of How People Change Their Organizations.* Boston, MA: Harvard Business Review.

4   Ibid.

5   Rosenfield, B., Wall, G., & Jansen, C. (n.d.). *Leading sustainable change: Wisdom from textbooks and trenches in post-quake Canterbury.* Christchurch, NZ: Grow Waitaha. Retrieved from www.growwaitaha.co.nz/media/1415/180504-leading-sustainable-change-ff-sf.pdf

6   Norrish, J. M., & Seligman, M. E. (2015). *Positive education: The Geelong Grammar School journey.* Oxford Positive Psychology Series.

7   Kwok, S. (2019, July 18–21). *The application of whole school positive education in Hong Kong primary school. Part of symposium: Whole-school wellbeing is caught and taught: Sustainable wellbeing change is cultural and curricular, and responsive to context.* Presented at the World Congress of Positive Psychology, Melbourne, Australia.

8   Rosenfield, B., Wall, G., & Jansen, C. (n.d.). *Leading sustainable change: Wisdom from textbooks and trenches in post-quake Canterbury.* Christchurch, NZ: Grow Waitaha. Retrieved from www.growwaitaha.co.nz/media/1415/180504-leading-sustainable-change-ff-sf.pdf

9   Itzchakov, G., & Kluger, A. N. (2018). The power of listening in helping people change. *Harvard Business Review.*

10 White, M. A., & Kern, M. L. (2018). Positive education: Learning and teaching for wellbeing and academic mastery. *International Journal of Wellbeing, 8*(1).

11 White, M. A., & Kern, M. L. (2018). Positive education: Learning and teaching for wellbeing and academic mastery. *International Journal of Wellbeing, 8*(1).

12 International Positive Education Network. (2017). *The state of positive education.* London: International Positive Education Network.

13   World Health Organization. (2017). *Depression and other common mental disorders: Global health estimates* (No. WHO/MSD/MER/2017.2). World Health Organization.

14   Slade, T., Johnston, A., Oakley Browne, M. A., Andrews, G., & Whiteford, H. (2009). 2007 National survey of mental health and wellbeing: Methods and key findings. *Australian and New Zealand Journal of Psychiatry, 43*(7), 594–605.

15   Kessler, R. C., & Bromet, E. J. (2013). The epidemiology of depression across cultures. *Annual Review of Public Health, 34,* 119–138.

16   Black Dog Institute. (2014). *Facts and figures about mental health.* Retrieved from www.blackdoginstitute.org.au/docs/default-source/factsheets/facts_figures.pdf?sfvrsn=8

17   Roffey, S. (2011). *Changing behaviour in schools: Promoting positive relationships and wellbeing.* London: Sage.

18   Cook, P. J., Dodge, K. A., Gifford, E. J., & Schulting, A. B. (2017). A new program to prevent primary school absenteeism: Results of a pilot study in five schools. *Children and Youth Services Review, 82,* 262–270.

19   Owens, M., Stevenson, J., Hadwin, J. A., & Norgate, R. (2012). Anxiety and depression in academic performance: An exploration of the mediating factors of worry and working memory. *School Psychology International, 33*(4), 433–449.

20   Frojd, A., et al. (2008). Depression and school performance in middle adolescent boys and girls. *Journal of Adolescence, 31*(4), 485–498.

21   Suldo, S. M., Thalji, A., & Ferron, J. (2011). Longitudinal academic outcomes predicted by early adolescents' subjective well-being, psychopathology, and mental health status yielded from a dual factor model. *Journal of Positive Psychology, 6,* 17–30.

22   Jonsson, U., Bohman, H., Hjern, A., Von Knorring, L., Olsson, G., & von Knorring, A-L. (2010). Subsequent higher education after adolescent depression: A 15-year follow-up register study. *European Psychiatry: The Journal of the Association of European Psychiatrists, 25,* 396–401. doi:10.1016/j.eurpsy.2010.01.016.

23   White, M. A., & Kern, M. L. (2018). Positive education: Learning and teaching for wellbeing and academic mastery. *International Journal of Wellbeing, 8*(1).

24   Howell, A. J. (2009). Flourishing: Achievement-related correlates of students' well-being. *Journal of Positive Psychology, 4,* 1–13.

25 New Zealand Government. (2013). *Wellbeing for success: Draft evaluation indicators for student wellbeing.* Retrieved September 3, 2019, from www.ero.govt.nz/publications/wellbeing-for-success-draft-evaluation-indicators-for-student-wellbeing/

26 New Zealand Government. (2016). *Wellbeing for success: A resource for schools.* Retrieved September 3, 2019, from www.ero.govt.nz/assets/Uploads/Wellbeing-resource-WEB.pdf

27 New Zealand Government. (2016). *School evaluation indicators: Effective practice for improvement and learner success.* Retrieved September 3, 2019, from www.ero.govt.nz/assets/Uploads/ERO-15968-School-Evaluation-Indicators-2016-v10lowres.pdf

28 Whitney, D., & Cooperrider, D. (2011). *Appreciative inquiry: A positive revolution in change.* ReadHowYouWant. com.

29 Waters, L., White, M., & Murray, S. (2012). Toward the creation of a positive institution. *The International Journal of Appreciative Inquiry*, *14*(2), 60–66.

30 Waters, L., & White, M. (2015). Case study of a school wellbeing initiative: Using appreciative inquiry to support positive change. *International Journal of Wellbeing*, *5*(1), 19–32. doi:10.5502/ijw.v5i1.2

31 White, M. (2018, April 6–7). *Building collective wellbeing: Integrating school culture, strategy, and curriculum.* 2nd Positive Education New Zealand Conference. Christ's College, Canterbury, New Zealand.

Watch

Simon Sinek – How Great Leaders Inspire Action. Retrieved from www.ted.com/talks/simon_sinek_how_great_leaders_inspire_action

Teresa Amabile – The Progress Principle. Retrieved from www.youtube.com/watch?v=CkN4w4V3FTU

Read

Amabile, T., & Kramer, S. (2011). *The progress principle: Using small wins to ignite joy, engagement, and creativity at work.* Harvard Business Press.

Cooperrider, D. L., & McQuaid, M. (2012). The positive arc of systemic strengths: How appreciative inquiry and sustainable designing can bring out the best in human systems. *Journal of Corporate Citizenship*, *46*, 71–102.

Grow Waitaha Leading Sustainable Change Guide. Retrieved from www.growwaitaha.co.nz/media/1415/180504-leading-sustainable-change-ff-sf.pdf

Listen

NZIWR podcasts are available from https://nziwr.co.nz/category/podcast/

NZIWR podcast: Stephen Eames.

NZIWR podcast: Nathan Riki.

NZIWR podcast: Adrienne Buckingham.

NZIWR podcast: Clive Leach.

Choosing a wellbeing model for your school

Introduction

Early on in their wellbeing journey, most schools grapple with the questions 'Why do we need a wellbeing model?' and 'Which model will be right for our school?' These are important questions that cut to the core of taking a whole-school approach to wellbeing. When we consider these questions, we engage with the purpose and process of developing wellbeing. We have to consider not just the validity of the model, but its relevance and appropriateness for context. These questions underscore the importance to whole-school wellbeing of:

- Building a shared understanding of wellbeing in your school community; and
- The people, place and processes in your school; a wellbeing model should reflect the shared goals of this community.

In this chapter, we review some of the wellbeing models most widely used in education and their application in different contexts. We explore how schools are innovating and adapting models to reflect their school priorities and values.

What the research says

A wellbeing model should 'support the process of whole-school wellbeing development and help your school embed wellbeing principles in the day to day life of your school'.[1] The model is not an academic justification for the wellbeing work that can sit in a folder on a shelf. It should be a tool every person in your school community is familiar with and which assists the school in moving forward with its wellbeing aims and goals.

What are the benefits of having a wellbeing model?

A school wellbeing model helps inform and educate, and motivate and evaluate.

Inform and educate

Most of us have absorbed the traditional public health messages of eating healthy foods, brushing our teeth, getting enough sleep and being physically active. However, the importance of managing our own psychological wellbeing has not yet fully permeated mainstream consiousness.[2] Likewise, most schools are strongly focused on their role in educating students to build their literacy and numeracy but are now starting to realise the importance of supporting and building wellbeing literacy.

Wellbeing literacy is defined as having the vocabulary, knowledge and skills that may be intentionally used to maintain or improve the wellbeing of ourselves or others.[3] This is an important life skill most parents and educators want students to develop both for school and throughout their adult lives, yet wellbeing literacy is still relatively low among many adults and students. A wellbeing model therefore has an important role to play in educating the school community about wellbeing. Wellbeing models typically contain a number of components reflecting the fact that wellbeing is multidimensional. A school wellbeing model sends a strong message to the school community that wellbeing is a valued good and provides a format for thinking about and discussing wellbeing.

The dimensions of wellbeing highlighted by the model become part of a shared language of wellbeing in the school. This means that, as well as educating individuals about wellbeing, a wellbeing model facilitates conversation about wellbeing. It literally provides the language for discussions to take place about wellbeing. Having a shared language of wellbeing is often one of the most valued benefits described by educators. They describe how this enables students to express how they are feeling and makes it easier for challenging situations to be shared. Where the extended family community is involved, this enables the language of wellbeing to be shared with school families, facilitating wellbeing conversations in the home. When the school and parent community have a shared understanding of wellbeing, it can contribute to a consistent message between school and home on student wellbeing.

In summary, a school wellbeing model can support development of wellbeing literacy for students, staff and the extended family community. The model provides an education aid or tool that supports learning in and beyond the school.

Motivate and evaluate

By providing a memorable visual reminder of wellbeing, a school wellbeing model serves to keep wellbeing front of mind for students and staff. These reminders make it easier for people to attend to their wellbeing; by providing specific actions and reminders, they motivate the school community to pay attention to their wellbeing. How many of us have great intentions to look after our wellbeing but get busy and forget to think about it? A wellbeing model is like having a coach beside you reminding you of your goals and priorities.

A wellbeing model also assists with evaluation at a personal and school level. Personally, I can look at the model and wonder how I'm doing. For example, how are the physical, emotional, social and spiritual/meaning aspects of my wellbeing going? I might check in and notice I've been very busy at work, and I'm scoring high on engagement, meaning and accomplishment, but low on relational/social wellbeing and even lower on physical wellbeing. In this way, a model provides the individual with a checklist against which they can easily evaluate their own wellbeing.[4] Likewise this thinking can be applied at the team, year group and classroom levels: What are we doing as a team (or house) to build positive emotions, how are our relationships, what is the purpose of this meeting, and is that obvious to everyone involved?

At a school level, the wellbeing model provides groups within the school with a clear set of priorities for use in decision-making. The wellbeing model provides a readily available yardstick against which a particular policy or decision can be evaluated. The model is a visible reminder that important decisions should be viewed through the lens of wellbeing as well as other strategic or financial perspectives.

Finally, a school can use its wellbeing model to 'join the dots' and track progress in developing wellbeing.[5] For example, a number of seemingly disparate activities underway across the school form a coherent approach to building social wellbeing and inclusion when viewed through a wellbeing lens. When pulled together under the rubric of social wellbeing, the school is seen to be making significant progress on this priority area.

Box 7.1: Benefits of adopting a school wellbeing model

Use this summary to help explain the benefits of having a school wellbeing model to your community:

- Helps develop a shared language of wellbeing within the school;
- Assists with communication with parents, students and the wider school community;
- Acts as a visual reminder of wellbeing around the school;

(continued)

> - Provides a framework against which you can track progress – the school can assess progress against each element of the model; and
> - Provides an accessible touchstone for prioritising and decision-making – activities that clearly fit within the model can be justified against this agreed framework.

Wellbeing models used in education

We briefly outline wellbeing models frequently used in education and where to find more information on them. Some are evidence based; others are effectively theories about what is most important for wellbeing. Many models reflect a lifetime's study and knowledge of an area. Used by schools to develop their knowledge and understanding of wellbeing, they often act as a springboard for schools who adapt these models (or develop their own) to respond to their context and culture.

Te Whare Tapa Whā *(the Four-Walled House)*

Te Whare Tapa Whā (the Four-Walled House) model of hauora/wellbeing was developed in New Zealand to support Māori Health and draws on an understanding of the aspects of wellbeing that are important within *te Ao Māori* (the Māori world).[6] New Zealand has a founding treaty (the Treaty of Waitangi) with its indigenous people which guarantees partnership, participation and protection for the Māori people. *Te Whare Tapa Whā* forms part of the New Zealand curriculum (health and physical education), which state schools are required to follow.[7]

The model has four dimensions: physical wellbeing (*taha tīnana*), emotional and mental wellbeing (*taha hinengaro*), social wellbeing (*taha whānau*) and spiritual wellbeing (*taha wairua*).[8] Each of the four walls of wellbeing contributes to the integrity and strength of the house. Unique among the wellbeing models we have examined is the fact that this house of wellbeing sits on the land (*whenua*), representing the importance of connections to place and planet: land, roots and ancestors.

For further information go to: www.ero.govt.nz/publications/wellbeing-for-success-a-resource-for-schools/useful-wellbeing-resources/ or see the resources we've developed at nziwr.co.nz.

The PERMA model

The PERMA model of wellbeing was developed by Dr Martin Seligman of the University of Pennsylvania, whose theory of wellbeing[9] proposes five domains of life people find naturally rewarding (i.e. they are intrinsically motivated to do them). One domain may be more important to an individual than another. These domains are positive emotions, engagement, relationships, meaning and purpose and accomplishment (PERMA). A growing number of schools now use this model, and specific measures have been developed using the domains, including the EPOCH[10] measure, and the PERMA-Profiler,[11] which has also been developed as the PERMA-H[12] (see Chapter 8 on measurement). For more information see: www.authentichappiness.sas.upenn.edu/learn/wellbeing or nziwr.co.nz.

For many users, this model was perceived as focusing on the cognitive aspects of wellbeing at the expense of physical wellbeing – a criticism which psychologist Chris Peterson characterised in his teaching as 'neck-up psychology'. The PERMA model is now often used in education as PERMA-V, with the suffix *V* standing for vitality (eat, sleep, move). Regular physical activity, a balanced diet and good sleep have long been recognised as vitally important for our overall wellbeing.

Geelong Grammar School's wellbeing model contains the five elements of PERMA plus positive health. Each domain is underpinned by character strengths, and the outer layer of the model contains the four key processes used to implement and sustain it, namely, learn it, live it, teach it and embed it. (These processes are described on page 18 of Chapter 2, What is whole-school wellbeing?) For more information, see: www.ggs.vic.edu.au/Institute/Resources/Our-Model; Norrish, J. (2015), the Geelong Grammar School Journey or nziwr.co.nz.

The Five Ways to Wellbeing

The five ways were developed by the New Economics Foundation (NEF) for Foresight, the UK government's future think tank, as part of the Foresight Project on Mental Capital and Wellbeing.[13] In a wonderful feat of synthesis, the NEF summarised over 4,000 scientific wellbeing articles onto a single postcard containing five evidence-based pathways to promote population wellbeing that were intentionally broad in their interpretation. This flexible and practical model is popular in public health promotion campaigns, providing users with practical real-world ideas of ways that they can improve their wellbeing. The Five Ways to Wellbeing are be active, give, take notice, connect and keep learning. For more information, see: www.gov.uk/government/publications/five-ways-to-mental-wellbeing, www.mentalhealth.org.nz/home/ways-to-wellbeing/five-ways-to-wellbeing-downloads/ or nziwr.co.nz.

The Mental Fitness model

The Mental Fitness model uses the familiar and accessible concept of 'fitness' to frame a wellbeing model used in mental health and wellbeing promotion across many contexts.[14][15] Developed by Drs Paula Robinson, Lindsay Oades and Peter Caputi at the University of Wollongong, this model, like physical fitness, highlights the intentional and repeated practice necessary to build mental fitness.[16] By using the concept of fitness, the model deliberately intends to destigmatise mental health and make it as accessible and open to discussion as our physical fitness. The Mental Fitness model focuses on four dimensions: strength (including sense of meaning and purpose), flexibility (psychological), endurance (self-efficacy and resilience) and team (social support and relationships). For more information, see: www.positivepsychol ogyinstitute.com.au/mental_fitness.html; Robinson, P. (2019). *Practising positive education: A guide to improve wellbeing literacy in schools.* 2nd edition, or visit the Positive Psychology Institute website at www.positivepsychology institute.com.au/.

The PROSPER wellbeing framework

The PROSPER wellbeing framework was developed by Drs Toni Noble and Helen McGrath in Australia.[17] The acronym PROSPER stands for positivity, relationships, outcomes, strengths, purpose, engagement and resilience. Each dimension of the framework represents evidence-based practices which schools can engage in to build wellbeing for their community. This model builds on the work of Noble and McGrath over several decades, supporting development of resilience and wellbeing in students and schools.[18] The PROSPER model is also consistent with the principles and approaches set out in their long-running Bounce Back resilience programme popular with schools in Australia and New Zealand.[19] For more information, see: Noble, T., & McGrath, H. (2015). *The PROSPER school pathways for student wellbeing: Policy and practices.* Springer.

The Mental Toughness model

Created to support a focus on psychological resilience (called mental toughness) in sport,[20] the mental toughness questionnaire (the MTQ-48) has since been validated as a robust measure of the concept, which is relevant to the numerous challenges we find ourselves facing in other areas of life.[21] Mental Toughness is associated with stress resilience and hardiness. Of interest to schools, use of the model with a teenage student population has also shown that a 'mindset of mental toughness enables an individual to cope successfully with the pressures and demands of life'.[22] The Mental Toughness model is based on the four Cs: challenge (embracing challenge and change), commitment (goal-focused 'stickability'), control (self-worth and managing self) and confidence (feeling competent and capable). For more information, see: https://aqrinternational.co.uk/category/ models-of-mental-toughness.

ASPIRE principles

The ASPIRE principles, developed by education psychologist and former special-needs educator Dr Sue Roffey, are based on the research evidence of what promotes wellbeing across the whole school.[23] Although they are given separately here, they are interactive in practice. The ASPIRE principles and circles solutions methodology have been used to deliver a successful, culturally responsive programme of social and emotional learning to young indigenous Australians.[24] The ASPIRE principles are agency (self-determination), safety (physical, emotional and psychological safety enables learning), positivity (fun, strengths-based language and solution-focused approaches), inclusion (belonging is critical for resilience and wellbeing), respect (demonstrated by active listening and not prejudging others) and equity (everyone can have access to opportunities and the chance to shine). For more information, see: https://growinggreatschoolsworldwide.com/how-we-work/the-aspire-principles.

Putting it into practice

We value and use the wellbeing models developed by our mentors and colleagues. However, we have deliberately chosen to give more space in this chapter to unpublished schools' wellbeing models as this is information not as readily available to readers.

Choosing a wellbeing model that 'fits' your school

There is no such thing as a perfect wellbeing model, but it is important to consider the 'fit' and appropriateness of a model for a school's culture and context at a given time. Some schools want to work with a model that's well known to their staff and local community, while other schools want to use an evidence-based model.

Choosing a wellbeing model is like turning an old-fashioned kaleidoscope; the particles within it stay the same, but once turned, a different picture appears. Most wellbeing models include elements of physical, emotion/mental, social/relational and spiritual wellbeing. In schools, we typically include a sense of meaning and purpose (or what makes life feel worthwhile) or connection to something bigger than yourself as part of the spiritual dimenson of wellbeing. Just as with a kaleidoscope, you can keep turning the wellbeing dimensions around until you find the picture that's right for your school.

How schools are working with wellbeing models

Some choose an 'off the shelf' wellbeing model, others create their own model reflecting school values, while others make wellbeing part of the school values framework. There is no right or wrong way to do this. Choosing a wellbeing model is, in and of itself, a wellbeing intervention. The engagment, learning and development of relationships through discussions about wellbeing are important acts of culture change that should not be underestimated.

What matters is:

- The school has a framework, aligned with school values, to guide school wellbeing practices;
- The school engages in discussion about what wellbeing is and what is most needed in the community. The process of adopting a wellbeing model is at least as important as the model itself, engaging people deeply in wellbeing learning; and
- The school community (staff, students and parents) supports the model which reflects their shared understanding of wellbeing.

For some schools, a wellbeing model is already well known in the school; it may be used in teaching health and PE (or PSHE in the UK) or may be widely known in the community (e.g. five ways to wellbeing). For these schools, rather than debating the value of including different wellbeing components, the focus of conversation can be, 'What does that mean to you?' The conversation shifts into unpacking the model and describing what it looks like in practice. This is an essential step to making a model 'come alive'. Where there is no clear preference for a model, discussion tends to focus more broadly on what wellbeing as a whole means to people. It is essential that the working definitions and models of wellbeing that schools adopt are inclusive and reflect the worldviews and practices of all the school community. At this point in the discussion, it is also helpful to provide wellbeing information to stakeholders so that discussion is informed by science and best practice.

Case study 7.1:   Engaging the school community in a vision for whole-school wellbeing

Upper Canada College (UCC) is an all-boys independent school located in the heart of Toronto, Canada. In the fall of 2016, under the leadership of Principal Sam McKinney, UCC set out to develop its new strategic directions, titled *Towards 2029* in recognition of its bicentenary year.

'A wide-scale community consultation identified wellbeing as a priority for our stakeholders. Discovery groups, including faculty and non-teaching employees, explored wellbeing research and best practice. Seligman's PERMA model was found to be meaningful and relevant for our school context. Tasked to develop a common understanding of wellbeing for the community, the new Wellbeing Team focused on "Feeling Good and Functioning Well"[25] as a starting point and added "Caring for Others". Our school mission statement speaks of providing transformational learning opportunities that foster the development of head, heart and humanity for our students. "Feeling Good" aligned with our domain of "Heart", "Functioning Well" aligned with "Head", and "Caring for Others" aligned with "Humanity". Thus, our framework came into being; positively received by our community, it will serve as a foundation for program development across the school'. See Figure 7.1.

Head	Heart	Humanity
Perspective	**Positive Emotion**	**Meaning**
Thinking critically, creatively and compassionately about situations to develop a wider range of thoughts, actions and reactions.	*Enjoying life and experiencing it through feelings like inspiration, peace, hope, gratitude and love.*	*Belonging to and serving something that you believe is bigger than you are.*
Growth-mindset	**Relationships**	**Other-mindedness**
Improving through learning, dedication, and hard work.	*Developing meaningful relationships with others.*	*Caring for other people and acting out of concern for them.*
Accomplishment	**Resilience**	**Engagement**
Building competence, mastering a skill, or achieving goals.	*Bouncing back from adversity and growing from struggle.*	*Committing to the people, activities, and initiatives that you care deeply about.*
Vitality		
Feeling healthy and capable and energetic.		

© 2019 Upper Canada College

Figure 7.1 Upper Canada College's wellbeing model

Source: Model definitions based on the work of Dr Martin Seligman, Dr Karen Reivich, Dr Carol Dweck, Dr Barbara Fredrickson, researchers associated with Greater Good (UC Berkeley) and Authentic Happiness (UPenn).

Case study 7.2:   Using psychological capital as a wellbeing model
for whole-school wellbeing

Mike Anderson, principal of Waimairi School, Christchurch, New
Zealand, has embarked on a wellbeing initiative aimed at building
the school's psychological capital, starting with staff.

'PsyCap is about filling our fuel tank so that when we hit challenging times we can cope without running out of gas'.

'Psychological capital (PsyCap) is an approach largely used in
organisations – to give them strong levels of capital. In our school,
we used a small business analogy, where a business with a strong
balance sheet has capital reserves so that it can weather a difficult
year. Our reserves might dip, but we can keep going. In education, a school can face emotional and psychological turmoil. This
approach is designed to build the school's collective psychological
resource to be stronger together to weather any storms.

The four pillars through which PsyCap is built are: hope, self-efficacy, resilience, and optimism. There is a lot of overlap with educational research on teacher self-efficacy which Hattie's research has
shown to have a large impact on learning.[26]

Our first priority was to develop understanding of psychological
capital and strategies to build it in staff. The shared leadership view
was that staff should not be discussing or aiming to develop a capacity in students that they were not already familiar with themselves.

A literature review confirmed that there was no previous application of PsyCap in education. We agreed that we would begin with
assessing and building staff PsyCap while working on developing
measures appropriate for students.

The school identified what psychological safety would look like in
the school and established a process that would feel safe for staff for
managing data and results. Staff PsyCap results were provided privately to individual staff and not shared with anyone in the school.
At this time, a number of staff with counselling skills were made
available for optional and confidential debrief or support for staff'.

Details of how Waimairi School has implemented PsyCap with staff
is included in Chapter 12 on staff wellbeing.

Case Study 7.3:   Rāroa School: Designing their own wellbeing model

Rāroa School has worked on wellbeing with staff for over two years. During that time, the school leadership committed to learning about wellbeing and dedicated time for all staff to learn about wellbeing. Deputy Principal Stephen Eames describes the process they have followed to develop their own wellbeing model.

'We want to support our students' wellbeing – and give them access to teachers who understand what wellbeing looks like. We want teachers to be looking after themselves so they're in the best possible condition to model what wellbeing and positivity look like.

We used existing models to help us learn about the science that underpinned all the models, but wanted to create something that worked for us. So we drew from all of them to create our own approach. After a lot of work and discussion staff developed a strong sense of ownership of actions that support their own wellbeing. This in itself meant teachers were in a stronger place to model what wellbeing looks like to students in the classroom.

Ultimately we constructed our model of wellbeing around our school vision – "ASPIRE to Achieve". Our teachers explored and identified the aspects of wellbeing that sit under each of those values and we co-constructed the actions and activities that would underpin each of the values.

Actively Involved: That might be healthy choices, ensuring that you have a chance to develop and live your passions.

Skilful Inquiry: Opportunity for self-driven learning for teachers, being able to be curious, to look into the profession.

Perseverance: It's easier to persevere when you have a strong sense of meaning and purpose. This is about making sure that teachers understand the things they do on a daily basis that positively affect students' lives.

Independence: This is about taking responsibility for your own wellbeing. The question that guides our wellbeing work is "How do we help others to help themselves?" We undestand the impact that we have as teachers and want to positively influence others.

Respect: This is about relationships and giving – relationships are our number one influence on wellbeing and learning.

Enjoying ourselves: This is about fun, joy and positivity in our lives. We talk about the power of purposeful reflection as a wellbeing tool. It's so important that we reflect on successes and on the people we're grateful for – purely to enjoy it without having a next step or an improvement (which we typically do in learning).

From staff to students

The key point now is that students are developing their understanding of wellbeing, and they're not developing it from the teachers' model, but rather from their teachers' understanding of that model. We are at the start of the process with students. And already we're seeing classes transforming. We're seeing calm, settled classrooms. We're seeing lots of reflection. I think a lot of the teachers are doing well-being and kindness inquiries. The students are practicing being grateful. There's a lot going on in the classrooms that has come about from the teacher learning before we even officially began the student wellbeing initiatives.

We restructured our staff room so that it was a welcoming place to come. It was about respecting staff and investing in their wellbeing. Teachers felt that all of these small things (plants, coffee machine, shoulder massage) added up to staff feeling valued. But nothing compared to the effect of working on this framework together'.

More detail on the design thinking process Rāroa used to develop their wellbeing model is in Chapter 9 on the sandpit phase.

Box 7.2: *Te Whare Mauri Ora*: An integrated bi-cultural wellbeing model for Aotearoa/New Zealand

Wiremu Gray, school counsellor and wellbeing facilitator, developed the *Te Whare Mauri Ora* wellbeing model in 2017.[27] *Mauri Ora* is a Māori language expression that means a healthy life force or life essence.

'The model is an integration of positive psychology, *Maori* methodology, bi-cultural understanding, Rangatahi (youth) voices and my own life story (See Figure 7.2). It draws on Te Whare Tapa Wha, PERMA-V, Five Ways to Wellbeing, and 7 habits of happy people.[28] Te Whare Mauri Ora was designed to help schools and other community organisations develop authentic cultural responsiveness to Māori. Mental health and well-being are presented through an indigenous lens that bridges knowledge from Te Ao Marama (a Māori world) and Auraki (a western world) with specific techniques and mental tools from Positive Psychology that are mana enhancing (acknowledge the worth of the person), personally and socially. The model explores the environmental influences and social determinants of health and wellbeing customised to local community and school contexts including staff relationships, leadership, student and staff interactions, parent community, and Boards of Trustees (Boards of Governors). Te Whare Mauri Ora is a solution-focused, strengths-based approach underpinned by the aspiration of Pae Ora[29] (a view of society encapsulating connections between the social determinants of health, and wellbeing for Māori whānau)'.[30]

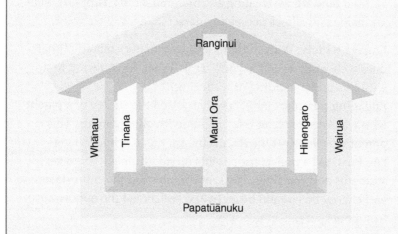

Figure 7.2 *Te Whare Mauri Ora* model. Copyright 2017 Wiremu Gray

Expert practitioner insight 7.1: *Clive Leach. Finding a strategy that suits your school*

Experienced teacher, executive coach and critical friend and change agent for school wellbeing, Clive Leach, shared this advice with us on finding a wellbeing strategy or model that suits your school.

- **'Work with school leaders [wellbeing leads] to unpack:** What does wellbeing mean for you, and what language will work for you? Let this inform your choice of strategy or model.

- **Wellbeing strategy and model:** It doesn't have to be a giant weighty strategic tome; it can be short and sharp. The purpose of the vision/strategy is to encourage the school to implement the wellbeing actions that support it. Schools I have worked with have used these strategies/themes/models to focus their wellbeing efforts:

  - **Five ways to wellbeing:** Sharing practical strategies to build each of the five ways.
  - **'Engage, relate and shine':** This is about shining from the inside out. How we look after our mental and physical wellbeing.
  - **People, process and place:** How do we engage with each other, how do the processes we use support our wellbeing and how are we creating an environment that supports well-being and allows people to interact in the way we want?

- **Engage widely:** With students and staff to understand "What does wellbeing mean for you?" and "What do you want to do with this understanding of wellbeing?"
- **Engaging parents:** One school harnessed the energy of a parent who was keen to share information with other parents. This parent, Sue Smith at the British International School Shanghai, Puxi, led a project for parents on mindfulness, character strengths and coaching. The school embraced the enthusiasm and energy this parent brought and welcomed the opportunity to support parents in this way'.

Case study 7.4:   Knox Grammar School's Total Fitness model (using Mental Fitness)

Knox Grammar School is a boys' school in Sydney, Australia, educating 2,400 day and boarding students from kindergarten to year 12 (ages 17–18). Paula Robinson, developer of the Mental Fitness model, has worked with Knox Grammar for over eight years, during which time the school has adapted the Mental Fitness model as the process underpinning their school wellbeing model. (We are grateful for permission to reprint elements of the story of the Knox Total Fitness model from Dr Robinson's book, *Practising Positive Education in Schools*.)[31]

'The Knox Total Fitness Program is a multi-level, strategic approach to creating a positive school climate that supports academic performance, mental fitness, and the wellbeing of staff and students. The program combines the science of Positive Psychology, Positive Organisational Scholarship, and Appreciative Inquiry supported by evidence- based coaching for sustainability.

Knox used Appreciative Inquiry to decide the key features of its program. . . . As the design phase continued, the Knox team started talking with students about the program. They quickly discovered a problem with language: words such as "positivity" and "wellbeing" were dismissed by students as "psychobabble" and difficult to relate to. Aware of the need to get students on board, the team began the search for a way to make the program more relevant and relatable. They opted for a physical fitness analogy based on Dr Paula Robinson's Mental Fitness Model[32][33] to engage the all-male student body.

Using the Mental Fitness Model as the foundation, the Knox Team created the Knox Total Fitness Model. Launched in 2014, the model includes both explicit and implicit approaches to support academic performance and increase mental fitness with the goal of significantly increasing wellbeing for all stakeholders . . . . All Knox staff members, including sport coaches, are trained in Positive Psychology. Under the program, each student is assigned a mentor to help them identify their strengths and set academic and personal goals. Students are introduced to activities and exercises scientifically proven to increase levels of wellbeing and performance. . . . The Knox Total Fitness Model is delivered through conventional classroom activities, technology platforms, the mentoring program, coaching and a specially devised online parenting program'.

Case study 7.5:   Creating *Te Haerenga* cross at Dilworth Rural Campus

Paul Tupou-Vea was a youth coach, teacher and outdoor instructor for seven years at Dilworth School Rural Campus, New Zealand, where students at the all-boy school have an outdoor-focused year 9 (age 14). 'Head of Personal and Social Growth', he led the development of the wellbeing programme and was part of the team that developed a wellbeing model for the Rural Campus.

'Encapsulating any deep and diverse learning community with a single model is a daunting task. It was important to the staff at our campus to be clearer and more structured with our work on helping students (boys) grow into holistically well men, of value to self and society. Referring to the rich language of the national curriculum key competencies, school values, motto, principles and a campus *whakatauki* (Māori proverb), created complicated messages for students. A model provided a simpler response with shared language for our community.

Dilworth has strong traditions in boys' education, Anglican faith, and a family atmosphere that the students know as brotherhood. The school's founder, James Dilworth, outlined his wishes for the school in a detailed will. For our context, "the will" anchored the process. Any discussions, actions and outcomes needed to align with the aims of the whole school, as outlined in the will. The process also needed to honour the traditions of the school, ensuring that the work that emerged was aligned with Dilworth's *kaupapa* (purpose) and *tīkanga* (culture).

We identified early that any model needed to be owned by all stakeholders in order for it to be sustainable. I worked closely with the senior management to facilitate appreciative inquiry–based conversations with whānau (extended family) about strengths, values, and goals. Students were primed to consider the best examples of adulthood and manhood, and asked to imagine their best selves. They were asked about different domains of adulthood they would like to have or develop. Finally, staff data was gathered, and a focused group of staff members gathered fortnightly over three terms to analyse the data and refine imagery and language, while staying anchored to the school's purpose and culture.

The project group examined different models of wellbeing, including Geelong Grammar's adaptation of Martin Seligman's PERMA, Carol Ryff's model of Psychological Wellbeing, and Mason Durie's *Te Whare Tapa Whā*. We wanted the model to encapsulate the learning competencies of the national curriculum, so that the language of this model could be used in any school setting – from the classroom to the sports-field, to the outdoors, to boarding and pastoral conversations with coaches.

Today, the model is used to guide curriculum planning across three curriculum strands at the Rural Campus: Academic; Personal and Social Growth; and Outdoor Education. Its use in pastoral and restorative conversations is invaluable, and the staff have built an accompanying rubric to guide the learning of sub-skills and behaviours associated with the model. As a successful pilot, the wider school community is currently progressing well in its creation of a model that speaks to and for Dilworth's larger network of campuses and communities'.

Reflection questions

- Is your school already using a wellbeing model(s) in different areas of the school?
- Have you asked your staff, students and parents, 'What does wellbeing mean to you?'
- Do you have a clear understanding of what these groups would like to see in a wellbeing model?
- How will a wellbeing model align with your school values?
- Is a separate wellbeing model the best approach for your school? (Could wellbeing be referred to in school values?)
- Is there interest from within the school community in developing your own wellbeing model, or would people prefer to adopt an existing model?
- Have you considered how you will use a wellbeing model?
- Is the model you want to use appropriate for the applications most important to you?
- Will your wellbeing model support and encourage development of a shared language of wellbeing?
- Is the model culturally appropriate for all your school community? Have you checked with different groups within the school?

Notes

1   Robinson, P. (2018). *Practising positive education: A guide to improve wellbeing literacy in schools.* Positive Psychology Institute.

2   Hone, L., Schofield, G., & Jarden, A. (2015). Conceptualisations of wellbeing: Insights from a prototype analysis on New Zealand workers. *New Zealand Journal of Human Resource Management, 12*(2), 97–118.

3   Oades, L. G. (2017). Wellbeing literacy: The missing link in positive education. In *Future directions in well-being* (pp. 169–173). Cham: Springer.

4   Robinson, P. (2019). *Practising positive education: A guide to improve wellbeing literacy in schools* (2nd ed.). Positive Psychology Institute.

5   Robinson, P. (2019). *Practising positive education: A guide to improve wellbeing literacy in schools* (2nd ed.). Positive Psychology Institute.

6   Durie, M. (2004). An indigenous model of health promotion. *Health Promotion Journal of Australia, 15*(3), 181–185.

7   Ministry of Education. (2007). *The New Zealand curriculum.* Ministry of Education. Retrieved from http://nzcurriculum.tki.org.nz/The-New-Zealand-Curriculum

8   Ministry of Health. (2019). *Māori health models.* Retrieved August 21, from www.health.govt.nz/our-work/populations/maori-health/maori-health-models/maori-health-models-te-whare-tapa-wha

9   Seligman, M. (2011). *Flourish.* North Sydney, Australia: William Heinemann.

10 Kern, M. L., Benson, L., Steinberg, E. A., & Steinberg, L. (2016). The EPOCH measure of adolescent well-being. *Psychological Assessment, 28*(5), 586.

11 Butler, J., & Kern, M. L. (2016). The PERMA-profiler: A brief multidimensional measure of flourishing. *International Journal of Wellbeing, 6,* 1–48. doi:10.5502/ijw.v6i3.526

12 Created by Peggy Kern and Michelle McQuaid, the PERMA-H Workplace Survey can be accessed at https://permahsurvey.com/about-us/

13 Jenkins, R., Meltzer, H., Jones, P. B., Brugha, T., Bebbington, P., Farrell, M., . . . Knapp, M. (2008). Foresight mental capital and wellbeing project. In *Mental health: Future challenges.* London: The Government Office for Science.

14 Robinson, P. (2017). Leading with mental fitness. In R. Koonce, P. Robinson, & B. Vogel (Eds.), *Developing leaders for positive organizing.* Bingley, UK: Emerald Group Publishing.

15 Robinson, P., & Oades, L. G. (2017). Mental fitness at work. In L. G. Oades, M. Steger, A. Delle-Fave, & J. Passmore (Eds.), *The Wiley-Blackwell handbook of the psychology of positivity and strengths-based approaches at work*. London: Wiley-Blackwell.

16 Robinson, P. L., Oades, L. G., & Caputi, P. (2015). Conceptualising and measuring mental fitness: A Delphi study. *International Journal of Wellbeing*, 5(1), 53–73.

17 Noble, T., & McGrath, H. (2015). PROSPER: A new framework for positive education. *Psychology of Well-being*, 5(1), 2.

18 Noble, T., & McGrath, H. (2012). Wellbeing and resilience in young people and the role of positive relationships. In *Positive relationships* (pp. 17–33). Dordrecht: Springer.

19 McGrath, H., & Noble, T. (2011). *Bounce back! A wellbeing & resilience program*. Melbourne, Australia: Pearson Education.

20 Clough, P., Earle, K., & Sewell, D. (2002). Mental toughness: The concept and its measurement. *Solutions in Sport Psychology*, 32–43.

21 Perry, J. L., Clough, P. J., Crust, L., Earle, K., & Nicholls, A. R. (2013). Factorial validity of the mental toughness questionnaire-48. *Personality and Individual Differences*, 54(5), 587–592.

22 Gerber, M., Brand, S., Feldmeth, A. K., Lang, C., Elliot, C., Holsboer-Trachsler, E., & Pühse, U. (2013). Adolescents with high mental toughness adapt better to perceived stress: A longitudinal study with Swiss vocational students. *Personality and Individual Differences*, 54(7), 808–814.

23 Roffey, S. (2017). The aspire principles and pedagogy for the implementation of social and emotional learning and the development of whole school well-being. *International Journal of Emotional Education*, 9(2), 59–71.

24 Dobia, B., & Roffey, S. (2017). Respect for culture – Social and emotional learning with aboriginal and Torres strait Islander youth. In *Social and emotional learning in Australia and the Asia-Pacific* (pp. 313–334). Singapore: Springer.

25 Keyes, C. L., & Annas, J. (2009). Feeling good and functioning well: Distinctive concepts in ancient philosophy and contemporary science. *The Journal of Positive Psychology*, 4(3), 197–201.

26 Hattie, J. (2012). *Visible learning for teachers: Maximizing impact on learning*. Routledge.

27 Gray, W. (2019). Te Whare Mauri Ora. Counselling Today/Nga Korero Awhina Newsletter of the New Zealand Association of Counsellors, part 1: May, and Part 2: June.

28 Setton, M. (2019). *7 Habits of Happy People*. Retrieved on 6 December 2019 from: https://www.pursuit-of-happiness.org/science-of-happiness/.

29 Inquiry into Mental Health and Addiction. (2019). *Oranga Tāngata, Oranga Whānau: A Kaupapa Māori Analysis of Consultation with Māori for the Government Inquiry into Mental Health and Addiction.* Wellington: Department of Internal Affairs.

30 *For more information contact: Wiremu Gray at manafacilitation@gmail.com.*

31 Robinson, P. (2018). *Practising positive education in schools: A guide to improve wellbeing literacy.* Sydney, Australia: Positive Psychology Institute.

32 Robinson, P. (2017). Leading with mental fitness. In R. Koonce, P. Robinson, & B. Vogel (Eds.), *Developing leaders for positive organizing.* Bingley, UK: Emerald Group Publishing.

33 Robinson, P. L., Oades, L. G., & Caputi, P. (2015). Conceptualising and measuring mental fitness: A Delphi study. *International Journal of Wellbeing, 5*(1), 53–73.

Watch

Five Ways to Wellbeing. Retrieved from www.youtube.com/watch?v=yF7Ou43Vj6c

Geelong Grammar School's wellbeing model. Retrieved from www.ggs.vic.edu.au/Institute/Resources/Our-Model

Prof. Martin Seligman on his PERMA model. Retrieved from www.youtube.com/watch?v=jqqHUxzpfBI

Read

Five Ways to Wellbeing: new applications, new ways of thinking. Retrieved on 5 December 2019 from https://neweconomics.org/2011/07/five-ways-well-new-applications-new-ways-thinking

Robinson, P. (2019). *Practising positive education: A guide to improve wellbeing literacy in schools* (2nd ed.). Positive Psychology Institute. This is a beautiful, accessible and enjoyable resource to have in your school library, reception area and staff room.

Listen

NZIWR podcasts are available from https://nziwr.co.nz/category/podcast/

NZIWR podcast: Paula Robinson (training for a fit mind).

NZIWR podcast: Stephen Eames (developing their model of wellbeing).

NZIWR podcast: Mike Anderson (psychological capital).

NZIWR podcast: Wiremu Gray (Te Whare Mauri Ora model)

Measurement and evaluation

Introduction

Given that 'what we measure affects what we do',[1] measuring is essential for building whole-school wellbeing, fulfilling several key purposes: providing a snapshot to understand how students/staff are functioning across a variety of domains (wellbeing, work satisfaction, work/life balance, stress, depression); identifying areas for improvement and assisting prioritisation; enabling evaluation of learning of wellbeing skills (mindsets, optimism, compassion) and curricula; assessing sub-group differences (year levels, departments) and school-wide issues/practices. Measuring your programme and its impact also helps convey the message wellbeing is important and can act as an intervention itself. Despite substantial demand for, and interest in, this important part of the wellbeing jigsaw, consensus around the best approaches remains largely lacking. While much attention has been focused on measuring the subjective wellbeing of students and staff, there is more to evaluation than self-report surveys assessing personal wellbeing. Next, we overview key aspects of measurement to consider and share what schools are currently doing.

How to measure

We are lucky enough to work with Dr Reuben Rusk, our in-house measurement guru at the New Zealand Institute of Wellbeing & Resilience. Reuben conducted his PhD research at the University of Melbourne with Professor Lea Waters and is known for his passion regarding wellbeing measurement. Here he shares tips and thoughts on how to measure carefully and produce meaningful, useful results.

Design

Have specific, well-reasoned objectives for measurement

Clarify the goals at the outset. As the programme progresses, these goals may change as a result of gaining experience. Schedule reviews every six months or year to ensure the objectives remain appropriate in the context of other school changes and challenges.

Develop a detailed plan for how the outputs will be used

Develop a clear vision for the outputs from the measurement programme: Who will receive them; what decisions or actions will they inform? That vision will help ensure your measurements are able to provide appropriate and useful outputs. Work forward from the objectives and backward from a clear picture of the desired outputs.

Establish a clear and well-reasoned measurement scope

Ensure this relates closely to the goals and desired outputs and justify all questionnaire content against them. The compromise between breadth and depth of measurement needs to be appropriate for your measurement requirements.

Ensure response burden is acceptable

Response burden is the overall time and effort required of respondents to complete the assessments. Ask a representative cross-section of the intended respondents what an acceptable completion time would be for them. Estimating completion time is difficult, so test out the questionnaires on a small pilot sample and adjust based on their feedback. Ask too little and you won't have sufficient information; ask too much and respondents will get bored, reducing the reliability of your data.

Programme engagement and support

Ensure stakeholder support

Measurement programmes are more likely to meet their objectives and inform real action when all stakeholders support them, so ensure all stakeholders understand the programme's rationale. Involving all stakeholders from planning to completion will help you be considerate and sensitive to their different concerns, challenges and values.

Identify your measurement champions among staff, students and the broader community

People who can cultivate and sustain interest and motivation to complete the questionnaires, analyse data and report results play an important role. Identify them early and keep them involved throughout.

Get respondents on board with the vision for the measurement programme

The responses will be more complete, accurate and trustworthy when respondents view the questionnaires favourably. Inspire them by sharing the background and goals of the measurement programme, helping them understand how it fits your school's broader wellbeing initiatives and goals.

Organise specific times and places for completion

Providing respondents with time set aside for completing the questionnaires is one practical way to improve response rates and quality.

Ensure responses are anonymous

Wellbeing information is often personal and sensitive, so programme coordinators need to deal with it carefully. Gather responses anonymously where possible, and ensure information that could identify individuals is not disclosed in reporting. Anonymity can make it feel safer to answer honestly and counteract the bias to respond in socially desirable ways. In small groups, anonymity can become compromised by guessing the identity of respondents. We recommend reporting average or aggregate results only.

Engage with respondents during the measurement programme

Keep them informed and provide real opportunities for them to contribute ideas. Before disclosing any summary results, consider their possible psychological, social and political implications.

Ethics

Respondents know how the data will be used and who will see it

Before providing responses, respondents must understand how their personal (and possibly sensitive) responses will be handled, stored and reported on.

The respondents have autonomy and choice

Wellbeing questionnaires can raise all sorts of emotions. It is important people have the choice to opt out and that no negative consequences are imposed on people who choose to not participate. This is tough, we know! But it is unethical to coerce people into responding.

Provide respondents with appropriate channels for psychological support

Responding to questions about personal wellbeing can surface questions, issues and emotions that may be difficult to deal with. This is especially true for children. Care must be taken to ensure respondents are provided with options for support. Provide a wide range of support, from informal conversations with peers, staff or discussion groups through to dedicated support staff and professional services, and ensure respondents are aware and sufficiently informed to use them by promoting these opportunities via a wide range of channels.

Measurement items and scales

Gather both qualitative and quantitative data

Qualitative data (focus groups and open-response questions) add a depth of meaning to quantitative results (numerical data) that can help knit the numbers together to form a cohesive and compelling story. The quantitative data add a crucial objectivity to that story, which helps to clarify changes over time.

Gather data at multiple levels, from individuals, year groups, departments, leaders and the whole organisation

These different levels of a school are interconnected. Gathering data relating to wellbeing at all these levels provides a more holistic picture as well as insights into what generates and sustains wellbeing within the school as a whole.

Each item (and scale) fits with the purposes and scope of the programme

Measure only what is relevant and needed to achieve the objectives of the programme. Some surveys will assess long-term changes in wellbeing outcomes; others will be used to evaluate individual programme effectiveness. In those cases, it may be useful to include items about specific thoughts and behaviours that lead to those wellbeing outcomes. Measurement programmes that span the spectrum from the current and the specific through to the long-term and the general can provide the fullest picture of change over time.

Keep questionnaires to a reasonable length

The respondents' expectations of response burden dictate what length is reasonable. However, long questionnaires can fatigue respondents, lead them to answer inaccurately in an effort to complete them quicker or reduce motivation to complete follow-up questionnaires. If the programme objectives demand a very large number of items, consider splitting them into multiple shorter questionnaires.

Ensure items (and scales) are appropriate and of high quality

Look for scales used successfully in a similar context and culture. Ideally, items would be supported by a body of peer-reviewed research demonstrating their validity, providing greater confidence that they will be sensitive to detecting change and provide repeatable responses in its absence. Plus, they should feature age appropriate language.

Ensure licensing obligations are met

While some scales are in the public domain, many require a license for use. The cost to license any particular scale does not necessarily imply its quality, and some scales are free to use provided certain conditions are met. See later in this chapter for our recommended list of psychometrically validated wellbeing scales frequently used in schools.

Implementation

Take one or more baseline measurements

Evaluation is best done by comparing responses during and after wellbeing initiatives with a set of baseline data collected before they commence. Control groups are often used in research to build confidence that changes are not due to other factors, but these are often impractical (and potentially unethical) in school contexts. If repeated baseline measurements establish a stable level, they can provide more confidence that changes seen during and after the initiative are not due to other factors.

Ensure repeat measurements are given in the same context

Responses can be affected by the context in which respondents give them. This context can include time of day, week of the term, recent experiences, the environmental and social setting or time pressure. Measurements will be more accurate when the context in which they are given is similar, and this consideration can guide how the measurements are facilitated. For the same reason, minimise changes in the format of the questionnaire.

Introduce personal assessments with care

Students tell us they want to know what the measure is for, why they are being asked to complete it, why this is important and what difference it will make. We recommend taking a look at Public Health England's publication *Measuring and Monitoring Children and Young People's Mental Wellbeing: A Toolkit for Schools and Colleges* which has a fantastic section on how to introduce wellbeing measures to young people. See www.annafreud.org/media/4612/mwb-toolki-final-draft-4.pdf.

Harness technology

Online platforms offer several advantages. Responses can be validated during submission to ensure required items are not missed. They also reduce the need for manual data entry (with associated data entry risks). However, paper copies do sometimes maximise participation. Also, be aware that, without care, the context in which an online survey is completed may differ widely between measurements. For example, via a mobile phone, a teacher might complete the initial questionnaire at school during lunchtime and complete the second questionnaire at home late one evening. Differences could arise due to the very different contexts in which the questionnaire is completed.

Analysis and reporting

Ensure analysts are qualified to interpret the data

Unless you are using an external provider, the gathered data will require analysis to summarise meaningful information. While sums and averages are easy to calculate, expertise is required to interpret those values. Differences could be due to meaningful change or simply random variation. Statistical expertise aids in determining their significance. Qualitative data can aid the interpretation process, but experience in this area also helps identify the most relevant and meaningful themes.

Tell a rich story

A report based on numbers alone will lack the impact that real stories provide. Weave the quantitative and qualitative results into a coherent story to help people make sense of the results. Ground the story visually through graphs, photographs and videos if possible. Seek to give insight at different levels of the story, from personal experiences and activities through to whole-school statistics. Finally, make the story accessible and interesting by connecting it to the goals, challenges and events that stakeholders already understand and value. Even the most well-intentioned leaders are not impartial and unbiased, and important decisions they make will depend not only on the actual results, but also on the quality of that story.

Box 8.1: Geelong Grammar School's measurement journey

'We didn't measure and we wish we had; measuring early on gives you an understanding if there's been a progress later on. We believed the research and decided to go ahead and implement across the board – we wanted to do something for the students. We now see that as one of the errors we made', explains Vice Principal, Charlie Scudamore.

Since then, GGS has invested heavily in measurement, conducting, among other things, a major longitudinal study in partnership with the University of Melbourne and Monash University.[2] Investigating the wellbeing of 383 year 9, 10 and 11 students from GGS and 138 sociodemographically equivalent students from a range of private schls in Melbourne (who weren't exposed to the GGS's PosEd curricula) showed the wellbeing of GGS year 9 students improved from the start to the end of the year, was stable in year 10 and declined in year 11. The improvements in wellbeing among year 9 students were significant and extensive (observed across all six domains of the GGS PosEd model – positive emotions, positive relationships, positive purpose, positive engagement, positive accomplishment and positive health – and other wellbeing and mental health measures). The fact that year 9 students from the control schools reported no such wellbeing gains led researchers to suggest that the benefits were a result of GGS's year 9 Timbertop programme. (It should be pointed out that year 9 is a special year at Geelong, with all year nine students boarding at Timbertop and engaged in an outdoor education programme placing a substantial emphasis on responsibility and cooperation. This makes it difficult to isolate the impact of the year nine PosEd programme from the rest of this unique experience.)

Qualitative data from focus groups also supported the beneficial effects of the Timbertop programme, with students showing insight into how the experience contributed to each domain of their wellbeing. Using mobile tablets to sample 50 students momentary daily experiences also suggested that students whose wellbeing improved over the year (62% of the cohort) showed a significant decrease in the use of negative strategies in response to negative events, while students whose satisfaction with life increased over the year (67% of the cohort) showed a significant increase in the use of positive strategies in response to positive events in their lives.

The absence of any significant improvements in year 10 – when positive education was comprehensive and explicit – was no doubt disappointing and surprising, but useful too. Focus groups conducted with year 10s identified aspects of the PosEd programme requiring change: students wanted the classes to be more interactive and experiential, less 'academic'; they wanted more real-world examples relevant to them and age specific; and they wanted more consistency across teachers in content delivery and modelling of aspired behaviours. In addition, the research also highlighted a need for a resilience 'booster' among year 11s, so the school now hosts an annual resilience retreat at the end of semester one in year 11.

Box 8.2: Issues to consider around measurement

We want to take this opportunity to express several concerns and important considerations around measurement.

- Assessment may have unintended consequences and even cause harm among both adults and students. We are concerned about schools electing to provide children with individualised wellbeing reports (with varying degrees of support) before the pros and cons of doing so have been properly debated by either the psychology or education communities. Schools need to carefully consider what best practice is in this area and what appropriate support for students should look like.
- When assessment is conducted as part of research through a university it is subject to ethical review. Assessment must be fit for purpose, and the protection of those involved is carefully considered – particularly for children, considered 'vulnerable subjects'. There is concern within the field that wellbeing assessment (whether online commercial assessment or within the school) is taking place without being held to the same standards.
- In the current data-driven era, data gathering is often not questioned. Understanding what data should and should not be

(continued)

collected, who benefits from data collection, where data is stored, who owns the data and what external contractors are doing with the data is vital.

- Like so much of education, the long-term impact of wellbeing promotion may not readily be detected, or even realised, until many years later. 'While boards should require evidence for positive education efforts, this needs to be tempered by an acknowledgement that the greatest impacts of supporting positive education may not be seen for many years'.[3] Most teachers we've worked with have stories about former students relaying the positive impact they had on them as teachers (many years later). The same may be true regarding the latent impact of wellbeing programmes.

- Be realistic about your hopes for wellbeing measurement (see the previous point). 'People will be surprised how little things move when it comes to wellbeing measurements', comments Georgie Cameron, who advises schools on measurement at the Institute of Positive Education. She also cautions schools to realise that free-to-use measures are not cost neutral: someone has to dedicate time and expertise to crunching the data, which are services reflected in the rates of paid-for services.

- Finally, we encourage schools to seek 360-degree feedback on subjective wellbeing and personal strengths and use observational data to provide a more valid, rounded story.

What to measure

Among well-resourced early adopters, measurement usually includes evaluation of specific programmes/professional learning, student/staff attitudes toward the programme, subjective wellbeing surveys (for staff, students and the wider community) and focus group and feedback forums, as well as observational and behavioural data. In order to keep things simple and practical, we have grouped the various measurement opportunities here.

Personal wellbeing

Assess subjective wellbeing among staff, students and the wider community using a multidimensional tool (such as EPOCH, AWE and the Well-being

Profiler as described next). This is far superior to traditional measures that focused on single aspects of wellbeing such as life satisfaction. We don't recommend using overly long measures or oversimplified measures. For example, many large health organisations have typically used the WHO-5 wellbeing survey, but with only five questions, this may aggregate top-line insights but won't provide sufficiently rich data to identify priorities for intervention. Additionally, schools may choose to use more 'fine-grained' or detailed measures that focus on evaluating single constructs, such as the Children's Hope Scale[4] or the Gratitude Questionnaire.[5] Try to go beyond self-report and incorporate teacher, colleague and parent input as well.

Listed here are some of the validated metrics we've seen used in schools to assess individual wellbeing among students, staff and parent communities. We encourage schools to use aggregated measures reporting group trends instead of providing individual reports. Not only is there limited evidence that individualised wellbeing reports have any tangible benefit for students, but there are also ethical concerns with this approach.

Warwick-Edinburgh Mental Wellbeing Scale (WEMWBS):[6][7] Measures positive mental wellbeing within the general population. The scale has been validated for use with children aged 13 and above but has been used with children aged 11 and above. The short form has 13 items and is free for use. For more details and permissions, see https://warwick.ac.uk/fac/sci/med/research/platform/wemwbs/.

The Well-being Profiler (University of Melbourne):[8] Provides domain scores on how young people (10 to 25 year olds) are faring across six categories of wellbeing (psychological, cognitive, social, physical, economic, emotional and strengths). Apart from positive indicators of wellbeing, such as engagement, life satisfaction, happiness, connectedness, physical health and stability at home, risk factors are also included. For example, negative emotional states such as anger, anxiety, depression and stress provide information about subjective experiences that might oppose the domain of emotional wellbeing and strengths. Other risk factors include loneliness, bullying, and negative peer pressure, which yield information about negative forms of sociality that could obstruct the domain of social wellbeing. Levels of sedentary activity are relevant to physical wellbeing. https://www.wbprofiler.com/

Assessing Wellbeing in Education (AWE): AWE provides a collection of validated scales wrapped up in an online survey for staff, students and parents – both individual and school reports – with qualitative and quantitative data, plus providing alerts regarding struggling students. The core adult survey features 52 items, the core junior student survey 14 items, and the core senior student surveys 29 items. One of the advantages of AWE is that it is customisable: Schools have the option of adding validated scales assessing specific aspects of wellbeing and adding open-response questions to suit their needs. We know of a large number of schools who have found AWE useful. Costs depends on the size of your school. As a guide, assessing up to 1,000 users will cost approximately NZ$3,000, US$2,100, UK£1,600, €1,800, and AU$2,750. See www.awesomeschools.com/.

The PERMA-Profiler:[9] A general measure, free to use, developed for adults, which measures flourishing (high levels of wellbeing) in terms of the five domains of Marty Seligman's wellbeing theory[10] (positive emotion, engagement, relationships, meaning, and accomplishment). It has been translated into multiple languages. The measure is available from Peggy Kern's website www.peggykern.org/uploads/5/6/6/7/56678211/the_perma-profiler_101416.pdf and can also be taken online through the University of Pennsylvania's Authentic Happiness website: www.authentichappiness.sas.upenn.edu/testcenter.

We've also heard of schools choosing to use Peggy Kern and Michelle McQuaid's PERMA-H Workplace Survey because of the PERMA profile report it provides, along with tips and ways to build wellbeing. See https://permahsurvey.com/.

The EPOCH Measure of Adolescent Wellbeing:[11] Adapting the PERMA scale for adolescents, EPOCH measures five positive psychological characteristics believed to promote flourishing: engagement, perseverance, optimism, connectedness and happiness. The 20 items have been adjusted to be developmentally appropriate for young people. It is free for use with permission: www.peggykern.org/uploads/5/6/6/7/56678211/epoch_measure_of_adolescent_well-being_102014.pdf.

Mental Fitness Index (MFI):[12][13] Robinson and colleagues developed the MFI as a reliable measurement tool to determine levels of mental fitness. The 69-item MFI survey provides a total score for each MF factor of strength, flexibility, endurance and team, allowing researchers or professionals to determine what specific areas of mental fitness may need improvement. Schools adopting the MF model and MFI survey tell us they like the physical fitness analogy. Each of the four high-level factors has sub-components which can be analysed individually: strength (strengths knowledge and use and meaning and purpose), flexibility (mindfulness, acceptance and reduced negative emotions), endurance (self-confidence, resilience, increased positive emotions, optimism, autonomy and competence) and team (positive relationships, relatedness and social support). While the MFI is not publicly available, Robinson and colleagues are happy to assist with any enquiries regarding mental fitness or the MFI and collaborating with and supporting any future research studies. Please contact them at info@appli.edu.au.

The Resilience Survey: An online survey for 8- to 18-year-olds, which collects, analyses and reports the resilience of young people in terms of their strengths, life satisfaction, hopefulness, anxiety and depression, coping style and risk and protective behaviours, incorporating four different measures. Schools are provided with a report which benchmarks their data against national Australian norms. The cost is AUD$4+gst per survey. All surveys are anonymous and students non-identified, with cohort-based reporting only. See www.resilientyouth.org.au/survey.

Australian Council for Education Research's Social-emotional Well-being Survey (SEW): Is a confidential online strength-based survey for students aged 3 to 18 years created by Michael Bernard. It provides schools with aggregated information about their student population at different levels (whole school, year levels, targeted groups). Costs depend on school size, and licences are for unlimited access to the survey and reporting for 12 months. See www.acer.org/au/sew.

If your school is undertaking comprehensive assessment of student and staff wellbeing and wants to include measures of mental distress, we strongly recommend you do so under the guidance and supervision of a qualified psychological researcher.

School-wide practices

We are constantly encouraging schools to put the large amount of school and education data they already have to good use when evaluating wellbeing. These include, but are not limited to, absenteeism, turnover/churn, stand downs, behaviour incident data, teacher observations (classroom, playground, assemblies), student profiles and portfolios, interviews with caregivers, reports to boards/trustees, school documentation (charter, policies, procedures), minutes from departmental meetings (guidance, pastoral, RTLBs etc.), staff room attendance and achievement/academic performance data.

In addition, a number of surveys are useful for measuring school climate and school-wide practices. For example, in NZ, the NZCER offers a variety of surveys evaluating school-wide practices (see https://hps.tki.org.nz/Tools-for-Schools/NZCER-surveys). Another good resource is Yale's InspireED (see https://inspired.fb.com/) website, which provides resources and surveys to enable student-led assessment of school climate and ideas for improvement.

In our work at the New Zealand Institute of Wellbeing & Resilience, we have collaborated with Reuben Rusk to create our own school wellbeing benchmark survey, evaluating personal wellbeing practices (for example, 'I have the skills to build wellbeing'); personal strengths knowledge and use ('I use my strengths effectively'); school-wide wellbeing practices ('Our leadership supports student wellbeing' and 'We have a school-wide model of wellbeing'); aspects of the school environment where wellbeing may be visible (prize-giving, classroom decorations, newsletter, assemblies etc.); school-wide strengths knowledge and use ('We focus on strengths in our contact with parents'); wellbeing in the classroom ('I feel competent discussing wellbeing with parents') and school challenges (how widespread stress, depression, suicidality, bullying etc. are in the school). The rapidly accruing dataset associated with this new scale means we should soon be able to test its psychometric validity. While this is not currently publicly available, please contact us (info@nziwr.co.nz) if your school is interested in using this benchmark survey.

Wellbeing literacy

We can also consider measurement of wellbeing literacy[14] levels (skills knowledge/competence on a wide range of wellbeing related concepts, such as strengths use/knowledge, self-determination theory and motivation, hope theory and goal setting). As no validated measure of wellbeing literacy currently exists, schools typically create their own surveys to investigate if levels of wellbeing knowledge and practice have shifted as a result of explicit efforts to teach wellbeing. These can include items such as 'In the past year, to what extent have your knowledge and understanding of the significance of wellbeing and resilience changed?'

Programme evaluation

The purpose of programme evaluation is to determine if the programmes you ran had the effect you expected and hoped for. Evaluation includes programme reach (e.g. number of staff attending professional development) as well as evaluation of subjective perspectives on professional development (Was it helpful, and do you use what you learned?). Specific wellbeing initiatives introduced to a school can be evaluated as part of ongoing review and commitment to continuous improvement. A large body of literature on evaluation within education already exists for schools to draw on.

Box 8.3: Education-led assessment of wellbeing

Many wellbeing assessment measures come from psychology. It's important for the field of wellbeing in education that we have measures grounded in educational frameworks and practice. The Ministry of Education in New Zealand and the Education Review Office (ERO; similar to OFSTED in the UK) have developed a framework of indicators to assist schools in their focus on student and staff wellbeing and evaluate progress. Resources include ERO's Wellbeing for Success: Draft Evaluation Indicators for Student Wellbeing (2013), Wellbeing for Success: A Resource for Schools (2016) and School Evaluation Indicators: Effective Practice for Improvement and

Learner Success (2016). Whether for ERO or their boards, schools need to document how they support wellbeing – the activities and practices they use to build a wellbeing culture. These are excellent resources forming the basis of NZIWR's wellbeing audit of existing school wellbeing practices. (See Chapter 6 on building ownership.)

ERO's document Evaluation Indicators: Effective Practice for Improvement and Learner Success (2016) provides guidance on how to achieve equity and excellence, focusing on both wellbeing and achievement. Wellbeing for Success: A Resource for Schools (2016) uses the same core concepts and focuses on supporting wellbeing. This document sets out the school leadership and management aspects shown to support wellbeing, as well as a pedagogical approach based on building effective relationships for teaching and learning, delivering a responsive curriculum, and providing effective teaching and opportunities to learn. Importantly for school practice, student voice in wellbeing decisions and monitoring of student wellbeing are highlighted as well as responding to wellbeing issues. See https://www.ero.govt.nz/publications/wellbeing-for-success-a-resource-for-schools/

Expert practitioner insight 8.1: *Institute of Positive Education: Implementing and sustaining positive education – a roadmap for schools*

In 2016 Geelong Grammar School created the multi-component rubric for tracking school progress in implementing whole-school wellbeing. With permission from GGS, we have included that roadmap here, with the intention of providing readers with an overview of all the processes involved in whole-school wellbeing promotion. As you look over the rubric, you will notice the different components of whole-school wellbeing identified by GGS and what they will look like in practice as your school moves from the left-hand side of the page as these practices are introduced, to the middle where they are consolidated, to the right hand side where actions are focused on sustaining. Using this rubric regularly to score your school's current wellbeing initiatives will provide you with quantitative assessments to look back on over time. We are most grateful to the IPE at GGS for so generously allowing us to publish it here.

Implementing & Sustaining Positive Education *a roadmap for schools*

INSTITUTE OF POSITIVE EDUCATION GEELONG GRAMMAR SCHOOL

	Introducing |1---------1|--------2|	Consolidating |3---------1|--------4|	Sustaining |1---------------5|	Totals
Learn				
Leadership support	Leadership explores possibility of school-wide implementation of positive education and appoints key staff	Leadership prioritises resources, provides support and champions Positive Education	Leadership ensures Positive Education remains prioritised through governance and innovation	
PosEd framework and infrastructure	Committee explores different wellbeing frameworks and audits existing wellbeing structures	Implementation of specific Positive Education framework across different areas of the school	Ongoing tailoring, integration and documentation of contextualised Positive Education framework	
Staff professional learning	Introductory professional learning for staff in key concepts of Positive Education	Introductory and further professional learning for all staff (teaching and non-teaching)	Regular, scheduled professional learning, internally driven and informed by specific school needs	
Parent & community education	Systematically inform parent community about key concepts and purpose of Positive Education	Provision of parent and school community education and establishing of formal parent-committee	Ongoing, scheduled parent education and contribution from formal parent-committee	
Resource library	Establish a foundation of support resources and connect with local and international networks	Systematically grow resource library including development and sharing of original materials	Ongoing collection, development, sharing and cataloguing of support resources	
Live				
Deliberate cultural practices	Introduce a range of opportunities for staff and students to participate in cultural wellbeing practices	Shared responsibility for development and maintenance of ingrained cultural wellbeing practices	Ongoing review and enhancement of embedded Positive Education practices	
Personal practices	Individuals explore, trial and share a range of personal wellbeing practices	General acceptance of the importance of maintaining and role modelling personal wellbeing practices	Whole school community actively nurturing wellbeing in self and others	
Teaching practices	Individuals explore and trial evidence-based teaching strategies to enhance student wellbeing and learning	Understanding and sharing of best practice pedagogy to enhance student wellbeing and learning	Common use of evidence-based pedagogy to enhance student wellbeing and learning	
Staff wellbeing	Gathering awareness of existing staff wellbeing levels and wellbeing needs	Implementation of targeted teaching and non-teaching staff wellbeing initiatives	Ongoing resources dedicated to actively supporting and growing staff wellbeing	
Student partnership	Seek student input in initial design of Positive Education curriculum and practices	Engage student representatives to provide informed feedback and lead student initiatives	Ongoing commitment to including student input in review, development and implementation processes	

	Introducing |----1----|----2----|	Consolidating |----3----|----4----|	Sustaining |----5----|	Totals
Teach,				
Sequenced curriculum	Trial new or tailor existing dedicated wellbeing lessons and activities	Staff and student feedback-informed refinement and customisation of curriculum sequence	Fully documented, comprehensive curriculum with ongoing review and enhancement process	
Explicit teaching	Allocate time and resources for delivery of explicit Positive Education teaching	Tailor and refine a comprehensive explicit Positive Education curriculum	Student and staff-informed feedback providing input into regular refining and customising of content delivery	
Implicit teaching	Identify pre-existing curriculum areas in which Positive Education concepts can be incorporate	Curriculum leaders regularly report on wellbeing integration and foster innovation and refinement	Fully documented and integrated implicit curriculum which complements explicit wellbeing curriculum	
Coaching of students	Training staff in coaching principles and practices to support student wellbeing	Development and refinement of coaching programme, activities and materials	Pastoral staff committed and experienced in coaching individual student wellbeing	
Sharing practices	Promote sharing of best practice and ideas within the school community	Support field of Positive Education by contributing to networks, events, publications	Formal process scheduled to facilitate ongoing sharing of best practice and ideas with appropriate networks	
Embed				
Wellbeing metrics	Identify wellbeing outcomes to be measured and appropriate measurement tools	Baseline data collected and used to determine specific areas of need and to guide Positive Education activities and interventions	Consistent measurement tool systematically utilised with data harnessed to inform Positive Education refinement and development	
Organisation policies	Review of organisational policies through evidence based, Positive Education lens	Amendment and communication of organisational policies to be aligned with Positive Education principles	Regular review of existing organisational policies and careful construction of new policies to ensure alignment with Positive Education principles	
Student policies	Review of student policies through evidence based, Positive Education lens	Amendment and communication of student policies to be aligned with Positive Education principles	Regular review of existing student policies and careful construction of new policies to ensure alignment with Positive Education principles	
Communications	Review of internal and external communication processes through Positive Education lens	Refine communication processes to align with Positive Education principles and to educate community	Internal and external communication processes fully aligned with positive education principles	
Student support services	Identify and connect all services within the school that support student welfare and wellbeing	Wellbeing infrastructure refined to ensure that all student services are integrated with Positive Education	Student support services fully integrated with school-wide Positive Education infrastructure	

institute@ggs.vic.edu.au

Figure 8.1 The Institute of Positive Education: A Roadmap for Implementing & Sustaining Positive Education

Case study 8.1:   Haeata Community Campus, New Zealand

Haeata has a strong commitment to wellbeing which is part of their annual goals and strategic direction.

Rebecca Wilson: 'As part of our strategic direction getting voice and feedback from our staff, *ākonga* and *whānau* was important. When you value wellbeing the way we do it is important to measure it; you measure what you value.

We began with the Wellbeing at School tool across the *kura* but on reflection should have begun with AWE. We chose to use the AWE tool as it measures wellbeing across all aspects of our lives instead of solely focusing on the school setting. We used AWE's 69 standard wellbeing questions (which included extra specific questions in the areas of Work Engagement and Stress) and added 8 questions specific to our school, five of these were free text and three scaled questions.

AWE assesses individuals' subjective wellbeing: experiences, feelings, functioning, and perceptions of how their lives are going – both what is going right, and what is going wrong.

The findings of the AWE staff survey were shared with all staff and Board of Trustees following strategic planning with Senior Leadership Team.

The AWE tool allowed us to look at what we were doing well and what our next steps could be. We looked for consistent messages that came out of the survey and decided to action three key areas to focus on and to communicate back to staff. These focus areas were embedded across the year and regularly reflected on in terms of making improvement across the school. The findings and actions from the survey have fed into the wellbeing strategy framework.

The important thing about measuring wellbeing is that you are informed and not making judgements that are not evidenced. Another positive thing around measuring wellbeing is that it increases buy-in as people can have a say'.

Expert practitioner insight 8.2: *Clive Leach. Considering measurement more broadly*

Clive Leach has worked with schools around the world for the past decade to support wellbeing. He shared these questions about assessment of wellbeing:

- For a lot of schools, wellbeing measurement has not been a priority. Schools are focusing on the work they want to do rather than on the measurement.
- It's always useful in schools to ask, 'What does success look like?' and 'How else might wellbeing change be tracked?'
- The stories that a school tells about itself are important markers of change and can be useful in showing how a school has moved forward. How can you curate stories?
- The language and vocabulary of young people around their use of strengths is another indicator of wellbeing change in a school. How might you evaluate this?

Reflection questions

- What's the purpose of measurement?
- What are you trying to evaluate in this particular instance?
- Who will be involved?
- How will you get a big enough sample that you can be sure the results are meaningful (i.e. representative of the broader population, not just unique to that particular sample)?
- Will the information be anonymous or otherwise?
- How will you assure participants of the confidentiality and security of their data?
- Do you have the correct consents (to gather data and use it)?
- How will you store the data?
- How and when will you share the data?
- What do you plan to do with the data?

- If you use an external provider, who owns that data? What can they do with it; where will they store it; who can they share it with?
- How will you communicate with various stakeholders the impact of your evaluation and the next steps? How will you tell the measurement 'story'?
- What steps will you take to ensure young people are comfortable with the assessments you are planning?
- Have you planned for quantitative assessment and qualitative (e.g. focus groups, interviews, or free text response)?
- How often will you measure?
- Who's going to analyse and report on the data?
- What will you do if the outcomes improve?
- What will you do if the outcomes decline?

Notes

1   Stiglitz, J., Sen, A., & Fitoussi, J-P. (2009). *Report by the commission on the measurement of economic performance and social progress.* Retrieved from www.stiglitz-sen-fit oussi.fr/documents/rapport_anglais.pdf

2   Vella-Brodrick, D. A., Rickard, N. S., & Chin, T-C. (2014, August). *An evaluation of positive education at Geelong grammar school: A snapshot of 2013.* Melbourne, Australia: The University of Melbourne.

3   White, M. A., & Kern, M. L. (2018). Positive education: Learning and teaching for wellbeing and academic mastery. *International Journal of Wellbeing, 8*(1).

4   Snyder, C. R., Hoza, B., Pelham, W. E., Rapoff, M., Ware, L., & Danovsky, M. (1997). The development and validation of the children's hope scale. *Journal of Pediatric Psychology, 22,* 399–421. doi:10.1093/jpepsy/22.3.399

5   McCullough, M. E., Emmons, R. A., & Tsang, J. (2002). The grateful disposition: A conceptual and empirical topography. *Journal of Personality and Social Psychology, 82,* 112–127. doi:10.1037//0022-3514.82.1.112

6   Clarke, A., Friede, T., Putz, R., Ashdown, J., Martin, S., Blake, A., . . . Stewart-Brown, S. (2011). Warwick-Edinburgh mental well-being scale (WEMWBS): Validated for teenage school students in England and Scotland. A mixed methods assessment. *BMC Public Health, 11*(1), 487.

7   Tennant, R., Hiller, L., Fishwick, R., Platt, S., Joseph, S., Weich, S., . . . Stewart-Brown, S. (2007). The Warwick-Edinburgh mental well-being scale (WEMWBS): Development and UK validation. *Health and Quality of life Outcomes, 5*(1), 63.

8   Chin, T-C., Jiang, J., Waters, L., Kern, M., Slemp, G. R., Oades, L., et al. (2016c). *Measuring youth well-being using the well-being profiler: Science background*. Melbourne, Australia: The University of Melbourne. Retrieved from www.wbprofiler.com/profile_well-being/science_ background

9   Butler, J., & Kern, M. L. (2016). The PERMA-profiler: A brief multidimensional measure of flourishing. *International Journal of Wellbeing*, 6(3).

10   Seligman, M. E. (2011). *Flourish: A visionary new understanding of happiness and well-being*. Simon & Schuster, New York, NY.

11   Kern, M. L., Benson, L., Steinberg, E. A., & Steinberg, L. (2015, August 24). The EPOCH measure of adolescent well-being. *Psychological Assessment*. Advance online publication. http://dx.doi. org/10.1037/pas0000201

12   Robinson, P. L., Oades, L. G., & Caputi, P. (2014). *Conceptualising and measuring mental fitness*, Doctor of Philosophy thesis, Department of Psychology, University of Wollongong. Retrieved from https:// ro.uow.edu.au/theses/4269

13   Robinson, P. L., Oades, L. G., & Caputi, P. (2015). Conceptualising and measuring mental fitness: A Delphi study. *International Journal of Wellbeing*, 5(1), 53–73.

14   Oades, L. G. (2017). Wellbeing literacy: The missing link in positive education. In *Future directions in well-being* (pp. 169–173). Cham: Springer.

Watch

Measuring Wellbeing in Schools: Anna Freud Centre (UK) video explaining why and what to measure in schools. Retrieved from www.youtube. com/watch?v=wkclI8y1MKQ

Professor Felicia Huppert. Retrieved from www.youtube.com/watch?v=_ RCVLcIIbPM

What is wellbeing and how can we measure it? UCL. Retrieved from www. youtube.com/watch?v=_RCVLcIIbPM

Read

Measuring and monitoring children and young people's mental wellbeing: A toolkit for schools and colleges. Public Health England. Retrieved from www.annafreud.org/media/4612/mwb-toolki-final-draft-4.pdf

The New Economic Foundation's Measuring Well-being: A Guide for Practitioners. Retrieved from https://neweconomics.org/uploads/files/8d-92cf44e70b3d16e6_rgm6bpd3i.pdf

The University of Pennsylvania's Authentic Happiness website also has a number of validated wellbeing and other mental health surveys. Retrieved from www.authentichappiness.sas.upenn.edu/testcenter

Listen

NZIWR podcasts are available from https://nziwr.co.nz/category/podcast/

NZIWR podcast: Clive Leach.

NZIWR podcast: Adrienne Buckingham.

The sandpit phase

Introduction

Once school leadership is fully on board and committed to the concept and philosophy of whole-school wellbeing and you have built a reasonable degree of buy-in amongst staff, then you want to start 'doing' – to move into implementation. This begins with empowering teachers and support staff to trial, adapt and pilot ideas and activities to nurture wellbeing across all areas of the school environment and their particular circles of influence. The wellbeing team and staff also need agreed frameworks or pedagogies to guide their implementation decisions.

Research on change is covered in more detail in Chapter 5 on understanding change dynamics, so we will turn first to practice and then to research of particular relevance to this topic.

Putting it into practice

Building wellbeing in complex school systems is messy. In our experience, it works best when the foundations have been laid carefully, with consideration to all stakeholders and by painting a compelling vision of change. At some stage, though, the time for talk and preparation is done, and the messy business of giving it a go is required. Much of the disappointment and disenchantment we see during implementation can be avoided by:

- **Equipping staff with the tools to implement and adapt.** 'Make it work in your classroom' is not sufficient support. Staff need agreed learning and pedagogical frameworks and tools to select these trial practices.
- **Clearly framing this stage as one of 'trial and error'.** This means removing any expectation of getting it right the first time, placing a

strong focus on learning from mistakes, putting timelines around how long a trial needs to run and agreeing how learning and review will be managed.

Wellbeing strategies have to be adapted and customised to each school context. That involves learning from failure as well as success. This stage is where staff get an opportunity to embrace the principles of growth mindset (Dweck, 2007) that are part of wellbeing learning.

Successful, sustainable wellbeing change responds to context and culture. To implement this kind of change, staff need to be able to critically and appreciatively evaluate their context, engage with the different people in it, and design strategies and tools (or choose curricula) that will be suited to the needs of these staff, students and community. Being asked to take on this work with no guiding principles or approaches is a bit like being asked to find your way to the South Pole with no map or compass. The result, most often, is a lot of floundering and wasted effort. Schools are full of people with a deep understanding of learning and the needs of learners. Most are familiar with approaches such as inquiry, design thinking, univeral design for learning (UDL) or SOLO taxonomy (Structure of Observed Learning Outcomes).

Stacking the odds in your favour: Increasing the likelihood of success in the sandpit

The schools we see really embracing this work share an excitement in learning and designing. Their teachers and staff are excited to apply learning/pedagogical approaches to this work. The sandpit phase for these schools is variously described as 'messy, exciting', 'the best thing I've done in school for years', or 'why I'm still in teaching'. In contrast, where schools have rushed to implementation without supporting staff professional development in wellbeing or without agreeing on the processes that will be used to guide the process, wellbeing change can become another burden on staff and a source of stress.

Three common sandpit pitfalls that we would like to help schools avoid are:

- **Ready, Fire, Aim.** Rushing to implement classroom wellbeing teaching before teachers are confident with the material can create significant stress and loss of self-efficacy for some of teachers. This can reduce staff wellbeing and is ultimately counterproductive;
- **Here's the information – go make it work.** Staff have been provided with wellbeing knowledge and training, but there is no agreed framework for how this work will be implemented. While decisions around curricula can be resolved with the purchase of and commitment to a validated

programme, decisions around how wellbeing will be 'caught' in a school are onoing and require as much careful evaluation and decision-making as decisions regarding wellbeing curricula.

- **You know this stuff already.** Neglecting ongoing professional learning can undermine the sustainability of wellbeing change. Professional development is vital to keep the concepts fresh and to ensure the community stays abreast of the latest developments in the relatively young and evolving field of the science of wellbeing.[1]

Having a team of wellbeing educators from across diverse departments is vital for embedding whole-school sustainable change. The research suggests you should take it slowly at first, allowing time for staff to get to know each other and build trust. Make sure that their willingness (or tolerance!) for sharing is applauded and that those brave initial sharers get the positive feedback they need and deserve. In a wellbeing community of practice we've worked with, establishing trust among educators was the first task. Once connections were established, we could ask educators whose work we knew to share what they had trialled. This proved to be an effective way to model sharing and build trust and rapport in the group. After a few sessions with different people sharing, we were then thrilled to hear one school suggest setting up a group Google drive to share resources freely.

The sandpit phase can be challenging and rewarding. In our experience with schools, expectations are of paramount importance. If you thought the wellbeing process could be done quickly and by "plug and play", then several years of trial-and-error learning will seem long and frustrating. When you have been clearly told that this is at least a five-year journey that will involve adapting different practices to find what works for you, then you are less likely to lose heart when you hit a roadblock after 18 months.

Here is some of the advice we share with schools:

- Giving it a go is messy. Forewarned is forearmed. By clearly articulating this phase as one of trial and error, you can build acceptance for the messiness;
- Understand and share what's working well. Where the school operates as part of a cluster (as happens in some countries), we encourage schools to share within and across school. Accelerate the learning process by sharing success tips and strategies;
- Don't expect everyone to come on board at the outset. Give them information and time;
- Teacher self-efficacy matters for wellbeing teaching. In addition to opportunities to fail (safely), teachers also need opportunities to learn (PLD, learning from students, self-reflection, sharing with peers);

- Encourage the emergence of mini-centres of expertise and excellence around the passions of particular staff or students. Then respect and share their expertise at staff professional learning days or in school newsletters;
- Failure is important: learn to be curious about what part of the failure actually worked and where it went wrong or for whom. The important question for wellbeing change leaders is 'What can we learn from this?'
- Find a good framework that you can use to help you plan and evaluate. Frameworks schools use to guide wellbeing work include SOLO taxonomy, inquiry learning, design thinking and universal design for learning. (See also the SEARCH framework in the research section.); and
- Identify existing opportunities for sharing wellbeing strategies between teachers and across departments, but don't just rely on these. Find or create new opportunities for sharing, as watching colleagues try things out accelerates the transition from wellbeing laggard to adopter. This sharing enables people to see wellbeing work in action and provides opportunities for 'first followers' to emerge.[2]

Box 9.1: Things schools say they got wrong

- One school commissioned an externally developed curriculum and asked staff to teach it with no wellbeing training. Staff stress and resistance took 18 months to overcome.
- Many schools put one enthusiastic and committed teacher in charge of wellbeing only to have that person burn out and leave. Wellbeing initiatives then grind to a halt as most wellbeing knowledge has left the school.
- Many schools start their wellbeing work at a sprint, expecting rapid change. Disappointment and disillusionment typically follow.
- One school focused solely on student wellbeing, putting more workload and stress on staff to deliver wellbeing programmes with no attention to staff PLD or wellbeing. Staff morale and trust in the leadership plummeted.
- One school committed to staff and student wellbeing removed the staff coffee machine as part of a cost-cutting exercise. This is not walking the talk.

What the research says

Learning, whether for a teacher or a student, involves risk, exposure, vulnerability and a willingness to make mistakes and learn from them. As educators, we encourage students to take risks and enter 'the learning pit'.[3] 'When I teach I always start the year saying, "If I was teaching you something that you already knew, that would be stupid, so therefore I am teaching you stuff that you don't know, and so therefore you are going to make mistakes. You don't know it, and in order to make mistakes, you have to be able to challenge yourself and you have to be able to give it a go. Part of that is making mistakes, and it needs to be a safe environment where you're not laughed at" and all that stuff'.[4]

As educators, while we encourage students to take risks, we are not always comfortable doing that ourselves. Many educators are reluctant to share their practice, out of fear of appearing incompetent and being shown up by better-performing colleagues.[5] One teacher in a study of effective leadership acknowledged the importance of trust: 'You do have to trust one another, you have to know that if you try something and it doesn't work, it's a safe environment to do that and no one's going to shoot you down and say "She's a really crap teacher" '.[6]

Encouraging staff to share honestly with each other helps avoid the thinking trap that everyone else's classroom operates more smoothly and successfully than their own.

Box 9.2: The SEARCH framework: An evidence-based and actionable framework for whole-school wellbeing

Lea Waters from the University of Melbourne's Graduate School of Education has been involved in a multi-year project to develop a new framework for positive education that is both data driven and evidence based, to help educators organise and evaluate wellbeing interventions in schools. The SEARCH framework covers six overarching pathways to wellbeing: strengths, emotional management, attention and awarenss, relationships, coping and habits and goals.

SEARCH provides a useful framework for schools wanting to design their own wellbeing curriculum – guiding lessons around the six pathways to wellbeing – and as a framework for auditing

---

(continued)

and evaluating existing programmes that tap into the six pathways. The SEARCH framework has been adopted by schools in Australia, New Zealand, the USA, Canada, Hong Kong and the United Arab Emirates.

The six different pathways are described in Table 9.1, which also suggests specific interventions for fostering wellbeing in each pathway. Given that research suggests interventions are more effective when designed to target multiple pathways,[7] Waters and Loton also hope the SEARCH framework will encourage educators to broaden the impact of specific wellbeing interventions, perhaps framing gratitude interventions as tools for fostering emotional management *and* building relationships. In this way, interventions become mutually reinforcing.

Table 9.1 The six different SEARCH pathways

SEARCH	Description of pathway	Sub-categories of interventions identified in literature
Strengths	Pre-existing qualities that arise naturally, feel authentic, are intrinsically motivating to use and energising.	Strength awareness interventions: These interventions help students identify their strengths, typically through surveys.
		Strength use interventions: These interventions help students set goals for how to put their strengths into action.
		Strength spotting interventions: These interventions teach students how to see when their peers are using strengths.
Emotional management	The ability to identify, understand and manage one's emotions by understanding how emotions operate through our thoughts, feelings and actions.	EI interventions: These interventions teach students how to perceive, understand, use and regulate emotions.
		Gratitude interventions: Gratitude interventions help students to notice, appreciate and acknowledge the positive in their lives.

Atten-tion and awareness	Attention is our ability to focus, either on inner aspects of self, such as emotions and physical sensations, or on external stimuli (e.g. the teacher's lesson in a classroom). Awareness refers to the ability to pay attention to a stimulus as it occurs.	Meditation interventions: Meditation is defined as the deliberate act of regulating attention through the observation of thoughts, emotions and body states. Meditation interventions in schools involve training a student's attention.
		Mindfulness interventions: Mindfulness is a state of focused awareness on one's thoughts, feelings and body sensations. Mindfulness interventions in school help students develop the skill of self-observation and be dispassionate about the self in the present moment.
Relation-ships	This pathway concerns the skills required to build and support supportive social relationships as well as capitalise on momentary social interactions.	Mentoring interventions: Mentoring is a process by which a more experienced person provides a less experienced person with guidance, support and caring over an extended period of time. The school-based mentoring interventions aim to provide peer support and or teacher-student support to enhance a sense of connectedness and belonging in the school.
Coping	Coping is defined as constantly changing cognitive and behavioural efforts to manage specific external and/or internal demands that are appraised as taxing or exceeding the resources of the person.	Resilience interventions: These interventions aim to help students develop the capacity for maintaining, recovering or improving mental health following life challenges.

(continued)

SEARCH	Description of pathway	Sub-categories of interventions identified in literature
Habits and goals	Habits are persistent and learned patterns and preferences in decision-making and behaviour. Goals are formal milestones, endpoints, achievements or aspirations that articulate what people desire, aim for and are willing to invest effort into.	Self-regulated learning (SRL) interventions: SRL interventions teach students the cyclical process of steps needed to persist through the learning process: self-evaluation, self-monitoring and goal setting along with strategy planning, implementation and monitoring. Goal interventions: These interventions teach students to set and strive for goals.

Source: Waters, L. & Loton, D. *International Journal of Applied Positive Psychology* (2019). https://doi.org/10.1007/s41042-019-00017-4

More putting it into practice: Case studies from schools

These pedagogies and frameworks have been used to plan and design work that supports staff and student wellbeing.

Case study 9.1:   Using an inquiry approach to develop wellbeing

Melinda Wilson, MAPP, is an educator researching and teaching wellbeing in schools in Australia and the USA. Her criteria for wellbeing work in schools are that it should be contextually appropriate, a rigorous learning experience, evaluated for effectiveness, and cost effective.

'I used the EPOCH characteristics of adolescent wellbeing as my guide. These are similar to PERMA but developed by Peggy Kern and associates (2016) to specifically indicate characteristics which point towards long-term positive well-being outcomes for adolescents. EPOCH stands for engagement, perseverance, optimism, connectedness and happiness. The synergy between EPOCH and inquiry-based learning is depicted in Figure 9.1.

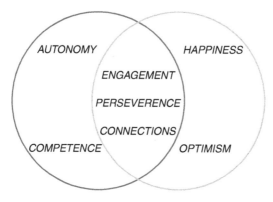

Figure 9.1 Synergy between goals of positive education and inquiry-based learning

Inquiry-based learning goals overlap with EPOCH in this way:

- There is challenge and thereby engagement and connection.
- It fosters a growth mindset encouraging students to find their passion and show perseverance and grit to achieve it.
- There is autonomy in the inquiry process; and
- Competence in the exhibition process where students use peer teaching to display their knowledge.
- Students need to connect with their peers and the wider world (relational).

I set a whole middle school year group the task of choosing one of their lesser strengths which they might want to grow. We used inquiry-based learning for this project: ask, investigate, create, discuss, reflect. Our objective was to show the students that strengths are dynamic. We started with a teaser video clip as the students already knew their strengths. The students were each to research that lesser strength and identify what it would look like when they were able to use it well. They then were asked to develop an intervention to use on themselves over the term to grow that strength.

At the end of term assembly, students had the opportunity to present their results to their peers, having been supported and mentored through the term. It was a lot of fun. Some students had worked hard to improve their humour or creativity, others kindness and gratitude. While everyone, achieved some level of competence, the best part was that they had autonomy in choosing the strength and the intervention and were therefore intrinsically motivated to learn that you can grow your strengths.

One student wrote that when she had begun the project she decided to work on her creativity. She reflected that it was hard work to start her task as she was not sure what creativity really meant. She persevered and developed an intervention she used each day to do her mathematics homework in a more creative way. By the end of term she had learned to be creative within an area of her life that she already enjoyed but had always approached in a very clinical and task-oriented way'.

Case study 9.2:   How Rāroa School used design thinking to develop a wellbeing model

Rāroa School has been working on wellbeing with staff for over two years now. Deputy Principal Stephen Eames describes how teachers used design thinking to build their own wellbeing model. More detail on Rāroa's wellbeing model is provided in Chapter 7 on choosing a wellbeing model.

'Many of our teachers use a design thinking approach with their students. When you design something, you design an experience or a product. To do this, you have to implement the new knowledge you're learning into something practical – and so you really embed the learning. We wanted to use the approach that we put our students through with our teachers – that way we're strengthening the teachers' understanding of the design process and their empathy for students using it.

The process of design thinking is about using our wellbeing knowledge to create the model. For each of the wellbeing indicators we identified, (for example, health and activity, learning and engagement), we developed what they looked like and then implemented it into a picture book. Each picture represents particular aspects of the model. You can see it visually and through an authentic design process you change, adapt, and adjust. The initial pictures didn't suit so we were continually in development and debating. One thing may work for one person, one piece may not work for the other. Students drew what they believed a healthy teacher looked like and teachers drew their version. We had lots and lots of discussion and debate. Every time it was implemented in the staff room there was scribbles and changes. It's a crazy process of just making it real. Teachers would email me. I'd say here's another picture and they'd say, "No that's not right". One of the pictures that changed at the last moment was around relationships. It changed from a happy couple to a woman with her grandmother because we thought that more people can relate to the connection.

We spent two years in the creation of our wellbeing model – to deveop our understanding of what wellbeing looks like – and it turned into a picture book for staff on what wellbeing looks like for an educator at Rāroa. This process helped us develop the shared language and understanding of what wellbeing looks like for our staff. Now we can take it to the students'.

Case study 9.3:   Universal design for learning (UDL) supports learning and wellbeing

Ara Simmons is an accredited facilitator, positive psychology practitioner and certified coach working with schools in New Zealand. She is passionate about UDL's ability to make learning more inclusive for all students.

'Universal design for learning (UDL) considers the outliers in any learning context – our ākonga (learners) who would need additional supports so that they could access the learning that is on offer. This ensures both an equitable approach plus the intentional design for diversity from the outset. Our context is a secondary school which serves a diverse population of students. The leadership have identified that UDL has to be a whole-school approach to have impact.

My first task was to appreciatively audit everything the school already did that used UDL, observing their practice using reflective questions from UDL's **access phase** (e.g. How will I support engagement for all? How can I make my materials adjustable and customisable? Will everyone be able to access all materials and spaces?).[8] The school's UDL Champion department was at the **building phase** with teachers able to surface the pedagogies they use in their deliberate acts of teaching. (Questions to probe these pedagogies include for example, How do I provide options for sustaining persistence and interest? How will I clarify understanding of vocabulary?)

As a team the teachers considered what their **current universal tools** looked like in their classroom. In other words, "What are your go-to teaching strategies?". These could be graphic organisers, completing an online quiz, or "think, pair, share". Teachers surfaced the unintended barriers they created for their students by their choices. With this awareness the team was able to move on and consider how to minimise these barriers.

In **the coaching and observation cycle** the following reflective questions were used to scaffold teachers' UDL planning:

1 What do we know about the learners and the context in which they like to learn?

2 What is the aim of the learning?

3 What potential barriers might there be to this piece of learning, considering some of the current ways I plan on delivering this?

4 What universal supports can I use that support access to learning for all?

5 Which of the UDL guidelines to learning am I considering (already referred to earlier)?

6 After teaching, what worked? What didn't work so well? What could I tweak?

Repeated iterations of these questions allow them to become part of the teachers' natural planning cycle. Benefits of UDL work are that teachers develop their relationships with their students, notice the significant barriers language can have, and the impact of making learning relevant. The language of teachers becomes more affirming and positively reframed. Students get to see themselves in the learning, feel more connected and able to ask the teacher for support because they feel the teacher cares enough to make the learning accessible. Collectively UDL supports the growth of a positive learning environment'.

Case study 9.4:   The Empathy Shoe Museum: A beautiful experiment

The sandpit phase is often associated with hard work, mistakes and 'do-overs' or the need to start again after setback or failure. Happily, it is also the place where beautiful experiments are made, which blossom and bear fruit in multiple ways.

One such initiative was the empathy inquiry led by Rāroa Intermediate School near Wellington, New Zealand. The inquiry was entitled 'Walk a Mile in My Shoes'. Students were invited to choose a pair of their shoes that represented their story and what was important to them.

In this cross-curricular inquiry, students then created and decorated models of their shoes (using technical and artistic skills). They told a story about themselves, what they used these shoes to do and something about themselves that would help the listener know and understand them (written and oral literacy skills). Students created their own team Empathy Museum for people to hear their stories and 'walk a mile in their shoes'. Parents were invited to come and view the students's work, thus enabling community engagement and learning on the topic of empathy and respect for the diverse experiences of those in their community. As the community viewed the shoes, they were able to use the QR codes in front of the shoes to access an audio autobiography on their mobile phones and to listen to the student telling their story.

Reflection questions

- Do staff in your school feel comfortable sharing their mistakes or asking for help?
- How will you acknowledge and support risk taking and failure?
- What plans have you to support staff to implement and share wellbeing practices?
- What teaching and learning frameworks does your school already use? Which of these might help with your wellbeing planning?
- Have you communicated the timeframe for implementing wellbeing change?
- How will you review, evaluate and make changes based on your learning through this stage?

Notes

1   Seligman, M., & Adler, A. (2019). Positive education. Positive education. In J. F. Helliwell, R. Layard, & J. Sachs (Eds.), *Global happiness and well-being policy report: 2019* (pp. 52–71). Global Council for Wellbeing and Happiness.

2   Sivers, D. (2010). *Leadership lessons from dancing guy*. Retrieved September 3, 2019, from www.youtube.com/watch?v=fW8amMCVAJQ

3   Nottingham, J. (2017). *The learning challenge*. Retrieved September 3, 2019, from www.jamesnottingham.co.uk/learning-pit/

4   Moir, S. J. (2013). *Teachers' perspectives of 'effective' leadership in schools.* Master's thesis submitted to the University of Melbourne, p. 34.

5   Moir, S. J. (2013). *Teachers' perspectives of 'effective' leadership in schools.* Master's thesis submitted to the University of Melbourne.

6   Moir, S. J. (2013). *Teachers' perspectives of 'effective' leadership in schools.* Master's thesis submitted to the University of Melbourne, p. 34.

7   Rusk, R., Vella-Brodrick, D., & Waters, L. (2017). A complex dynamic systems approach to lasting positive change: The Synergistic Change Model. *Journal of Positive Psychology*. Available first online.

8   CAST. (2018). UDL Guidelines version 2.2 by CORE Education. Retrieved September 4, 2019, from http://udlguidelines.cast.org/

Watch

Darfield High School's wellbeing journey. Retrieved from https://vimeo.com/325355695

Shirley Boys' High School's 'slow burn' approach to whole-school wellbeing. Retrieved from https://vimeo.com/325355750

The Learning Pit/Challenge. Retrieved from www.jamesnottingham.co.uk/learning-pit/

Read

Amabile, T., & Kramer, S. (2011). *The progress principle: Using small wins to ignite joy, engagement, and creativity at work.* Harvard Business Press.

Listen

NZIWR podcasts are available from https://nziwr.co.nz/category/podcast/

NZIWR podcast: Sonya Papps (spending time in the sandpit).

NZIWR podcast: Charlie Scudamore (lessons from ten years of positive education).

NZIWR podcast: Stephen Eames (using design thinking to create a model of wellbeing).

Building an effective team

Introduction

Principals certainly play a critical role in leading change, but successful, sustained and embedded change is never made by one person alone. The spectre of the sole individual who carries school wellbeing on their shoulders has been observed at numerous schools. It usually ends with teacher burnout, departure from the school and the collapse of the wellbeing programme. The creation of a broad-based representative team is vital: leading wellbeing change is the responsibility of many, rather than the early adopting few. Empowering others to lead change is both desirable and achievable, making relationship and capacity building key.[1] This chapter looks at the role of teams in building support across different interest groups and how to inspire and nurture your early adopters, maintain morale and momentum and ensure continuity.

What the research says

Research examining the ingredients of successful change in educational contexts demonstrates that it starts with, but goes well beyond, the principal.[2] Having generally come from a teaching background, school principals are well positioned to lead change efforts; they understand the complexity of schools as organisations. But their leadership style, not background, is the key factor determining their success as change agents. To implement wholeschool wellbeing change, the principal, board of trustees and senior leadership all have to view wellbeing as a necessary and urgent priority. But their motivation alone is insufficient. Successful implementation requires distributed leadership (as opposed to top down) and intrinsic motivation (as opposed to transactional or extrinsic motivation).[3] As one principal observed:[4] 'You can't achieve [change] on your own. Senior leaders and team leaders – these people really drive the change'. Top-down leadership stifles educator initiative; teacher leadership flourishes in collaborative settings.[5]

Table 10.1 Checklist: Building an effective team

How many of these team-building practices take place in your school?	Tick those occurring in your school
• Involve others in the decision-making. • Respect and value all staff members as individuals and professionals, all students as having a valuable contribution to wellbeing change. • Share the load by allocating responsibilities across all stakeholders (inviting them to volunteer to take on different projects increases autonomy). • Bring together a small team of people across stakeholders who are enthusiastic about coming on this journey with you and willing to commit three years. • Challenge your organisational structures – are they appropriate for the change you want to lead? • Encourage staff (or teams) to create/write their own MATES (mutually agreed team essentials) agreements. • Encourage risk and innovation by developing a 'no-blame' culture where everyone feels confident that what they share will be viewed via a learning lens. • Model the behaviour and thinking you want to see in others (as individuals and teams). • Develop a wellbeing professional learning community and encourage all stakeholders to participate and lead the learning. • Make initial professional learning voluntary – volunteers are more motivated than those who are 'voluntold'. • Provide multiple and diverse opportunities for everyone to share. (This can be, but should not be limited to, professional learning and staff meetings.) • Provide opportunities for feedback. • Identify multiple and varied opportunities to share what's going well.	

McKinsey and Company has found effective change management requires three components: senior, middle and frontline employee involvement; clarity around responsibilities and a good understanding of the reasons for change throughout the entire organisation.[6]

Whatever their role in the school, leaders need to demonstrate excellent relationship skills, a clear sense of direction, an ability to respond to context, a desire to serve others and good strategic decision-making and also be inspirational, confident, effective communicators capable of fostering trust, belonging and commitment.[7] This large and broad leadership skillset is more easily found across a team than in a single individual. To develop these skills, educators need opportunities to work collaboratively in a supportive and nurturing team environment, with time to reflect on their professional practice.[8]

Putting it into practice

A study of educational leadership in post-quake Christchurch[9] shared the importance of shifting school culture from a 'just tell us what to do and we'll get on with it' culture to a 'let's try stuff and learn so we are better able to make decisions'. 'It is important that staff can volunteer to participate, rather than be told or asked to do so, as the act of choice promotes ownership and sustained interest. This can be difficult at times for leaders, who want to proactively create diverse teams to ensure all relevant perspectives are incorporated. But . . . creating structures and allowing staff to opt in (and choose with whom they worked) resulted in high-quality work as well as high morale'.[10] The advice we've heard from schools that have put wellbeing front and centre for some time now suggests that, while you may choose to make one introductory session mandatory for all staff, volunteering is a more effective long-term strategy than being 'voluntold' when it comes to building an effective team. Yes, it takes more time, but autonomy is more powerful than coercion in the long run.

When we work with schools, most of the professional learning we run is with their wellbeing team. These are the early adopters, the people who are intrinsically drawn to the work. They don't need much convincing; they volunteer and view the work as a calling. Ideally, you want to gain a long-term commitment from these people – suggesting three years is one way of testing the genuineness of their expressed commitment!

Over time, the trick is to expand this team from the seeding group to include a range of voices and opinions, knowledge and experience. The best way to do this is to provide frequent and diverse opportunities for further learning, inquiry and discussion around wellbeing, incorporating a range of formats and durations delivered via different media and at a variety of times. Adults, as well as students, like to learn in different ways, after all. To make this easier, we've included podcasts, research papers, websites, blogs and other readings, videos, and books at the end of each chapter.

Rhiannon McGee, head of positive education at Geelong Grammar School, agrees: 'Whether it's coaching, or Positive Education, always start with Professional Learning. Cultivate your champions – draw on the energy of those who are prepared to dedicate their time to that Professional Learning so you can come back as a core group and decide what's going to work for our context. Asking what are our change levers? What do we want to focus on? From my experience, don't bring in a whole programme that you impose on every staff member, look for ways in through already existing approaches'. GGS currently offers staff a three-day discovering PosEd on-boarding programme for new staff hires (compulsory); once-a-term PosEd 4 U session (open to all); optional term-long opportunities to take a deeper dive on single-focus topics such as mindfulness and access to the Institute of Positive Education's insight series, which features visiting fellows; regular opportunities for additional top-up in professional learning are also available to all staff throughout the year on a voluntary basis.

To ensure the long-term viability of whole-school wellbeing, your school will need to continue to invest in building the capacity of a number of colleagues to lead and drive the ongoing delivery of wellbeing training – particularly among new staff members, new parents and new students. Succession planning for the departure of key staff is also vital.

Insights informing our approach to building effective teams come from various sources. We respect Derek Sivers's wisdom on how to start and grow a movement. Sivers's emphasises the key role played by your 'first followers': 'The first follower is actually an under-estimated form of leadership, it takes guts to stand out like that. The first follower is what transforms the first nut into a leader. A movement must be public, it's important to show not just the leader, but the followers, because new followers emulate the followers and not the leader', he explains in his very popular TED talk (see the 'Watch' section at the end of this chapter). Likewise, Brene Brown's Dare to Lead offers pratical support and advice to anyone leading change (see the 'Read' section at the end of this chapter).

We'd add to this three further pieces of really useful advice. The first comes from Chris Eyre, suggesting the three people everyone needs on their personal team: a critical friend, a confidante and a cheerleader. 'The most important criterion is that your confidant (i.e. key supporter) cares more about you than about the issues at stake', writes Eyre, also suggesting educators find supporters outside their school as well.[11] The next comes from the late, great Chris Peterson (co-author with Martin Seligman of the VIA character and strengths and virtues framework), who suggested in a lecture many years ago that it was more important to have a friend than a fan – in other words, don't surround yourself with yes men! Third, and in direct contrast, we constantly remind wellbeing change agents to not get dragged down by the naysayers. There will be opposition to your plans; that's an inevitable part of change! We find watching the three carriage train video really useful here (see 'Watch' section); it reminds us to not take disagreement and dissatisfaction personally. It is not you they hate, just the prospect of 'another' change. Focus your attention on your second wave of followers, make them the change agents and share their endeavours as broadly as you can.

Expert practitioner insight 10.1: *Linda Tame, experienced education leader, on building an effective team*

Linda has 35 years' experience working as an educator in schools. She has been a secondary school principal for 18 years, working at three schools: Lincoln High School, Linwood College and in her current role at Golden Bay High School.

'Schools are all about conversations and relationships. No matter how good the theory, if the relationships aren't strong and the conversations focused on what matters, then progress will be slow, shallow and unsustainable. Here are some considerations I have found useful.

1   Take the time to gather data, have conversations, and then decide what it is you are going to develop or change. This requires leadership. Principals have an overview and likely more knowledge of what the range of possiblitities are. Choosing the best programme for the current context is critical. Use a combination of personal leadership knowledge, experts and within school voice. Keep the why at the centre.

2   Once a decision has been made this programme must be a primary focus in the school. The leaders' job is to protect this focus. New ideas come into our inboxes and from staff, students and the community daily. They have the great potential to dilute. I keep and share a list of good ideas we are not currently working on!

3   Ensure the Board of Trustees know what is going on and support the programme. Governance support for significant initiatives makes a difference.

4   Decide how this programme will be supported. Considerations include

- Who will lead it? Having principal support initially sends a strong message.
- What external expertise will be used?
- How will there be time to implement it? eg Can Kāhui Ako within/across school teachers be used for leaders? How will teachers and students find the time? What will they stop doing so they can focus on this?
- Timetable staff times at least a term out, so that the programme is given the support it needs.
- Help team members to understand there will be successes and failures along the way; this is all part of embedding change.

5   Set up an evaluative framework, so data and voice are being gathered to answer the question: is the programme having the impact on students outcomes we expected? If, overall, the programme isn't working, make changes or stop doing it. Too often schools carry on with "their foot on the accelerator in the sand".

6   When the time is right (maybe at the beginning, maybe not) call for volunteeers for the team. Shoulder tap if necessary. Be brave and include students! Picking the right time for creating the team is important.

7   Find ways for the team to 'form' and 'storm' ideas, e.g. have an in-school retreat and provide rolls and soup for lunch. Set up agreed working protocols such as Google Docs, agendas, notes, prompt start and finish times etc. If team members feel valued, and that their work is important and making a difference, the team will fly.

8   Decide at what point your relational trust of the team is such that you can loosen your control. Initially they will likely need external leadership to build the focus.

9   Take the time to pause and celebrate little successes along the way.

10 Keep a close eye on the team. Support and challenge them. Acknowledge their work'.

Case study 10.1:   Introducing wellbeing at Worser Bay Primary,
                      Wellington, New Zealand

The principal's perspective: Jude Pentecost's interest in wellbeing
began seven years ago, prompting her to complete the 18-month
Certificate in Wholeperson Positive Psychology through the Wholebeing Institute (with lectures by psychologist Tal Ben Shahar and
residentials at Geelong Grammar).

'From that time on I have continued to engage in a lot of personal
and professional learning which I take back to staff and work with
leaders in other schools. This has included: qualifications in Executive
and Organisational coaching, formal accreditation as a Strengths
Profile coach, neuroscience-mBraining cert (I'm still working on this).

Early on we adopted the Geelong Grammar School model of flourishing and made it our own by tying it into what we were doing, what we
felt our children needed, and aligning with cultural competencies and
Māori health models including *Te Whare Tapa Whā, Te Pae Mahutonga*
and Te Wheke. Using Geelong's 'Learn it, live it, teach it, embed it'
framework I realised we needed to first of all focus strongly on the
learn and live aspects among our staff for this to truly become a philosophy not a programme. Teacher Only days always have a large PosEd
component – we've just had two days with GGS's Institute of PosEd in
the last holidays which was great for reminding us about the science,
as this is something I have to constantly do. Although hard asking staff
to do PLD in the holidays these two days really highlighted to my staff
how embedded PosEd is in our school, so was great for them.

Our learning and wellbeing journey is ongoing, multifaceted, and
has to be kept front of mind – not just by me but my leaders and all
staff – so here's an overview of what we do to keep "the living it"
principles alive at WBS.

Strengths

When coming for an interview all staff – teachers/support staff –
come ready to talk about their VIA character strengths and how
we would see these in action/dialled up/dialled down etc. The
Board of Trustees are also familiar with these and we map and refer
to strengths regularly. Character strengths are often touched on in
coaching sessions, along with strengths that have been highlighted

through the Strengths Profiler debrief. My leadership meetings always have a starting question about strengths/what's working well and incorporate a lot of language about 10% better, 10% more. We also refer to strengths in conversations about performance.

Meetings with parents about "tricky" behaviour start from a strengths perspective (often using Robert Biswas Diener's sailing boat metaphor as we see sailing boats from our school).

The character strengths have been developed by the children and whānau into artworks: little plaques can be found in obscure places around the playground and staff and students alike go hunting and reminding themselves of what they need. For instance, when one staff member had to do a lengthy whaikorero at the powhiri he was found on the adventure playground focusing on the bravery plaque.

Concepts like growth mindset are also embedded and highlighted in staff conversations.

Meetings

Whole staff meetings always start with a WWW (what went well) and a PosEd starter to shift mindset. At the moment we have a focus on Positive Emotion/Music so the first ten minutes of the staff meeting will be a movement – meditation, singing, dancing, clapping – whatever the teacher for that session decides.

SPIRE goals and buddies

Staff set SPIRE goals (Spiritual, Physical, Intellectual, Relational, Emotional) and meet regularly with coaching buddies to keep these alive.

Weekly emails from me

I send a Friday email which is often loaded (not tooooooo much!) with messages, links, thoughts, research etc. My weekly blog post to the community is also strengths/wellbeing based.

Language

My project for the Wholebeing Pos Psych course was all about language so this is highlighted with staff and we work to be deliberate in the words we choose, for example encouraging ourselves and students to be "80% good enough". What we say, how we say it is key. I model this with staff and have provided PLD focused on effective listening, being present and reminding them that there is no such thing as multitasking. We practice how to pay attention and tune in to others, to truly listen to the language they are using and not talk too much! We have also enjoyed learning more from the leaders in this work and found sound and communications expert Julian Treasure's TED TALKS fascinating.

Small things

- Appreciation jars in the staff room where staff place messages to each other.
- Gratitude wall in the foyer that can be added to.
- Appreciation cards for whānau.
- A short walk before a meeting/ at morning tea/lunch is encouraged.

Class Programmes

- Teachers will often be found in a downward dog, breathing, meditating, alongside children. I would like to see this more actually.
- Basically, we are attempting to build resilience in staff so they have optimal functioning to be able to do the best for the kids and each other'.

The wellbeing lead perspective: Gillian Towie found introducing staff to strengths a useful way to start:

'Each of us learning about our own strengths was a really nice first step. It provided shared language and something that everyone could connect on. From there we began to be strength spotters in ourselves, each other and with the students. Another effective strategy that helped to distribute the leadership was having people roster themselves for PosEd starters at our meetings on a Monday and a Thursday. This served a few purposes – building leadership and accountability making us all responsible for doing some research and learning hands-on tools, but also allowed us to trial these tools and build a resource bank. We worked through building a mindfulness toolbox that utilised visualisation, breathing, meditating and movement and moved onto building our knowledge and understanding of positive emotion through music'.

The staff's perspective

- 'I have found the SPIRE framework really helpful in thinking about my own wellbeing and how to keep all areas in balance. This has made me connect to the PosEd framework when thinking about planning for children. It has helped me see the need for balance in all areas and the real meaning of educating for the "whole" child'. **Gillian.**
- 'It's been great to see how PosEd links to neuroplasticity and brain theory. Being able to have new ideas to boost my own wellbeing and the classroom is really rewarding too. It helps me and the learning environment'. **Ximena**
- 'The fuzzy jars have been a great way to acknowledge the small things we do daily for each other and the students. SPIRE buddies have helped to strengthen working relationships and establishing connections between one another. Mindfulness activities have had a positive effect on students and provided me with strategies to deal with challenging situations. PosEd starters as a staff have been great fun and a lot have been used in class to start the day or as an intro to a new lesson/activity'. **Scott**
- 'Acknowledging that the skills and exercises which we practice with the kids are helpful and relevant to us as well. The PD sessions we do around our own wellbeing help make it more meaningful when delivering it to the kids, I find it important that the kids see us not only preaching but also using these. I think it's awesome that we as a staff value walking the walk not just talking the talk. Workplace wellbeing becoming addressed more in all professions, especially relevant in a profession where dropout rates are high although many schools wouldn't address it. The idea of positive education being a proactive means of addressing the well-being issues we see growing, rather than the ambo (ambulance) at the bottom of the hill (traditional psychology), really resonated with me when Jessica phrased it'. **James**
- 'Really interesting to note how reframing things so that the flourish model is at the centre of what we do affects students

positively. "Words create worlds" and much of this is becoming entrenched with kids, talking about Growth Mindset etc as part of their language. Making mistakes as part of learning, being patient with themselves and this is a model we can use as staff also. Using SPIRE as a framework for thinking about my own wellbeing is really useful and feels like a good template for an organic discussion'. **John**

- 'In my own journey, the focus of PosEd in staff means that I feel happy and supported at work. When talking to other PRTs (at other schools) I realise how lucky I am, and how everyone should have this!' **Jenny**

Reflection questions

What does leadership mean to you?

- Key words, characteristics, process and qualities?
- Are there differences specific to leading wellbeing change or not?
- When have you seen effective leadership in your school community before?
    - Share stories; what did you experience?
    - What are the common characteristics and themes of effective leadership/change management?
    - Who were the 'first followers' involved in those initiatives? Watch Derek Sivers's TED talk (see 'Watch' section at the end of this chapter).
    - Who are most likely to be your 'first followers'?
    - What/who will persuade others to join the movement?

- When have you experienced ineffective leadership?
    - What were the characteristics?
    - How can you avoid these pitfalls?

- Who will support you as change leader/s?
    - Within your organisation support?
    - External support?
    - Thinking of these people individually, what specific types of guidance might be helpful from them?

- How can your team help develop the leadership capacity of others?
- How can you get purposeful about developing leadership capacity through team environments?
- How will you communicate your wellbeing priorities to new staff?
- How will you build in time for staff to constructively discuss the strategies and practicalities with other staff and students?
- What initial professional learning is required?
- What other opportunities for learning can you provide? (Different entry points, diverse topics, times, duration, formats: e.g. podcasts, videos, lunch and learn, newsletters etc.)
- Who in your wider community can you draw support from?

Notes

1   Ministry of Education. (2008). *Kiwi leadership for principals: Principals as educational leaders.* Wellington, NZ: Professional Leadership: Schooling Group.

2   Rosenfield, B., Wall, G., & Jansen, C. (2017). *Leading sustainable change: Wisdom from textbooks and trenches in post-quake Canterbury.* Christchurch, NZ: Grow Waitaha.

3   Hallinger, P. (2003). Leading educational change: Reflections on the practice of instructional and transformational leadership. *Cambridge Journal of Education, 33*(3), 329–352.

4   Rosenfield, B., Wall, G., & Jansen, C. (2017). *Leading sustainable change: Wisdom from textbooks and trenches in post-quake Canterbury.* Christchurch, NZ: Grow Waitaha.

5   Muijs, D., & Harris, A. (2006). Teacher led school improvement: Teacher leadership in the UK. *Teaching and Teacher Education, 22,* 961–972.

6   LaClair, J. A., & Rao, R. P. (2002). Helping emoployees embrace change. *McKinsey Quarterly.* Retrieved May 21, 2019, from www.mckinsey.com/ business-functions/organization/our-insights/helping-employees-embrace-change

7   Bryman, A. (2007). *Effective leadership in higher education.* London: Leadership Foundation for Higher Education.

8   Southworth, G. (2004). *Primary school leadership in context: Leading small, medium and large sized schools.* London: Falmer.

9   Rosenfield, B., Wall, G., & Jansen, C. (2017). *Leading sustainable change: Wisdom from textbooks and trenches in post-quake Canterbury.* Christchurch, NZ: Grow Waitaha.

10 Rosenfield, B., Wall, G., & Jansen, C. (2017). *Leading sustainable change: Wisdom from textbooks and trenches in post-quake Canterbury.* Christchurch, NZ: Grow Waitaha.

11 Heifetz, R., Grashow, A., & Linsky, M. (2009). Leadership in a (permanent) crisis. *Harvard Business Review, 87*(7–8), 62–69.

Watch

How to lead innovation, the three carriage train. Retrieved from www.youtube.com/watch?v=HEPinFBcBgU

How to start a movement, TED talk by Derek Sivers (the lone dancing guy on the hill). Retrieved from www.youtube.com/watch?v=V74AxCqOTvg

Read

Brown, B. (2018). *Dare to lead: Brave work: Tough conversations: Whole hearts.* Random House. New York, NY.

Cameron, K. S. (2012). *Positive leadership: Strategies for extraordinary performance.* Berrett-Koehler Publishers, Inc. San Francisco, CA. Retrieved from http://search.ebscohost.com.ezproxy.aut.ac.nz/login.aspx?direct=true&db=cat05020a&AN=aut.b12588362&site=eds-live

Quinlan, D. (2017). Transforming our schools together: A multi-school collaboration to implement positive education. In C. Proctor (Ed.), *Positive psychology interventions in practice.* Springer. Cham, Switzerland.

Listen

NZIWR podcasts are available from https://nziwr.co.nz/category/podcast/

NZIWR podcast: Charlie Scudamore (Positive Education Leadership)

NZIWR podcast: Dr Chris Jansen (Leading Change)

CHAPTER 11

Cultural responsiveness and wellbeing

Introduction

Culturally-responsive practice addresses the challenges faced by ethnically and linguistically diverse (ELD) groups in many countries for whom mainstream education is not working. A growing global body of research demonstrates the harm caused by mainstream practices and effective alternatives to them. Frameworks and practices to support cultural responsiveness (CR) bear similarities to evidence-based wellbeing practice. Leadership and staff development in this area are essential to be able to implement culturally responsive practice. A critical part of this work involves schools engaging with and learning from their ELD communities, partnerships which will form an important part of schools' professional development.

What the research says

Having one's cultural identity seen, understood and valued is an important influence in health care and education,[1] with the non-dominant groups in many societies being under-served and experiencing lower health[2][3] and education outcomes.[4][5][6] In many countries, indigenous people and ethnic minorities report lower levels of educational engagement and achievement, with higher levels of school suspension.[7] Disparities in education and health between indigenous and dominant societal groups do not appear to be reducing in Australia, Canada or New Zealand, despite programmes aimed at 'closing the gap'.[8] The challenge for indigenous peoples, as succinctly put by Berryman, Macfarlane and Canavagh, is that, in mainstream education and health systems, 'eurocentrism can actively legitimise and perpetuate inequality'.[9] The gap to be closed has to date been defined in terms of deficits indigenous and minority populations are expected to rectify to meet govern-ments' mainstream targets.[10] The field of cultural responsiveness challenges this view and provides an alternative approach to supporting the health and wellbeing of indigenous and minority populations.

Angus Macfarlane spells it out clearly in his book title: *Kia hiwa ra: Listen to Culture*.[11] To build an effective learning relationship, the learner has to feel that who they are is seen and valued – that the school and teachers recognise, understand and respect the cultural identity, traditions, practices and values that come with being part of that cultural group. Critically, this means let-ting go of pervasive deficit thinking about indigenous or minority cultures, embracing a strengths-based perspective and working in a model emphasising empowerment and co-construction.[12]

In addressing issues of responding to students from diverse backgrounds, terms used include: 'cultural safety', whose aim is an environment that is safe for people;[13] cultural responsiveness, defined by Geneva Gay as 'teaching to and through [students'] personal and cultural strengths, their intellectual capabilities, and their prior accomplishments';[14] and Paris's concept of cul-tural sustainability, 'which has as its explicit goal supporting multilingualism and multiculturalism in practice and perspective for students and teachers'.[15] All these approaches share a recognition of the importance of being guided by culture in designing or co-creating teaching and learning experiences.

Two different dimensions to cultural responsiveness in education

In many countries with a history of colonisation, there are substantial bar-riers for first nation or indigenous peoples to overcome as a result of their history, which can include forced loss of traditional lands, loss of language and cultural practices and even forced removal of children from their birth families by the state.[16] [17] [18] [19] Increasingly, in countries with a colonial history, the moral obligation to remove barriers to wellbeing and acheivement for indigenous peoples is acknowledged. In education, there has been a growing awareness of, and demand for, culturally responsive structures and practices.

A second driver of cultural responsiveness has been the growing multi-cultural nature of contemporary society. Many schools, even in small towns far from international capitals, have students from around the globe.[20] These multi-cultural communities now often include refugees, as the last decade witnessed a huge wave of people forced to leave their war-torn homes in search of refuge and security. To support all these students to learn and be able to achieve and function as contributing members of the society in which they now live, schools must be able to provide the sense of connection and belonging enabling the academic engagement and wellbeing we have already described.[21]

Why does cultural responsiveness matter for wellbeing?

For students from minority ethnicity groups, school can be an unsupportive environment where the 'cultural toolkit' students bring with them is not acknowledged or valued – where teaching is not designed to respond to their culture. Belonging and connection to school are important for student wellbeing and for achievement. Connectedness in the classroom predicts engagement, which in turn predicts achievement. Having a group of students routinely feel disconnected from their school, classroom, teachers and many of their peers has substantial consequences for wellbeing and learning.

> *'If we look at a child's colouring book, before it has any colour added to it, we think of the page as blank. It's actually not blank, it's white. That white background is just* there *and we don't think much about it. Not only is the background uniformly white, the lines are already in place and they dictate where the colour is allowed to go. This is the setting for our Whitestream schools – that white background, and its unspoken privilege, is the norm'.* Ann Milne.[22]

To support Māori learning and achievement, New Zealand academics and educators in the field of cultural responsiveness have been advocating for teachers get to know and value the whole child – including the cultural tool-kit they bring with them to school – and engage with their culture to connect with and engage the student. This approach is closely aligned with the relational approaches advocated to support student wellbeing.[23] Like many traditional cultures, Māori culture encourages a holistic view of development, focusing not on the deficits a child may present with, but the strengths and gifts they also have.[24] Macfarlane and colleagues emphasise this strengths-focused tradition, focusing their research on the factors enabling Māori student success[25] (in contrast to research examining deficits, achievement gaps and failure). Connection to cultural identity was identified as an important factor supporting student success in this research.[26] This work aligns closely with the strengths-focused appoached within positive psychology and whole-school wellbeing promotion.

Creating a culture of caring

Cultural responsiveness research emphasises the importance to students of feeling they belong and are cared for. Intervention strategies implemented and replicated between New Zealand and the USA[27] have demonstrated the effectiveness for learning and classroom behaviour of a two-fold approach of creating a culture of care (based on holistic caring for students and restorative approaches to repair harm to relationships) and implementing culturally responsive pedagogies in the classroom.

'Schools and classrooms that embody a culture of care understand safety not only as freedom from harm but also as having the freedom to be who and what we are. Being who and what we are within classrooms and schools implies being able to maintain and enhance our ethnic and cultural knowledge and identities – and values and beliefs – while at the same time interacting peacefully with students and teachers from different ethnicities and cultures'.[28] Cavanagh, Glynn and Macfarlane and Macfarlane emphasise the importance of a restorative, rather than a punitive, approach when working with students from different cultures: 'Restorative practices are particularly important where the person or persons harmed, and the person or persons causing the harm, come from different ethnic or cultural groups. Different ethnic or cultural groups will have a different understanding of what constitutes harm, and a different understanding of what constitutes an effective and acceptable way of repairing the harm'.[29]

Findings from this research project found two themes most important for a culture of care: building and maintaining relationships and exercising holistic care. Students want and need to be cared for as people, as well as for their learning. Research from this project highlights the importance of sustained professional development supporting educators to implement these practices.

The educultural wheel and the Hikairo rationale from Aotearoa/ New Zealand

Schools appreciate frameworks to help guide their practice in the area of cultural responsiveness. Professor Angus Macfarlane's educultural wheel provides a framework for engaging with a Māori perspective in schools.[30] Although based in Māori culture, the principles of relationship, self-leadership, caring and commitment resonate across cultures. The wheel is based on core Māori principles and values: building relationships, whereby students and teachers get to know each other as people (*Whakawhanaungatanga*); becoming an effective and competent teacher and also enabling autonomy and agency for the student (*Rangatiratanga*); an ethos of caring, respect and kindness for others (*Manaakitanga*); unity and coming together as one (*Kotahitanga*) and the beating heart (*Pumanawatanga*) that is the effort and commitment to making the other four concepts live in the school.

The Hikairo rationale,[31] which provides a bi-cultural approach to working with students who present challenging behaviour in schools, is based on a core concept of *aroha*, or love and caring, and involves:

- Establishing meaningful relationships;
- Setting clear and fair boundaries;
- Encouraging consensus and collaboration in decision-making;
- Infusing genuine caring and respect into classroom routines and processes;
- Building a school climate of support and caring based on fairness, integrity and compassion;

- The student, teacher and *whānau* (extended family) being collectively involved in and responsible for resolving challenges at school and in the community; and
- Presenting a vision of wellbeing to students that involves giving and receiving love, achieving self-worth, having fun and becoming self-disciplined.

Evaluating the cultural responsiveness of SEL programmes for indigenous populations

Part of the work of this field involves confronting mainstream approaches. Researchers Brenda Dobia and Sue Roffey have challenged the 'universality' of social and emotional learning (SEL) programmes, despite their widespread popularity.[32] Dobia and Roffey point out that a) much of the work with students from these groups operates with a deficit lens, where shortcomings of the students are to be overcome; and b) very few educators involved in teaching SEL have any engagement with Aboriginal and Torres Strait Islander culture. Thus, they are concerned that 'SEL programs based on explicit classroom teaching of formal skills that privilege non-Indigenous ways of thinking, feeling and behaving may reinforce rather than challenge a deficit lens'.[33] This is particularly concerning given 'the crucial role of culture and identity in mediating self-awareness and social development for Aboriginal and Torres Strait Islander youth'.[34] Recommendations to promote cultural responsiveness in SEL teaching include:

- SEL programmes must acknowledge and work with differences in communication and relationship styles between indigenous and non-indigenous populations;
- Planning and co-facilitation of SEL programmes should be shared between Aboriginal and Torres Strait Islander and non-indigenous teachers.

Greater success was experienced with a pilot for the Aboriginal Girls Circle (AGC), a SEL intervention which aimed to increase participation, social connection and self-confidence among Aboriginal girls attending high school. Based around the Circle Solutions methodology,[35] the AGC incorporated a strengths-based approach, community-based project work and cooperative learning strategies. This approach demonstrated respect for Aboriginal culture and interest in learning from it. The programme was well regarded by students and school leaders for the results it achieved for the students involved, but also for the flexibility of delivery and cultural fit. Dobia noted that 'the provision of space and support to explore a sense of cultural identity, with direct involvement of community Elders, was essential to building the girls' sense of agency and cultural pride'.[36] She recommends that SEL programmes for indigenous populations include two-way learning – with indigenous and non-indigenous cultures learning from each other – including addressing the issue of racism faced by indigenous youth.

The behaviours of culturally responsive leaders

For school leaders wanting to implement evidence-based practices, Muhammad Khalifa, Mark Gooden and James Davis have identified a set of indicators derived from best-practice culturally responsive school leadership (CRSL).[37] Schools can use the behaviours in Table 11.1 as a checklist to monitor progress.

Table 11.1 Checklist: Culturally responsive school leadership behaviours (CRSL)

How many of these CRSL practices are in place at your school?	Tick those occurring in your school
1. Critically reflects on leadership behaviours. - Has commitment to ongoing learning of cultural knowledge. - Is conscious of practice in and out of school. - Measures CRSL using school data. - Measures CRSL using parent and community voice. - Uses equity audits to measure inclusion policy and practice.	
2. Develops culturally responsive teachers. - Develops teacher capacities for culturally responsive pedagogies. - Creates culturally responsive PD opportunities for staff. - Creates a CRSL team that looks for ways to develop CR in school. - Looks for ways to change school curriculum to be more culturally responsive.	

- Models culturally responsive teaching. - Uses culturally responsive assessment tools for students.	
3. Promotes culturally responsive inclusive school environment. - Accepts local identities. - Builds relationships and reduces anxiety for students. - Models CRSL in interactions with students. - Articulates a vision for inclusive practices. - Challenges exclusionary practice, policy or behaviour. - Values and uses the indigenous cultural and social capital of the students. - Uses student voice to build cultural responsiveness. - Tracks disparities in academic and disciplinary trends in school.	
4. Engages students, parents, and indigenous community contexts. - Develops meaningful positive relationships with local community. - Finds overlapping spaces for school and community. - Advocates for community-based causes in school and community. - Adopts a strengths focus with students and their families (and counters deficit images of students or community). - Uses community to inform school's understanding of students and their families. - Connects directly with students. - Nurtures and cares for others and shares information.	

Source: Adapted from Khalifa, M. A., Gooden, M. A., & Davis, J. E. (2016). Culturally responsive school leadership: A synthesis of the literature. *Review of Educational Research*, *86*(4), pp. 1272–1311.

Putting it into practice

The field of cultural responsiveness contains many frameworks and practices ready to be adopted to support student belonging and wellbeing. This section includes frameworks and case studies from New Zealand and around the world. Although they may be designed with one specific group in mind, these practices can often be universally applied to support a culture of caring.

Te Pikinga ki Runga: *Raising possibilities by applying the three Ps*

Sonya Macfarlane's framework *Te Pikinga ki Runga*: Raising Possibilities[38] provides an assessment, analysis and programme-planning framework for teachers and special education practitioners working with Māori students presenting with learning or behavioural challenges. Again, we believe this work has wider application for learners from ethnically and linguistically diverse (ELD) groups.

Te Tiriti ō Waitangi (the Treaty of Waitangi), contemporary bi-cultural New Zealand's founding document, has been interpreted as intending three foundational principles: partnership, protection and participation, which apply to protection of Māori students and culture within the education system.

Based on the three Ps, *Te Pikinga* articulates how these principles can look in practice:[39]

- **Partnership:** Lifelong partnerships are most effective when power is shared and balanced. Schools need to learn how to do this with *whānau* (extended family).
- **Protection:** This must include 'protecting and enhancing student self-concept and cultural identity by utilising strengths-based and holistic approaches to overall health and wellbeing'.
- **Participation:** 'Enhancing the classroom curriculum to support presence, participation and learning' for the student. This includes supporting the student to make meaning, think, relate to others, manage self, contribute and participate – all core competencies for learners of the 21st century, articulated in the New Zealand curriculum.[40]

Macfarlane identifies four domains across which teachers can support the engagement and wellbeing of the student: relational (*hononga*), psychological (*hinengaro*), physical (*tinana*) and self-concept (*mana motuhake*) and provides reflective questions for educators to consider how they can better understand and support the student they are working with. The *Te Pikinga ki Runga* model in Figure 11.1 encourages educators to consider how they can open doorways (*huakina mai*) between school and family, consider the tamaiti (child) from a holistic and culturally responsive perspective and help them develop the core competencies described earlier.

Figure 11.1 *Te Pikinga ki Runga*: Raising the possibilities

Box 11.1: Indicators of Success in culturally responsive education: *Mātauraka Mahaanui*

Mātauraka Mahaanui is the advisory board guiding education renewal in the Christchurch area (post earthquakes) and brings together education, Māori *iwi* (tribe), *Pasifika*, and community interests. Its role is to innovate Māori inclusion in the 'spaces, curricula, hearts and minds of education providers'.[41] *Mātauraka Mahaanui* has developed a framework for evaluating progress in achieving positive outcomes for Māori learners[42] with respect to: teaching *te reo Māori* (the Māori language), engagement with *whānau* (extended family) and planning and implementation of culturally responsive pedagogy and leadership. Based on their cultural-responsive practice, schools can use the framework's behavioural indicators to place themselves at one of four stages of progress: Building, emerging, strengthening or championing. The indicators of success can be downloaded from the *Mātauraka Mahaanui* website: www.matauraka.co.nz/resources.

Case study 11.1:   One educator's practical strategies for building cultural responsiveness

Nathan Riki is a *Kāhui Ako* (school cluster) lead teacher based at Breen's Intermediate School in Christchurch, New Zealand. Nathan actively supports schools to become culturally responsive, emphasising the importance of partnership with families. While Nathan's work specifically focuses on cultural responsiveness to Māori, the underlying wisdom of his advice can be applied more broadly. He encourages schools to collaborate with *whānau* from the start: 'We need to involve each other in what we are doing in a school. We need whānau in our schools helping us making decisions'. He shares what has worked for him:

- *'Explore the "why" of cultural responsivesness with staff.* Have a clear "why" and a vision of what you want to achieve for Māori students. Break the work down into small steps and scaffold the process for our teachers. I use the five values of the Tātaiako framework which have specific practices associated with them:[43]

  - *Whanaungatanga* – relationships. Schools need to understand how important this is and have practical ways to build relationships with students, their families, other staff, and the community.

- *Manaakitanga* – is about care and respect not just for students but for Māori beliefs, values, and customs (*tikanga* and *te Ao Māori*).
- *Tangatawhenuatanga* – is about valuing the land and ensuring that we know about the place that we belong to. This helps to build identity and is important for Māori students who might have moved away from their traditional *kainga* (home place).
- Ako – the reciprocal nature of teaching and learning. The teacher is learning alongside the students. *Tuakana/Teina* is a Māori concept of the older and the younger learning from each other.
- *Wānanga* – is about the quality of interactions with all the stakeholders. It's about the way you invite *whānau* (extended family), *iwi* (tribes), or *hapu* (sub-groups of tribes) into your school, and how you engage in discussions with them.

- *A* **whānau** *class* – a place for Māori students to come together twice a week to learn about their culture and its customs, protocols, and language. I did this at my school with *kai* (food) together, *korero Māori* (speak in Māori) and an opportunity for them to celebrate being Māori. The students in this class ran a *noho marae* (*marae* overnight stay) and taught the other students about the protocols and customs to follow. This earned a lot of *mana* (respect and appreciation) from students all round the school.
- **Whānau hui** (family meetings) – see Nathan's 'recipe' for a successful *whanau hui* in Chapter 14 on connecting with parents, caregivers and the community.
- *Physical expressions of a commitment to bi-culturalism* – You should be able to stand in any part of a school and know that you are standing in a bi-cultural country. Walk through your school with the lens of a *whānau* (Māori family) member – what will they see? How will they answer the question, 'will my children be able to learn *in, through*, and *about their culture* at this school?'
- *Learning in, through, and about Māori culture.* Schools are doing reasonably well at learning "in" (introducing *te reo Maori* language frameworks) and "through" (teaching about Māori *tikanga*

(protocol and customs). The challenge is the "about". How do we connect our Māori students with their history, place, and people, especially when they are far away from these?

Building cultural responsiveness in the staff room

- **Developing capabilities and confidence** so that more teachers are equipped and confident to teach Māori language and customs. Otherwise, we will be relying on one teacher to carry it all and that is not sustainable.
- **Value and share knowledge.** Where a school has a staff member who really cares and is expert in this *kaupapa* (purpose), these staff need to be valued and looked after. Don't task this person to do all of the work. Make it a collaboration and a shared goal for the entire school.
- **If you get the staff room right, the classroom will follow.** Get the feeling right in the staff room – build the relationships and caring in the staff room first. Staff do the same activities I do with students: the "in, through, and about" of learning about Māori culture has to take place in the staff room as well.

  - **Whānaungatanga** – staff stand near the compass points in the room that represent where they feel most at home and comfortable, and then tell someone else about that place. Staff describe learning more about each other when they do this.
  - **Karakia** (traditional Māori prayers) – before staff meetings.
  - **Te reo Māori** (Māori langugae) – used in the staff room.
  - **Tikanga followed in the staff room** (Māori protocol and customs) – the learning about Māori culture has to take place in the staff room as well'.

Box 11.2: A teacher's reflections on ethnocentricity and place-based learning in Aotearoa/New Zealand

Leanne Whitfield, assistant principal at Khandallah School, Wellington, New Zealand, shared reflections on her personal journey in cultural responsiveness.

Dysconsciousness and ethnocentricity

Samu defines dysconsciousness as "an uncritical habit of mind . . . that justifies inequity and exploitation by accepting the existing order of things".[44] I first became aware of my own dysconsciousness when I heard Ann Milne[45] speak of the perspectives of her students at Kia Aroha College. She showed a film of them speaking of their experiences, and I had the opportunity to see the world through their eyes. For me, this was the beginning of a journey that I'm still on, towards a better understanding of racism in Aotearoa (NZ) and how racism can hide in plain sight in every aspect of society and be perpetuated by dedicated, caring professionals just like me.

Dysconsciousness (also referred to as ethnocentricity) is by nature hard to detect or quantify, and functions as a significant barrier to understanding and development of culturally responsive practice (CRP) for many teachers. Milne quotes Peggy McIntosh: "I enjoy unearned skin privilege and have been conditioned into oblivion about its existence, unable to see that it put me 'ahead' in any way, or put my people ahead".[46] 2018 statistics show that the overwhelming majority of teachers in Aotearoa are female and NZ European/Pakeha.[47] This lack of diversity amongst education professionals signals that dysconsciousness is likely to be pervasive and unchallenged in many settings.

When embarking on improving CRP, teachers should start with deep reflection about their own cultural perspectives and how these affect their thinking and actions as professionals.

Place-based education

While the field of place-based education (PBE) is well-established around the world, particularly within indigenous communities and environmental contexts,[48] in my own context of a high-decile 74% Pakeha (NZ European) suburban school, the importance of local Māori history for our students is barely understood by our teachers. Māori history encompasses the history of all the people of Aotearoa/ New Zealand and the recommended pedagogy of the study of history promotes the development of many of the skills identified for

(continued)

21st-century learners.[49][50] More importantly, the study of Māori history through PBE can go some way towards addressing inequality in our education system, with New Zealand currently ranking in the bottom third of OECD countries in terms of equity in education.[51]

Wally Penetito identifies a number of strands of place-based curriculum, including the necessity of challenging your own taken-for-granted world. Penetito reflects that Māori history was 'invisible' in his own schooling experience.[52] While our local area has a rich Māori history, our teachers are unaware and therefore ill-equipped to have culturally responsive teaching practice that upholds their Te Tiriti responsibilities. When teachers are unaware of the events of history that have created the physical space and social context in which they work, their practice is even more susceptible to dysconsciousness. If Māori history is "invisible" in our curriculum – and if our teachers know little about it, then it must be – it is impossible for the school to play its part in dismantling the social inequities that Bolstad et al. identified as being perpetuated by the education system in New Zealand.[53]

Milne cautions against "shading" the White spaces in education through the use of one-off or isolated cultural experiences which consign culture to the margins of school life.[54] Sleeter also identifies "cultural celebration" as an activity that has the side effect of relegating culture to the margins of what a school is doing, rather than being at the centre of all decision-making.[55] A fuller understanding of Māori history helps students to understand that they as individuals are part of a larger story of the place where they are.[56] Learning and practising pepeha is an example of practice that enables all learners (including Tauiwi – non-Māori – who have come in more recent migrations) to develop understanding of who they are, and how they fit into their context. This is relevant to both Māori and non-Māori learners'.

Case study 11.2:   Facilitating multi-cultural wellbeing

Ara Simmons is an accredited facilitator, positive psychology practitioner and certified coach, whose family came from Bangaladesh to the UK where Ara grew up. She is an advocate for work that respects the sometimes complex identities that students and staff bring to school. Working in New Zealand, she says, we are always working from the Treaty of Waitangi, and it's important to be responsive to identity and culture.

Having spent more than ten years working in a multi-cultural setting in the UK, Ara was very used to creating a family-like feeling with her diverse students. In the UK, where school lunches are provided and teachers are expected to sit with their students, Ara really got to know her students as people and hear about their lives. Sharing food was an important practice in her family's home culture of Bangaladesh and felt very natural when she worked with Māori students in New Zealand.

Many students and staff have multiple cultural identities and need to be able to express these in their schools. Ara comes from a *whānau* that has multiple cultural identities, including Bangaladeshi, Pakeha and Māori, and this has helped her look at things from multiple perspectives. She encourages people to ask open questions that offer the other person the space to lead and share the information that they choose. Asking a student or a colleague, 'Tell me about you. What's important to you? What would you like me to know about you in order to understand you and work well with you?' Ara acknowledges the teacher of her youngest child who asked just such an open question that gave this child the opportunity to share their multi-cultural background and to feel really seen. This question placed the adult in a place of curiosity, wanting to know, but gave the child the choice of what they chose to share.

Some of the work that Ara does to help students engage with and share their identity is directly relevant to wellbeing constructs such as meaning, purpose and spirituality. Ara has successfully helped young people construct a helpful narrative about their lives – through constructing personal 'life books' or thinking about their journey on the life *waka*. (The *waka* or canoe is a potent symbol from Māori culture for journey, challenge and community/team.) These books 'help students uncover their personal why', learn 'who you are for yourself' – in other words, to help develop a sense of identity and personal value and to foster a sense of direction and purpose.

Case study 11.3:   Connecting across cultural differences to find our
                      shared humanity

Dr Tayyab Rashid is a clinical psychologist and researcher who
has worked with people from ethnically and linguistically diverse
groups (ELD) experiencing complex mental health issues for over
15 years. The developer of Positive Psychotherapy for adults and
children and the Strengths-Based Resilience programme (SBR) for
high school and university students, he is an active clinician and
researcher in the field of wellbeing in education. He shared these
reflections on cultural responsiveness:

- **'Culture is a veneer under which sits our common humanity.**
  I have worked with marginalised youth in Jersey City, Brooklyn,
  and Toronto; with journalists and social workers in the Lebanon,
  and with families bereaved after 9/11 in the USA. With all of
  these people I find a common humanity – a realisation that there
  is good in all of us.
- **Cultures are dynamic.** We have to remain curious about differences between individuals within the same culture. There
  can be wider differences between people from within the same
  culture than between two people of different cultures.
- **Curiosity and respect are two strengths that can help us approach
  and make our way in new cultural territory.** Being open-minded
  and curious, and having people or processes to help us navigate
  new places, can help us become familiar with new cultures.
- **Empathy has two components – emotional and behavioural.**
  You don't have to be able to empathise to be culturally responsive, but you can be respectful because of the historical injustices
  that have been suffered by another group. That's a behavioural
  rather than an emotional response but it's important.
- **Visual signs can signify welcome and belonging.** We live in
  an era where millions of people have been forced to leave their
  homes and to seek refuge across the world. Any signs we can
  give that signify, "You are welcome and you belong here" are
  culturally responsive'.

**How can schools respond to and include families from Islamic
culture?**

- **'Muslims come from many hetergenous backgrounds** – just
  being Muslim doesn't mean we're the same. A Muslim from

Africa can have a very different culture to a Muslim from Bangaladesh. The Islamic faith is what brings these very different groups together. Beyond those shared religious beliefs, you can gently ask and explore their different practices.

- **A hybrid model of culture.** In most Muslim cultures, the obligation towards family is very important and the agency (sense of ability to act) is collective. Many people from these collectivist cultures now find themselves raising children in very different cultures, navigating multiple cultural domains. The home is largely managed by parents with little control by children, until they step out of the home, where they enter a very different culture. Let's be patient with these young people as they learn to manage these culture transitions.

- **What are the important strengths of the Islamic faith and of the Muslim community?** Muslim communities across the world are now living in secular societies where they have the opportunity not to practice their religion. Their strength is to remain connected to the faith but also their flexibility to adapt to their new societies. They are contributing to the societies where they live, and through their behaviour, demonstrate, despite media fears, that they are not terrorists, but people who get up and go to work, and dream about how they will help their students or patients'.

Reflection questions

- Would a visitor to your school see signs of the different cultures at school represented in each area of the school? In New Zealand, which is a bi-cultural nation, would a visitor see signs that remind them of that fact in each school area?
- What culturally responsive school leadership behaviours are in place in your school?
- How does your staff room reflect a commitment to cultural responsiveness? Are relationship and belonging nurtured in the staff room as well as the classroom?
- Is responsibility for cultural responsiveness spread throughout the school staff, or is it all left to the one staff member from an indigenous or minority culture?
- How does your school communicate with parents and students from non-majority cultures?

- Are extended families made to feel welcome at school meetings? Are they consulted to find times that work best for them? Is is easy to bring small children with the family? Is there care or space for them to play?
- Do students at your school learn 'in, through and about' their culture? How does the content of your teaching reflect our students' culture – including their history, customs and language?
- How are staff at your school developing their knowledge of and commitment to cultural responsiveness?

Notes

1   Durie, M. H. (2003). The health of Indigenous peoples: Depends on genetics, politics, and socioeconomic factors. *British Medical Journal, 326*(7388), 510–511.

2   King, M., Smith, A., & Gracey, M. (2009). Indigenous health part 2: The underlying causes of the health gap. *The Lancet, 374*(9683), 76–85.

3   Larson, A., Gillies, M., Howard, P. J., & Coffin, J. (2007). It's enough to make you sick: The impact of racism on the health of Aboriginal Australians. *Australian and New Zealand Journal of Public Health, 31*(4), 322–329.

4   Marie, D., Fergusson, D. M., & Boden, J. M. (2008). Educational achievement in Maori: The roles of cultural identity and social disadvantage. *Australian Journal of Education, 52*(2), 183–196.

5   NMSSA Project Team, including Gilmore, A., Allan, R., Jones, L., Darr, C., Asil, M., Quinlan, D., . . . Lancaster, D. (2015). *Māori student achievement in English: Reading: Key findings 2014* [National monitoring study of student achievement (NMSSA) report 5.2]. Dunedin and Wellington, New Zealand: Educational Assessment Research Unit & New Zealand Council for Educational Research, 30p.

6   NMSSA Project Team, including Gilmore, A., Allan, R., Jones, L., Quinlan, D., Gilmore, J., White, J., . . . Darr, C. (2014). *Mathematics and statistics* [National monitoring study of student achievement report 4]. Dunedin and Wellington, New Zealand: Educational Assessment Research Unit & New Zealand Council for Educational Research, 167p.

7   Savage, C., Hindle, R., Meyer, L. H., Hynds, A., Penetito, W., & Sleeter, C. E. (2011). Culturally responsive pedagogies in the classroom: Indigenous student experiences across the curriculum. *Asia-Pacific Journal of Teacher Education, 39*(3), 183–198.

8   Mitrou, F., Cooke, M., Lawrence, D., Povah, D., Mobilia, E., Guimond, E., & Zubrick, S. R. (2014). Gaps in Indigenous disadvantage not closing: A census cohort study of social determinants of health in Australia, Canada, and New Zealand from 1981–2006. *BMC Public Health*, *14*(1), 201.

9   Berryman, M., Macfarlane, S., & Cavanagh, T. (2009). I: Indigenous contexts for responding to challenging behaviour: Contrasting Western accountability with Maori restoration of harmony. *International Journal of Restorative Justice*, *5*(1), 1.

10   Pholi, K. (2009). Is 'Close the Gap' a useful approach to improving the health and wellbeing of Indigenous Australians? *Australian Review of Public Affairs: Journal*, *9*(2).

11   Macfarlane, A. H. (2004). *Kia hiwa ra: Listen to culture: Māori students' plea to educators*. Wellington: New Zealand Council for Educational Research.

12   Bishop, R. (2003). Changing power relations in education: Kaupapa Māori messages for 'mainstream' education in Aotearoa/New Zealand [1]. *Comparative education*, *39*(2), 221–238.

13   Papps, E., & Ramsden, I. (1996). Cultural safety in nursing: The New Zealand experience. *International Journal for Quality in Health Care*, *8*(5), 491–497.

14   Khalifa, M. A., Gooden, M. A., & Davis, J. E. (2016). Culturally responsive school leadership: A synthesis of the literature. *Review of Educational Research*, *86*(4), 1272–1311. doi:10.3102/0034654316630383

15   Paris, D., & Alim, H. S. (2014). What are we seeking to sustain through culturally sustaining pedagogy? A loving critique forward. *Harvard Educational Review*, *84*(1), 85–100.

16   Bishop, R. (2003). Changing power relations in education: Kaupapa Māori messages for 'mainstream' education in Aotearoa/New Zealand [1]. *Comparative education*, *39*(2), 221–238.

17   Haebich, A. (2015). Neoliberalism, settler colonialism and the history of Indigenous child removal in Australia. *Australian Indigenous Law Review*, *19*(1), 20–31.

18   Lawrence, B. (2003). Gender, race, and the regulation of native identity in Canada and the United States: An overview. *Hypatia*, *18*(2), 3–31.

19   Whitbeck, L. B., Adams, G. W., Hoyt, D. R., & Chen, X. (2004). Conceptualizing and measuring historical trauma among American Indian people. *American Journal of Community Psychology*, *33*(3–4), 119–130.

20   Elliott, S., & Yusuf, I. (2014). 'Yes, we can; but together': Social capital and refugee resettlement. *Kotuitui: New Zealand Journal of Social Sciences Online, 9*(2), 101–110.

21   Sleeter, C. E. (2001). Preparing teachers for culturally diverse schools: Research and the overwhelming presence of whiteness. *Journal of Teacher Education, 52*(2), 94–106.

22   Milne, A. (2017). *Colouring in the white spaces: Reclaiming cultural identity in whitestream schools.* New York: Peter Lang Publishing.

23   Roffey, S. (2010). *Changing behaviour in schools: Promoting positive relationships and wellbeing.* Sage.

24   Habib, A., Densmore-James, S., & Macfarlane, S. (2013). A culture of care: The role of culture in today's mainstream classrooms. *Preventing School Failure: Alternative Education for Children and Youth, 57*(3), 171–180. doi:10.1080/1045988X.2013.798777

25   Macfarlane, A., Webber, M., McRae, H., & Cookson-Cox, C. (2014). *Ka Awatea: An iwi case study of Māori students' success.* Te Rū Rangahau, University of Canterbury.

26   Macfarlane, A., Webber, M., McRae, H., & Cookson-Cox, C. (2014). *Ka Awatea: An iwi case study of Māori students' success.* Te Rū Rangahau, University of Canterbury.

27   Cavanagh, T., Macfarlane, A., Glynn, T., & Macfarlane, S. (2012). Creating peaceful and effective schools through a culture of care. *Discourse: Studies in the Cultural Politics of Education, 33*(3), 443–455. doi:10.10 80/01596306.2012.681902

28   Cavanagh, T., Macfarlane, A., Glynn, T., & Macfarlane, S. (2012). Creating peaceful and effective schools through a culture of care. *Discourse: Studies in the Cultural Politics of Education, 33*(3), 443–455. doi:10.10 80/01596306.2012.681902

29   Cavanagh, T., Macfarlane, A., Glynn, T., & Macfarlane, S. (2012). Creating peaceful and effective schools through a culture of care. *Discourse: Studies in the Cultural Politics of Education, 33*(3), 443–455. doi:10.10 80/01596306.2012.681902

30   Macfarlane, A., Glynn, T., Cavanagh, T., & Bateman, S. (2007). Creating culturally-safe schools for Māori students. *The Australian Journal of Indigenous Education, 36*(1), 65–76.

31   Macfarlane, A., Glynn, T., Cavanagh, T., & Bateman, S. (2007). Creating culturally-safe schools for Māori students. *The Australian Journal of Indigenous Education*, *36*(1), 65–76.

32   Dobia, B., & Roffey, S. (2017). Respect for culture – Social and emotional learning with aboriginal and Torres strait Islander youth. In *Social and emotional learning in Australia and the Asia-Pacific* (pp. 313–334). Singapore: Springer.

33   Dobia, B., & Roffey, S. (2017). Respect for culture – Social and emotional learning with aboriginal and Torres strait Islander youth. In *Social and emotional learning in Australia and the Asia-Pacific* (pp. 313–334). Singapore: Springer.

34   Dobia, B., & Roffey, S. (2017). Respect for culture – Social and emotional learning with aboriginal and Torres strait Islander youth. In *Social and emotional learning in Australia and the Asia-Pacific* (pp. 313–334). Singapore: Springer.

35   Roffey, S. (2014). *Circle solutions for student wellbeing*. London: Sage Publications.

36   Dobia, B., & Roffey, S. (2017). Respect for culture – Social and emotional learning with aboriginal and Torres strait Islander youth. In *Social and emotional learning in Australia and the Asia-Pacific* (pp. 313–334). Singapore: Springer.

37   Khalifa, M. A., Gooden, M. A., & Davis, J. E. (2016). Culturally responsive school leadership: A synthesis of the literature. *Review of Educational Research*, *86*(4), 1272–1311. doi:10.3102/0034654316630383

38   Macfarlane, S. (2009). Te Pikinga ki Runga: Rising possibilities. *Set: Research Information for Teachers (Wellington)*, *2*, 42–51.

39   Macfarlane, S. (2009). Te Pikinga ki Runga: Rising possibilities. *Set: Research Information for Teachers (Wellington)*, *2*, 42–51.

40   Ministry of Education. (2017). *The New Zealand curriculum*. Retrieved September 2, 2019, from http://nzcurriculum.tki.org.nz/The-New-Zealand-Curriculum

41   Mātauraka Mahaanui. (2019). *Our kaupapa*. Retrieved August 20, 2019, from www.matauraka.co.nz/

42   Mātauraka Mahaanui. (2019). *Indicators of success*. Retrieved August 20, 2019, from www.matauraka.co.nz/resources

43   Teaching Council New Zealand. (n.d.). *Tātaiako: Cultural competencies for teachers of māori learners.* Retrieved September 2, from https:// teachingcouncil.nz/content/tataiako

44   Samu, T. W. (2011). Understanding the lines in the sand: Diversity, its discourse and building a responsive education system. *Curriculum Matters*, 175–194.

45   Milne, A. (2019, February 6). *Swimming with Sharks – Our covert white spaces.* Retrieved August 28, 2019, from Ann Milne Education www. annmilne.co.nz/blog/2019/2/6/swimming-with- sharks

46   Milne, A. (2017). *Colouring in the white spaces: Reclaiming cultural identity in whitestream schools.* New York: Peter Lang Publishing.

47   *Teacher Workforce.* (2018). Retrieved August 28, 2019, from education counts www.educationcounts.govt.nz/statistics/schooling/workforce/ teacher-workforce

48   Penetito, W. (2009). Place-based education: Catering for curriculum, culture and community. *New Zealand Annual Review of Education, 18.* Retrieved July 15, 2019, from https://ojs.victoria.ac.nz/nzaroe/ article/view/1544/1389

49   Scott, C. L. (2015). *The futures of learning 3: What kind of pedagogies for the 21st century?* Paris: UNESCO Education Research and Foresight.

50   Ministry of Education. (2015). *Te Takanga O Te Wa – Maori History.* Wellington, New Zealand: CORE Education.

51   UNICEF. (2018). *An Unfair Start: Inequality in children's education in rich countries.* Retrieved 2019, from UNICEF Office of Research – Innocenti www.unicef-irc.org/publications/series/report-card/

52   Penetito, W. (2019). Place-based education and Maori history. *Maori History in the New Zealand Curriculum.* CORE Education. Retrieved July 15, 2019, from Maori History in the New Zealand Curriculum http://maori history.tki.org.nz/en/programme-design/place-based-education/

53   Bolstad, R., Gilbert, J., McDowall, S., Bull, A., Boyd, S., & Hipkins, R. (2012). *Supporting future-oriented learning & teaching – a New Zealand perspective.* Wellington, New Zealand: Ministry of Education.

54   Milne, A. (2017). *Colouring in the white spaces: Reclaiming cultural identity in whitestream schools.* New York: Peter Lang Publishing.

55   Sleeter, C. E. (2012). Confronting the marginalization of culturally responsive pedagogy. *Urban Education, 47*(3).

56   Ministry of Education. (2015). *Te Takanga O Te Wa – Maori History.* Wellington, New Zealand: CORE Education.

Watch

10 Ways to Teach Me: Brigham Riwai-Couch. Brigham shares his perspective of the top 10 things that make a difference for him as a learner. This video focuses on Māori achieving educational success as Māori, drawing on student voice. Retrieved from https://vimeo.com/325105212

Core Education's video on how schools can show respect for the Treaty of Waitangi in New Zealand and 'our beautiful bi-cultural history'. Retrieved from https://edtalks.org/#/video/giving-mana-to-tiriti-o-waitangi-in-our-schools

Documentary about Learning Ground, a culturally responsive programme for high risk youth. This programme was evaluated by Dr Brenda Dobia, Senior Researcher in the Centre for Educational Research, University of Western Sydney. Retrieved from https://vimeo.com/267926611/a29f130509

Janina Konia describes how a secondary school community of practice in Christchurch, NZ, aimed at promoting citywide wellbeing, recognises the fundamental links between cultural belonging and connection for students and their wellbeing. Retrieved from www.youtube.com/watch?v=7j5Apr6KnVU

Read

Cavanagh, T., Macfarlane, A., Glynn, T., & Macfarlane, S. (2012). Creating peaceful and effective schools through a culture of care. *Discourse: Studies in the Cultural Politics of Education, 33*(3), 443–455.

A guide for ECE centres and schools to determine levels of capability in relation to achieving positive outcomes for Māori achieving education success as Māori. https://static1.squarespace.com/static/5b5653d5b27e39c-c700a025f/t/5cd54019e79c70d453a15b32/1557479452022/Indicators+Framework+FINAL+Updated+February+2019.pdf

Milne, A. (2019, February 6). *Swimming with Sharks – Our covert white spaces.* Retrieved August 28, 2019, from Ann Milne Education www.annmilne.co.nz/blog/2019/2/6/swimming-with-sharks

The reflective questions in Sonja Macfarlane's Te Pikinga framework should be on every educator's must-read list: Macfarlane, S. (2009). Te Pikinga ki Runga: Rising possibilities. *Set: Research Information for Teachers (Wellington), 2,* 42–51.

Listen

NZIWR podcasts are available from https://nziwr.co.nz/category/podcast/

NZIWR podcast: Nathan Riki (The Mahi: Cultural Responsiveness in Schools)

NZIWR podcast: Ara Simmons (Cultural Responsiveness, multi-cultural perspectives).

NZIWR podcast: Brenda Dobia (Cultural Responsiveness, Indigenous Australia).

NZIWR podcast: Tayyab Rashid (Cultural Responsiveness, Islamic perspective).

Promoting educator wellbeing

Introduction

Teacher and principal wellbeing are essential parts of whole-school wellbeing; there is no whole-school wellbeing without educator wellbeing. Teachers lead by example and are role models – whether they like it or not. Research has demonstrated in education (and workplaces generally) that those with higher wellbeing tend to be more engaged, more productive and enjoy higher job satisfaction. By deliberately building their wellbeing literacy and developing and implementing personal wellbeing strategies, teachers can model wellbeing and resilience strategies to their students, share this learning experience with them and hopefully perform their roles more enjoyably and effectively. The same applies for principals who play a vital role in supporting educator wellbeing. As Coleman wrote a decade ago, it's just plain obvious 'that the emotional health of one half of a community will be influenced by the emotional health of the other half'.[1]

What the research says

While there are a multitude of definitions of teacher wellbeing, we like McCallum and Price's definition that 'wellbeing is diverse and fluid respecting individual, family and community beliefs, values, experiences, culture, opportunities and contexts across time and change. It is something we all aim for, underpinned by positive notions, yet is unique to each of us and provides us with a sense of who we are which needs to be respected'.[2]

Given the high levels of stress and burnout in the profession, protecting and promoting the wellbeing of educators is vital for the education landscape globally. There is an abundance of international research demonstrating that teaching is a highly stressful profession, and stress and poor working conditions are linked to teacher attrition.[34] For example, an OECD survey reported that half the countries were seriously concerned about the supply of quality teachers.[5]

Grenville-Cleave and Boniwell found British teachers rate their wellbeing significantly lower than those in other occupations, including health, social work, human resources and finance.[6] An Association of Teachers and Lecturers (ATL) study reported that 55% of teachers felt their job was having a negative impact on their wellbeing.[7] A quarter of teachers report adverse student behaviour as the primary reason for burnout.[8] A current teacher shortage in New Zealand is driven by declining retention rates, an ageing workforce and the lowest number of students enrolled in teacher training in ten years.[9]

> *'Investment in teacher wellbeing contributes to improved health and wellbeing for teachers and students, and ultimately to positive learning outcomes'.*[10]

Staff wellbeing relates to student success. Briner and Dewberry (2007) found average levels of teacher wellbeing within schools to be linked to student performance (as assessed by SATs), even after controlling for other factors known to influence academic performance.[11]

While much of the extant empirical research relates to negative aspects of educator wellbeing – burnout and stress; relationships with students, parents, colleagues and leadership; workload and having to respond to ongoing change – researchers have now begun to unpack the strategies and initiatives promoting educator wellbeing. In their review of the teacher wellbeing literature, Faye McCallum and colleagues identify the strategies adopted by individual teachers (both personal and professional) likely to influence wellbeing in a sustainable way.[12] They recommended adopting Bronfenbrennner's ecological model[13] to identify whole-school and organisational initiatives that complement individual measures promoting generativity, motivation, energy and teacher self-efficacy. Table 12.1 sets out a checklist of research-supported teacher wellbeing initiatives based on McCallum and colleagues' work.

Although there is a dearth of both descriptive and predictive studies at present,[14] what is apparent is that teacher engagement in professional learning groups (PLGs) has been shown to be an effective strategy for supporting changes in teacher beliefs and practices. Gibbs and Miller's research shows that colleagues and school leadership play a significant role in supporting teachers' beliefs in their efficacy in managing children's behaviour.[15] A Finnish study investigating factors promoting or hindering educator wellbeing, involving nine different comprehensive schools,[16] also found educator wellbeing was

Table 12.1 Checklist of teacher wellbeing initiatives

Checklist of teacher wellbeing initiatives (and how they can help teacher wellbeing)	Tick those areas you actively practise
- Reflection strategies (insights regarding professional practice). - Mindfulness training (for managing stress). - Emotional management strategies. - Coaching psychology (building learning communities). - Growth mindset approaches (problem solving). - Self-care habits (recovery and restore). - Celebrating achievements and success (feeling valued).	

Source: Adapted from Faye McCallum, Deborah Price, Anne Graham, Anne Morrison (2017). 'Teacher wellbeing: a review of the literature'.

influenced by the emotional support of colleagues and recommended that teachers may benefit from seeing themselves as 'active collaborative learners' within their teaching communities. Owen[17] suggests 'professional reinvigoration and teacher wellbeing' can be promoted by ongoing professional learning in a supportive context. According to Owen, PLGs provide opportunities for 'challenging ideas to increase potential for success, gaining greater accomplishment through joint work and nurturing positive emotion and sharing of good feelings'.

Research also identifies the considerable influence of principals on the wellbeing of teachers. Heidmets and Liik[18] found that the way teachers think and feel about their school is strongly related to leadership style, suggesting transformational leadership style (versus a transactional leadership style) was related to lower levels of reported job insecurity, burnout or considerations for leaving among teachers.

Putting it into practice

The sources of stress are diverse, many of them unique to teaching. As Chris Eyre, author of *The Elephant in the Staffroom: How to Reduce Teacher Stress and Improve Teacher Wellbeing*, observes: 'A day in teaching contains hundreds of interactions. A child misbehaving, a student in tears because of events at home, another student who still doesn't get an equation despite three explanations, another is 5 minutes late again, another is quiet and subdued – all in lesson 1, and there are 4 more lessons to go. There are interactions with staff, angry parents and the 30 emails that arrived during the day whilst you were teaching. All these interactions engage us to some degree on an emotional level; it may not even be conscious. A day in teaching is a mental health roller coaster, and it can take its toll'.[19]

There's so much pressure in teaching to get everything done (marking, admin, planning); challenging behaviour (from students, colleagues and parents); student progress (or lack of it); constant performance reviews (senior management, parents and student 'rate my teacher' sites); the rapid pace of educational reform; numerous out-of-classroom commitments (clubs, meetings). School days are long, not to mention all the hours of overtime clocked each week. Eyre reminds educators, however:

1   It could be worse. If you weren't a teacher, what job would you do? Would it match teaching for variety, challenge and fulfillment?

2   Teaching is a tough profession with a compressed and intense workload. Don't allow the uninformed outsider put you down.

3   The struggle is mainly psychological. Find ways of dealing with the stressors.

Chris Eyre is right. Every educator needs a plan to manage stress.

Personal stress plans

Self-awareness and having a plan are your best defences against stress. At the New Zealand Institute of Wellbeing & Resilience, we organise personal stress plans into traffic light colours, providing a simple framework that's suited to stressful times! We've found this step-by-step process useful for helping us and those we train to view and navigate tough times.

Everyone's stress signals and triggers are different, so step 1 is a good exercise to do with Post-it notes in the staff room. It may reveal symptoms you weren't previously aware of.

Step 1 (SEEING RED):

• Know your stress symptoms and identify your triggers. Write them down.

Step 2 (YELLOW = PRESS PAUSE):

- Before you send that email or bite back at the deputy head or persistently unreasonable parent, make a conscious effort to put your response on hold. Count to ten, go for a walk: give your thinking, rational brain time to take over from your emotional, irrational brain.
- Find someone to discuss the situation with: it overcomes isolation and gives you another perspective. Challenging your 'worst case' thoughts rather than accepting them is good psychological practice.
- Make a determined effort to focus your attention on the things you can change, and (somehow) accept or let go those you cannot. Sounds simple, but this kind of mental agility lies at the heart of resilience.
- Prioritise. First ask:
  - Is this something that truly matters?
  - Is this something that only I can do?
  - Is this something I can actually exert influence over or change?
    Once you've identified the tasks that rightfully demand and deserve your attention, write them all down and then ruthlessly prioritise them for both urgency and importance.

- Learning how to say 'no' is also a vital learnable skill for teachers.[20] Try these variations on 'no':
  - 'Can I get back to you later on that?' Hit the 'pause' button and buy yourself some time.
  - 'Not now but next week/month'. Similar to the previous point, leaving the door ajar.
  - 'I have already . . . ', pointing out when you've already done something similar, and they've clearly forgotten.
  - 'I would love to, but I'm currently focusing on . . . ' You're not lazy; you just have other priorities.
  - 'I'm mainly focused on/concerned with my students; they need me right now'. Another priority reminder that points out the negative impact of doing something else.

Step 3 (GO GREEN): Some stress is inevitable and unavoidable. All educators need to know their go-to stress-busting strategies. We recommend these:

- Burn it off: Any form of physical acitivity. (Doesn't have to involve Lycra!)
- Connect: With others.

- Tune it out: Any kind of activity that truly engages you and distracts your mind from the issue in question. (Nothing good ever comes from 'ruminating' on a problem for more than a minute!)
- Tune it out: Any kind of mindfulness, 'box breathing', or other relaxation activities.
- Turn it off: Unplug from technology (particularly emails when not at work – it's hard but vital to avoid burnout).
- Make a break: Have a ritual that puts a boundary between work and home for your mind (shower, change of clothes, leave your laptop in the car).
- Recover: Take your sleep seriously (leave your phone by the front door).

Planning for staff wellbeing

'Professional learning efforts targeting teacher wellbeing should aim for more than simply reducing stress and burnout – they should also strive to cultivate positive patterns of thinking and feeling'.[21]

Dedicating one week a year to staff wellbeing is not sufficient to support educators in an effective way. Educators at all levels will benefit from a greater understanding of psychological processing at the individual level – the way our thoughts, actions and emotions interact has a massive impact on our day-to-day experience.

Over the past two years we have run numerous principal and educator wellbeing workshops at regional education conferences across New Zealand. Using a whole-school view of wellbeing influences, we encourage educators to consider barriers and enablers to wellbeing at the personal, classroom, staff, school, and state/national policy levels. (See Chapter 2, Figure 2.1, page 16.)

An important wellbeing strategy is to avoid overwhelm and focus attention where it can have greatest effect. We suggest that 'does it matter?' and 'can I control it?' are two important questions that can build wellbeing. At the systemic level, most staff say something like, 'These factors matter, but I can't change it. My union are working on this for me'.

Using the worksheets in Figure 12.1 on page 213 (Wellbeing planning worksheets: Focusing and prioritising wellbeing), we encourage staff groups to identify the classroom and school factors that *support wellbeing* (e.g. supportive community, great staff room, generous professional development budget) and those that *hinder wellbeing* (e.g. unwieldy administrative system, old computers, non-cohesive staff group). After staff have identified their wellbeing supports and hindrances, we ask them which ones a) matter and b) they can control. One of the 'aha' moments for many educators was

Personal factors influencing your wellbeing (e.g. friendships, strengths, optimism, kindness, gratitude, sense of purpose, mindfulness, volunteering, sleep and leisure activities)	
Factors that support my wellbeing	**Factors that challenge my wellbeing**
Factors to appreciate/nurture	**Factors I can influence/change**
Wellbeing and resilience strategy: Appreciate the good, and focus your efforts on things you can influence.	

Organisational factors influencing your wellbeing (e.g. admin, colleagues, supervisor, clients, structures, policies, resources, work culture, location, environment)	
Factors that support my wellbeing	**Factors that challenge my wellbeing**
Factors to appreciate/nurture	**Factors I can influence/change**
Wellbeing and resilience strategy: Appreciate the good, and focus your efforts on things you can influence.	

Figure 12.1 Wellbeing planning worksheets: Focusing and prioritising wellbeing

Skills/strategies proven to support wellbeing (Check that they are part of your wellbeing plan)	Making it stick: Embedding wellbeing in your daily life

• Practice **gratitude** – notice '3 Good Things' daily or Hunt the Good Stuff (#htgs).
• Adopt a **strengths focus** – look for what is right in yourself, others, organisations, meetings and situations.
• Avoiding **thinking traps** (disputing your unrealistic pessimistic thinking).
• **Mindfulness** – at least once a day, practice being present and noticing without judgment.
• **Relationships** benefit from all the listed strategies.
• **Self-compassion** – be as kind to yourself as you are to your best friend.
• **Rest and recover** – give your body and mind time out from work each day and longer breaks each year.
• Develop a **growth mindset** – 'I can't do that YET'.
• Remember the **iceberg of success** – look for the learning in every setback/failure.
• Remind yourself of the 'why' of your work – What makes it feel most **meaningful or worthwhile** to you?
	• **People with specific and written goals are more likely to achieve them.** This applies to wellbeing too. For each wellbeing action, ask:
	  ✓ **Who** can I do this activity with?
	  ✓ **When** will I do it in my day?
	  ✓ **Where** will I be when I do this activity?
	• Make wellbeing **a regular part of your day** – diary it, commit to action with others.
	• One small action is better than a big plan.
	• How can you **bring wellbeing to work**?
	  ✓ Walking meetings (or first ten minutes of a meeting).
	  ✓ Start meetings with WWW (what went well).
	  ✓ End meetings with 'one thing I'm looking forward to'/gratitude.
	• If you set an alarm to get up, why not set one for rest/sleep?
	• Who could be your wellbeing buddy?

'It's better to go for a walk than not go for a run'. Billy Graham, Naenae, Wellington, New Zealand	

Figure 12.1 (Continued)

My personal wellbeing action plan			
Physical wellbeing (eat, sleep, move)	**Emotional/ mental wellbeing** (psychological)	**Social wellbeing** (relationships)	**Spiritual wellbeing** (meaningful/ worthwhile)
For each action on your plan:	• **Who** will I do it with?	• **When** will I do it?	• **Where** will I be?
What's the smallest change I can make that will make the biggest difference to my wellbeing? Who will I ask to be my wellbeing accountability buddy? Who is my confidant/key support?			

Figure 12.1 (Continued)

realising they could 'let go' of hindrances that they couldn't control, that worrying or complaining wasn't making change happen and, if anything, was adding to their stress.

We encourage staff, as a group, to dedicate time each term to identify the issues they want to change, considering:

- Where they have influence and control;
- Which issues matter most (i.e. make the biggest difference);
- Prioritising ruthlessly; and
- Sharing the burden by allocating roles and supporting each other.

Staff use the same process to focus on personal wellbeing factors, identifying what's already working well and where future efforts may be most helpful. This process helps personalise and contextualise wellbeing planning. It avoids 'randomly picking things from a list' and ensure strategies are prioritised and personal. A list of evidence-based wellbeing strategies, however, is also provided – we can all do with some reminders of what works.

Box 12.1: Educator wellbeing activities (McCallum and Price)

These creative and practical activities come from leading researchers in educator wellbeing.[22]

- Decide whether you would like to make a classroom for early childhood, primary or secondary school students. Create your ideal classroom or learning space, one that establishes, promotes and sustains positive wellbeing. You can draw it, make a diorama or decorate an actual room and take photos. Write a 1,000-word reflective essay or poem telling us about your space and why it would be a positive learning environment for students and teachers.
- *Two stars and a wish.* Identify two areas of your wellbeing that you believe are faring well; give yourself a gold *star*. Identify one *wish* that you have to improve an area of wellbeing, and identify strategies to achieve this. Share with colleagues.
- What artefact represents wellbeing to you? It could be an object, drawing, photo, poem or song. Share with a colleague.
- Ask yourself, *'What's the worst that can happen?'* Make a list of your own strengths and accomplishments and refer to it to boost confidence. Don't waste energy worrying. Take action on what you can control, and minimise risks for what you can't.
- A strategy to help your wellbeing as you transition to a new school environment to teach is to consider if you are 'community ready', 'school ready' and 'classroom ready'. In a table, list your relative strengths and weaknesses with respect to these three areas. This is a good strategy to help you identify the resources you need to help in your preparation.

Source: McCallum and Price (2015, Chapter 6).

Box 12.2: Chris Eyre's top tips for educator wellbeing

The Elephant in the Staffroom addresses educator wellbeing in a practical, realistic and psychological way. As a teacher himself, Eyre knows the pressures of modern-day teachers well. He offers a framework for building collective understanding of staff wellbeing barriers and enablers and good material for staff room discussion. Insights from Chris:

- **Well teachers teach well.** Wellbeing is not a side issue. Remember to manage energy just as much as you manage time. There are lots of demands on us as teachers, but we can't do any of them if we've collapsed in a heap somewhere. You are the number one resource that your students have.
- **Teach well and be confident.** Whatever is going on, our main priority is planning, teaching and marking. If we teach well, it does wonders for our confidence and puts the admin into perspective. Teach badly and we become convinced that we are no good at anything. The number one priority and the thing that most affects our confidence is our teaching.
- **Go easy on the guilt.** Try to keep it in perspective. So one particular lesson didn't go so well? it's not the end of the world. Don't succumb to perfectionism; accept that you will never complete the list.
- **Rest.** Physical and mental energy levels are important. Make sure yours are topped up. Take at least one midweek evening off completely and have at least one full day off at the weekend. Your energy levels are the most important thing in determining how things go in the classroom.
- **Look after yourself – stay positive.** It's easy to overlook the fact that most things have gone well. Remind yourself of what you can do (or get others to remind you). Celebrate success. And don't listen to the grumbling voices in the staff room who try to convince you that the life of a teacher is the hardest life known to man.
- **The long game.** Teaching is a long game: a marathon, not a sprint. It's not about the first week or the second week. It's about the whole year in colleges or, in schools, several years. We would

love to deliver outstanding lessons all the time, mark two essays for each student every week, run three after-school clubs etc., but we have to be realistic. Being organised means hassle at the start of the year for long-term gain.

- **Stick to your values and principles.** Decide what matters and what doesn't. Try not to be moved. The question 'Why?' is the most powerful one you can ask. Some things are valid and good, but not for you.
- **Help.** Ask for help when you need it, and take advantage of any that is on offer. Just because we are often on our own in the classroom doesn't mean that we have to do everything on our own. Use the wider team, and play your part in that team.
- **Significant others.** Make time for family and friends. Remember that you are not just a teacher. Make sure your relationships stay healthy and strong, and don't be tempted to spend all the weekend in the spare room preparing.
- **Grow and have fun.** Finally, grow as a person and as a teacher. Try to be as good as you can at what you do, but remember that your mental health matters more. How we think about ourselves and our role as teachers is crucial in determining whether we survive and succeed in the job. Look for things to enjoy each day; schools and colleges are quite often hilarious places.

Case study 12.1:   Using psychological capital to support staff wellbeing

Waimairi School uses psychological capital as a lens through which staff explore wellbeing. PsyCap 'micro-interventions' aim to build the four pillars of psychological capital (hope, efficacy, resilience, optimism).

PsyCap cafe – teacher-led self-reflection session

Staff members with high levels of PsyCap meet weekly in a cafe after school to share their understanding of the four pillars, using worked examples of issues they've dealt with during the week. Teachers share the things that have added to their capital balance or drawn down on it. During the cafe period, the school experienced a significant event, going into lock-down while a significant terror attack took place in the city. The school responded to this stress by advocating self-care and shutting down all non-essential events and meetings. In this environment, staff chose to maintain PsyCap cafe because it was a 'tank filler', providing a valued resource and support for all involved.

Building your PsyCap might prevent burnout

The school's work on staff burnout showed how burnout gets in the way of building PsyCap. For example, empathy, de-personalisation, and performance accomplishment burnout will undermine the ability to build PsyCap. When teachers explored burnout, they realised the potential of PsyCap to act as a preventative approach to teacher wellbeing. One staff member who recognised she was at risk of empathy burnout focused on it and took action. As a result, at a later team session on preventing burnout, this teacher was an outlier – the only teacher not at risk of empathy burnout.

Case study 12.2:   A self-determination theory (SDT) lens on staff wellbeing

Self-determination theory (SDT) suggests people perform at their best when their basic and universal psychological needs for competence/mastery, autonomy and relatedness are "supported versus thwarted".[23] SDT provides a useful framework for promoting and protecting educator wellbeing. Here are some examples of how schools have used SDT.

- **Flexible time outs:** St Catherine's School in Sydney changed from a set 'time out' period every fortnight (when teachers could leave early if they wanted) to the creation of 'on call' periods (when teachers could be asked to cover a lesson), enabling the creation of flexible time outs. If a teacher was not teaching or on call, they could leave school early or arrive late. Used by teachers at all levels, it communicates respect for staff to complete their work and manage their time.

In her work with UK schools, Gilda Scarfe has seen the following:

- **'Do-it-yourself conference'**: Established by a group of head teachers at UK schools to reduce feelings of isolation and provide support for tough decisions. A problem or concern is shared at the twice-yearly conference with experienced and expert colleagues who guide a plan of action. Members are trained in a solution-focused coaching approach.
- **Wellbeing photo display:** One school asked staff to share a photo and brief sentence explaining how they look after their wellbeing at the start of the year. Photos are displayed in the corridors, providing talking points for staff and students.
- **Video feedback:** Staff replaced marking with video feedback to reduce workload. This reduced stress and created more connectedness between parent, teacher and students.

SDT-based questions to foster staff wellbeing

- How much autonomy do individual staff/teams already have in their roles?

  - Is there room for more?
  - Can there be a choice in the way they approach tasks?
  - Do all staff need to do things in the same way?

- Where and how can you give staff more trust and freedom? How can you explain your thinking around this to them?
- How would you know if staff craved more autonomy? Or if they felt they were being micro-managed?
- What can you do to increase your staff sense of relatedness:

  - Across the whole staff?
  - Across various teams?
  - Between senior management, teachers and support staff?

- How can you encourage your staff to find trusted friends at work?
- What simple, practical acts of kindness can you personally (or as a team) do for staff?
- What kindnesses do your colleagues already do? Have you noticed and drawn attention to them?
- What routine opportunities have you set up to share good news, positive observations/reflections and classroom wins among your staff?

- What casual opportunities do you take to share good news, positive observations/reflections and classroom wins among your staff?

Case study 12.3:   A community of learning focuses on staff wellbeing

The Palmerston North East *Kāhui Ako* (community of learning) includes ten schools focusing on staff wellbeing in their first year of wellbeing work. Some of the practical strategies and innovations they have implemented include:

- Enabling a team of 'creative' staff to re-organise and plan the staff room during a teacher-only day. The design crew made the staff room more welcoming and friendly. The school caretaker built five tables on zero budget, and a *whānau* wall (family wall) was created to share family photos. Different pods (groups of three teachers who work together) take turns running a quiz in the staff room during Friday break time. The staff room is now used more with teachers mixing more.
- The wellbeing teams of each school attending a termly book group on staff wellbeing. Reading *Onward* by Elena Aguilar, teachers discuss the strategies and share them in staff meetings.
- One school is embedding wellbeing practices in short tips shared with staff at weekly staff meetings. Linked to the school's values, they are becoming part of 'the way things are done here'.
- One school prioritising inclusion and belonging among staff and focusing their activities on social meetings: a family day at year-end rather than a staff party and lots of opportunities for the staff to get to know each other and their families.
- Staff taking on a '40-Day Wellbeing Challenge' using the five ways to wellbeing, reporting back and sharing progress and activities. After a staff survey revealed staff were low on the 'be active' dimension of the five ways, staff organised within school activities including yoga, boxing and a walking group.

Case study 12.4:   A wellbeing survey that is an individual wellbeing
plan

Rāroa School Deputy Principal Stephen Eames describes how staff at
the school have been encouraged to reflect on their own wellbeing as
part of work to develop staff engagement and wellbeing.

An individual wellbeing plan rather than a survey

'Many wellbeing surveys invite staff to critique the senior leadership
team. We do want feedback on what we can get right and how we can
support our teachers, but we've introduced an annual survey we call
an Individual Well-being Plan (IWP). It's an opportunity for teachers
to reflect on, and evaluate, their own wellbeing so they can make some
positive goals or actions, which are then part of a coaching process.
Teachers have time to think about how they can improve and flourish.

There was a little bit of pushback when we created the IWP questionnaire. But you can't expect everybody to have complete buy-in –
particularly at the start. The first time it went out there was some
interesting comments because people actually wanted the opportunity to tell us what they think about the leadership. There were a few
people that used it as an opportunity to critique. One comment said,
"This is a very one-sided questionnaire". Yes, of course it's one sided,
it's about you and how we can help you. So that took a little while.

Results from this year's IWP indicated that 100% of our teachers
report feeling supported by the school leadership. That's an outcome we're very proud of. Staff genuinely support each other at our
school. One teacher reflected that, "I feel comfortable approaching
anybody with my problems. . . . they offer guidance and advice and
they will always be willing to offer time to do this. As the beginning
teacher at the school, it is something I really value and appreciate"'.

Reflection questions

- How does your school invest in staff wellbeing?
- How many of Faye McCallum's successful teacher wellbeing initiatives
  (see page 209) are underway in your school?
- How would staff in your school rate the emotional support they receive?

- How much support do staff gain from collaborative working and learning?
- Is staff wellbeing supported by an inclusive and transformational leadership style?
- Do staff in your school have strategies to manage stress?
- Have staff in your school been able to ask for help when they need it?
- Do staff in your school have wellbeing plans?
- Does your staff room support your wellbeing?

Notes

1   Coleman, J. (2009). Wellbeing in schools: Empirical measure, or politician's dream? *Oxford Review of Education, 35*(3), 281–292.

2   McCallum, F., & Price, D. (2016). *Nurturing wellbeing development in education* (p. 17). New York: Routledge.

3   Leithwood, K. & McAdie, P. (2006). *Teacher working conditions that matter: Evidence for change, elementary teachers' federation of Ontario.* Education Canada. Toronto, Ontario.

4   Kyriacou, C. (1987). Teacher stress and burnout: An international review. *Educational Research, 29*(2), 146–152.

5   OECD. (2005). *Teachers matter: Attracting, developing and retaining effective teachers.* Paris: OECD Publishing.

6   Grenville-Cleave, B., & Boniwell, I. (2012). Surviving or thriving? Do teachers have lower perceived control and wellbeing than other professions? *Management in Education, 26*(1), 3–5.

7   Sellgren, K. (2014). Teachers report rise in mental health fears. *BBC News Education.* Retrieved May 6, 2019, from www.bbc.com/news/education-26990735

8   Fernet, C., Guay, F., Senécal, C., & Austin, S. (2012). Predicting intra-individual changes in teacher burnout: The role of perceived school environment and motivational factors. *Teaching and Teacher Education, 28*(4), 514–525.

9   Post Primary Teachers' Association. (2016). *Theory of secondary teacher demand and supply.* Retrieved from www.ppta.org.nz/dmsdocument/180

10   McCallum, F., Price, D., Graham, A., & Morrison, A. (2017). *Teacher wellbeing: A review of the literature.* Retrieved from Analysis and Policy Observatory Website https://apo.org.au/node/201816

11   Briner, R., & Dewberry, C. (2007). *Staff well-being is key to school success.* London: Worklife Support Ltd/Hamilton House.

12   McCallum, F., Price, D., Graham, A., & Morrison, A. (2017). *Teacher wellbeing: A review of the literature.* Retrieved from Analysis and Policy Observatory Website https://apo.org.au/node/201816

13   Bronfenbrenner, U., & Morris, P. A. (2007). The bioecological model of human development. In *Handbook of Child Psychology, 1.*

14   Cenkseven-Onder, F., & Sari, M. (2009). The quality of school life and burnout as predictors of subjective wellbeing among teachers. *Educational Sciences: Theory and Practice, 9*(3), 1223–1235.

15   Gibbs, S., & Miller, A. (2014). Teachers' resilience and wellbeing: A role for educational psychology. *Teachers and Teaching, 20*(5), 609–621.

16   Soini, T., Pyhältö, K., & Pietarinen, J. (2010). Pedagogical wellbeing: Reflecting learning and wellbeing in teachers' work. *Teachers and Teaching: Theory and Practice, 16*(6), 735–751.

17   Owen, S. (2016). Professional learning communities: Building skills, reinvigorating the passion, and nurturing teacher wellbeing and "flourishing" within significantly innovative schooling contexts. *Educational Review,* 1–17.

18   Heidmets, M., & Liik, K. (2014). School principals' leadership style and teachers 'subjective wellbeing at school. *Problems of Education in the 21st Century, 62,* 40–50.

19   Eyre, C. (2016). *The elephant in the staffroom: How to reduce stress and improve teacher wellbeing* (p. 22). Routledge.

20   Eyre, C. (2016). *The elephant in the staffroom: How to reduce stress and improve teacher wellbeing.* Routledge.

21   Cook, C. R., Miller, F. G., Fiat, A., Renshaw, T., Frye, M., Joseph, G., & Decano, P. (2017). Promoting secondary teachers' wellbeing and intentions to implement evidence-based practices: Randomised evaluation of the achiever resilience curriculum. *Psychology in the Schools, 54*(1), 13–28.

22   McCallum, F., & Price, D. (2016). *Nurturing wellbeing development in education* (p. 17). New York: Routledge.

23   Deci, E. L., & Ryan, R. M. (2008). Self-determination theory: A macrotheory of human motivation, development, and health. *Canadian Psychology/Psychologie Canadienne, 49*(3), 182.

Watch

Burnout Blockers for Teachers series. Retrieved from www.youtube.com/watch?v=_kZHqddEA-A

Rankin, J. G. (2018). First Aid for Teacher Burnout. Retrieved from https://vimeo.com/255557770

Read

Aguilar, E. (2018). *The onward workbook: Daily activities to cultivate your emotional resilience and thrive.* Jossey-Bass, a Wiley Brand. And its associated workbook and website. Retrieved from www.onwardthebook.com/

Eyre, C. (2017). *The elephant in the staffroom: How to reduce stress and improve teacher wellbeing.* Oxford, UK: Routledge.

Faye McCallum and colleague's Literature Review of Teacher Wellbeing. Retrieved from https://apo.org.au/sites/default/files/resource-files/2017/10/apo-nid201816-1133141.pdf

The Five Ways to Wellbeing at Work Toolkit (from the Mental Health Foundation, NZ). Retrieved from www.mentalhealth.org.nz/home/our-work/category/42/five-ways-to-wellbeing-at-work-toolkit

Glasgow, P. (2014). *Teach, love, life: From stress to success. A practical guide to teacher wellbeing.* Victoria, Australia: Busy Bird Publishing.

Steve Francis' Happy Schools newsletters. Retrieved from www.happyschool.com.au/

Teacher, Agi Enyedi, on burnout. Retrieved from www.britishcouncil.org/voices-magazine/how-can-teachers-avoid-burnout

www.amazon.com/Onward-Workbook-Activities-Cultivate-Resilience/dp/1119367387/ref=dp_rm_title_0

Zonneyvlle, S., & Armstrong, D. (2019). *The forty-hour principal: Provocations for the discerning educator.* Copy Press Books. Nelson, NZ. Retrieved from https://40hourprincipal.com/ See their blog too on FB: The Forty Hour Principal.

Listen

NZIWR podcasts are available from https://nziwr.co.nz/category/podcast/

NZIWR podcast: Sonya Papps (Educator Wellbeing)

NZIWR podcast: Mike Anderson (PsyCap for Educator Wellbeing)

Partnering with students

Introduction

The fact that this chapter is one of the slimmest in this book is no coincidence. While student voice has been a growing theme in academic research since the 1990s and schools across the world are endeavouring to engage authentically with students around wellbeing, most acknowledge they are struggling to do so or taking their first fledgling steps.

Partnering with students is, however, essential. Being heard is a fundamental human right. According to the United Nations Convention Rights of a Child: 'Parties shall assure to the child who is capable of forming his or her own views the right to express those views freely in all matters affecting the child'.[1] As a result, governments globally are making student voice part of curricula. Educators and school administrators have a responsibility to incorporate student views, and best practice goes way beyond merely asking students for feedback on educator-devised programmes. Wellbeing initiatives are much more likely to be welcomed, be effective and become embedded if they are born out of active participation with shared decision-making reflecting young people's concerns, hopes, interests, frustrations and opinions.

What the research says

Authentic student engagement should involve young people at every stage of the process: initial research and scoping, design, implementation, feedback and review. Yes, this is messy and definitely challenging to do, but systems theory is quite clear that 'real social change only occurs when the boundaries of who is included when defining problems, generating solutions, and affecting change is expanded to include all relevant voices'.[2]

While there is very little consensus in the academic literature as to what defines student voice,[3] [4] research does suggest that engaging with students is beneficial for schools.[5] [6] [7] [8] [9] Cook-Sather's review of international practices and literature reminds researchers and educators that when they translate themselves into 'partners with students', they are no longer the 'distanced, authoritative, sole authors of the meaning', and students are 'no longer objects of study' but 'primary actors'.[10]

While literature relating student voice to wellbeing practices specifically is nascent, some researchers are starting to explore this important topic. For example, a team from AUT University[11] recently asked 361 year seven and eight students (11- to 13-year-olds) how they conceptualise wellbeing and found students consider enjoyment/having fun, feeling safe and being kind/helpful as key (central) components of wellbeing and sense of satisfaction as a less essential component. Low socio-economic status adolescents considered comfort/being wealthy, being focused, good physical health, good values and success/achievements as more important for wellbeing than high-socioeconomic status adolescents. Consistent with previous studies, supportive family relationships, positive friendships and physical activity/sport were the most frequently reported pathways to wellbeing among this sample of NZ adolescents.

Action research by Nottinghamshire Educational Psychology Service asked 4- to 11-year-olds their views (via talking and drawing) on various aspects of wellbeing, including school environment, how other people in school helped them feel good about themselves, what happened when someone was upset, what helped them look after themselves in school and when they enjoyed joining in.[12] 'One of the most striking aspects of conducting these focus groups was the skills demonstrated by the children both in relation to participation and mental health and wellbeing', commented the researcher, Jane Hall. Not only did the research report the noticeable emotional vocabulary demonstrated by the children, but it also linked this to the social-emotional learning undertaken at school. Ultimately, Hall reported on how useful student voice was in guiding school staff to make changes to support wellbeing in their school.

Having voice gives the speaker access and opportunity to express their beliefs and ideas and influence decisions,[13] and evidence shows schools providing opportunities for student voice report lower incidence of challenging student behaviour.[14]

As Holdsworth and Blanchard warn, however, student voice should not be about 'providing data for others to use in making decisions, but as one of encouraging young people's active participation in shared decisions and in consequent action about their own present and future'.[15] To assist the process of going beyond using students to provide data, various models of student voice have been developed over the years including Hart's,[16] Mitra's[17] and Fielding's.[18]

Researchers urge educators to pay attention to the purpose of engaging students' opinions, ensure the representativeness of the input, and be mindful of the limits around what changes are actually possible. Don't over-promise and under-deliver! We particularly like Bernstein's recommendation that we pay attention to the 'acoustic of the school',[19] drawing attention to who's voices are being heard – and missed. For instance, an Australian review of student engagement, voice and mental health discovered that students at risk of having high mental health support needs were less likely to voice their opinion and concern to adults, meaning less is known about what engages them with school.[20]

Researchers[21][22] have suggested several good questions to review before engaging with young people, which we've included in the reflection questions at the end of the chapter (see page 237).

The NZ Education Review Office (ERO) reports that schools with good wellbeing practices provide students with opportunities to develop confidence as leaders, learners and valued members of the school community.[23] Specifically, schools identified by ERO as having good wellbeing practices shared the following characteristics: young people actively contributed to the planning, implementation and review of wellbeing initiatives; many schools adopted a buddy system between older and younger students to foster student-to-student relationships and leadership roles and responsibilities in these schools included mentoring, coaching, leading interest groups and representing the school in the local community. 'Students were viewed as inherently capable. Their views, ideas and decisions were sought and valued. They were trusted to take on the leadership roles that contributed to their wellbeing'. The changes shown in Table 13.1 were evident in the schools where students were actively involved in promoting and improving their wellbeing and the wellbeing of others.

Putting it into practice

Giving young people a say in their educational experience is recognised for having engagement and educational benefits for individuals, as well as the wider community, via encouraging collaboration; supporting a positive school environment and culture; building respectful relationships, connections and a sense of belonging; developing interpersonal and intrapersonal capabilities and capacity; teacher reflections and valuable learning for educators; and enhanced relationships between teachers, school leaders, students and families.

Table 13.1 Changes evident in schools where students were actively involved in promoting wellbeing

Changes observed in schools with students actively involved in wellbeing		
Area of focus	**From**	**To**
Student voice	Schools relying on surveys as the means to seek students' perspectives.	Schools using a range of ways to involve students in decision making and leadership of their wellbeing and learning (for example, focus groups, class discussions, quality circle time and 'think tanks').
Student leadership	Leadership opportunities only available to an 'elite' group of students.	Opportunities for all students to take on leadership roles and responsibilities.
Student involvement in decision-making	Limited or no opportunities for students to make decisions about things that affect their wellbeing.	Students actively involved in decisions that have an impact on their wellbeing through the curriculum, pastoral care processes and identification of wellbeing priorities.

Source: Education Review Office (ERO, 2016)

There are a number of ways schools can engage students as partners in the wellbeing journey. They can provide opportunities for students to get involved in decision-making on matters that affect them (student wellbeing councils, action groups), collaborate with students to co-create wellbeing resources (such as student journals, diaries, curriculum, websites, radio, plays, information sheets), practices (leading wellbeing-focused assemblies, peer-support and buddy groups, Check and Connect, restorative relationships/disciplinary and communications, coaching, leadership roles), environment, relationships and pedagogy.

The best way to understand how students want to learn about and promote wellbeing in their schools is to ask them. That means including them in the research, planning, implementation and review processes. This involves partnership and participation.

One of the key lessons shared by Geelong Grammar School, gleaned from over ten years of promoting whole-school wellbeing, is the importance of 'doing wellbeing *with* students, not *to* them'.[24]

We are lucky enough to have been involved in a citywide community of practice (COP) around wellbeing over the past three years, involving every secondary school in Christchurch, NZ. We facilitated this COP for a whole year – inviting each school to send staff making up its wellbeing team to ter-mly *hui* (mini learning conferences/meetings) – before it occurred to us how ridiculous it was not inviting students to join the community. Having young people participate in the COP has transformed it – now we're all learning side by side, and it's easy to see that the changes schools are making are more likely to be embedded when they are genuinely co-created with their own students.

Case study 13.1:   Getting students to 'own' wellbeing: Wellbeing badges and ambassadors at St Peter's Cambridge

In 2019, St Peter's Cambridge created wellbeing badges and a new wellbeing ambassador role to boost awareness of and support for wellbeing. Dr Micheal Brown, director of wellbeing at St Peter's, explains:

'The Wellbeing badge serves as an expression of wellbeing connect-edness across both the student and staff population. The badge – designed and endorsed by students and staff – links the school house colours in an image associated with inclusiveness. Worn in a democratic way by anyone who wants to wear one, the St Peter's wellbeing badge is a fabulous indicator of the support the students have for wellbeing.

As the weeks have gone by, more students have moved into the newly created Wellbeing Ambassador role. This has allowed for social awareness of wellbeing to unfold via an organic approach enabling a positive expression of wellbeing in both individuals and across the school population. Both the badges and the Ambassa-dors reveal the instant connectedness and ongoing supportiveness within our student population, serving as a symbol of inclusion and acceptance of wellbeing within our school, and identifying that inclusion and acceptance is a significant element of a student's jour-ney during their time at school. Wearing the badge shows support and recognises students/staff as champions for wellbeing. Students (and staff) wearing the badge have emerged as leaders of change, based on their own journey and experiences, while also reflecting the individual methods employed to increase personal understanding of wellbeing and the understanding others have of wellbeing. These badges are democratic (like Yellow Daffodil, Purple Ribbons) designed to promote awareness and encourage dialogue. As we move towards having 50 Wellbeing Ambassadors at school, the importance and value of individual wellbeing experiences and sharing these has emerged'.

Box 13.1: What students want in wellbeing learning

Early feedback from students at GGS as part of an evaluation study bears noting by all educators.[25][26] Students wanted:

- Less didactic teaching and worksheet filling in and more experiential activities;
- More peer-to-peer learning, as they value their peers' experiences;
- Good connections with their teachers: teacher connection was an important factor in students' enjoyment of their positive education lessons;
- Wellbeing learning that is directly relevant to their real-world experience; and
- Teaching to emphasise the individual, dynamic and multifaceted nature of wellbeing and so to 'describe' rather than 'prescribe' wellbeing.

Expert researcher/practitioner insight 13.1: *Dr Sue Roffey, Director of Growing Great Schools Worldwide. Engaging with student voice*

Nine reasons to engage student voice:
- Participation gives children and young people a sense of inclusion and belonging;

- Engagement in your community enhances resilience and wellbeing;
- When young people are given agency, they are more likely to take responsibility for the decisions they make;
- Optimal adult-child relationships include authentic consultation;
- Seeking someone's opinion makes that person feel good about themselves and positive towards the person involved;
- Giving students opportunities to contribute increases their motivation to collaborate, encourages their creativity and thinking skills and develops a more positive self-concept;
- Adults' views of young people may change if we provide opportunities for students to identify and demonstrate their strengths;
- Children are often marginalised in our society and in our schools: they do not have an automatic 'voice' in matters that concern them and sometimes behave in ways that are attention seeking in order to be 'heard'; and
- Children have a right to be heard in matters that concern them.

Source: Sue Roffey, *Changing Behaviour in Schools* (2011, p. 120)

Case study 13.2:   Creative student-led solutions to wellbeing challenges

Clare Erasmus, head of the technology faculty and head of whole-school mental health and wellbeing at Brighton Hill Community School in Hampshire, UK, has spent the last five years supporting her school to build positive mental health and wellbeing, sharing her learning in *The Mental Health and Wellbeing Handbook for Schools: Transforming Mental Health Support on a Budget* (Jessica Kingsley Publisher, 2019).

A wellbeing space

Clare began with a series of student focus groups that revealed students wanted to know where, when and from whom they could access mental health support. Drop-in support that moved location and key contacts was not working. Clare has set up the Wellbeing Zone in one school and the Wellbeing Square in another, places where students can gather to discuss wellbeing, support each other or gain access to support. Student wellbeing ambassadors, who staff the spaces, were trained in providing support, including listening without judgment, safeguarding procedures and support for their own wellbeing if they are upset by what they've heard. Her approach is summarised here.

How wellbeing is supported in the school

- 'Students can self-refer. The process is led by student mental health ambassadors, who are overseen by staff trained as mental health first aiders. The school wellbeing space is the place where students can come and talk to the wellbeing ambassadors.
- Referral. All staff are trained on the signs to look out for – particularly longevity and impact. They know the referral procedures but are also trained and encouraged to have the first conversation as they probably already have a relationship with that child.
- Lessons. These are rolled out in personal and social health education (PSHE); there is a curriculum setting out the areas that must be covered.'

Students supporting teachers to teach wellbeing

Wellbeing teaching is part of PSHE, with many teachers required to deliver wellbeing lessons. That includes some teachers who were less confident with this material and reluctant to teach. Clare engaged the students in her media class to create wellbeing podcast interviews on the required topics. These eight-minute recordings worked at a number of levels: staff could focus on the class discussion following podcast content; staff interviewed for the topics shared personal stories, 'humanising' staff for students and making connection easier; students enjoyed the audio content – Clare hypothesises that it's a welcome break from their regular video diet. Clare is now focusing her efforts on training teachers in facilitating discussion and holding a safe space for all students.

Giving students voice and agency

Approached by a group of students concerned that they were subject to homophobic bullying, Clare tasked them with making (as part of their schoolwork) a ten-minute investigative documentary on homophobic bullying in the school. With the support of the principal, the students accessed resources and support to do this, uncovering a problem with homophobic language in the school. The students presented their work and led discussions at the school assembly and neighbouring primary schools. Interest in their work led to students presenting at the teachers' union national conference and a request for their video from the House of Commons. Students were proud of the challenge they led and change they brought about by their activism.

Engaging parents and students in wellbeing

Clare developed strategies to support a diet of mental health for families using the GREAT values (give; relate; energised family; aware of self, others and surroundings; try something new). The MH5aDay 30-Day Challenge was a way to engage families in building mental health using the GREAT values. Year seven took the challenge home in the five weeks coming up to Christmas. Equipped with a list of activities under each of the GREAT values (one for students and one for parents), families took on the challenge, sending photos, and signing off on completed challenges. Parents enjoyed it, saying it helped their families focus on wellbeing. Concerned about excluding students who don't have families willing or able to engage in this activity, Clare now encourages students to do the challenge with friends and is adapting the language to be more inclusive.

An app that's a conversation starter

Media studies students developed the app Teen Mind for their school to provide information on mental health and wellbeing concerns. With external support from app developers, students researched what the app should include. With basic information on each topic (e.g. anxiety, self-harm), warning signs to look out for and places to go for help, the app became a useful resource for teenagers and for their parents. One unexpected benefit reported by parents was that they used the app to raise a topic of concern with their teen.

Case study 13.3:   Onewhero Area School – The benefits of involving students in programme creation

Paul Tupou-Vea, director of Clifftop Wellbeing, has been working alongside Onewhero Area School in a range of media over the last two years. His general work at the school is in developing staff capacity and co-designing their wellbeing strategy and curriculum. Paul describes the evolution of the programme:

'Onewhero Area School caters for students from year 1 to year 13 and is the social hub of a relatively small rural community. The school first gained exposure to wellbeing science through a two-day professional development programme I led, based on positive education. The programme created an even platform for all school staff (including non-teaching staff) to share language and tools for staff and student wellbeing. A senior leader was responsible for wellbeing and post the two-day training programme, the school created a focused team of teachers and support staff from across the school. This team still meets regularly to plan and initiate the schools' work and professional development around wellbeing.

After a year, the wellbeing team was busy in the work of implementing new lessons and tools for students and at the same time began building a curriculum for it. At this point a brave decision was made. Rather than continuing on the path of teachers determining students' learning and then justifying it – they decided to engage the community. This meant allowing more time to plan how they would interact with parents and families, as well as students themselves. While it was clear that this would take more time than 'Plan A', there was a shared desire for wellbeing to be comprehensive, intentional and integrated into the school's culture and practice.

The wellbeing team and I co-designed and facilitated an appreciative inquiry (AI) summit, focused on wellbeing. While it was compulsory for staff to attend, invitations were given to students, parents and members of the Board of Trustees. The result was a conversation about past and present successes, as well as future hopes for the wellbeing of Onewhero's young. Conversations crossed social boundaries and gave all people a voice and a forum to be heard. Parents and board members valued the chance to contribute their thoughts and just to see and hear that their kids were valued. Students appreciated the opportunity to have agency over their education and environment. Staff valued the solution-focused conversations and planning.

Currently, the wellbeing team is in the process of synthesising the rich data gathered into a curriculum and model that truly represents the aspirations of their school community. Concurrently they are able to move with more certainty in teaching skills they know are important to their students and are aligned with core goals. Finally, the wellbeing team has increased their support base significantly. Students wanted to lead projects to increase social connection and improve physical environments, while staff at the summit highlighted other areas for focus in and out of the classroom. There is a distinct feeling at Onewhero that their community is being thoughtful and considered in their approach to whole-school wellbeing. Where there may have been a race to flashy lesson plans in classrooms, there is now a sense that meaningful change will be achieved by the whole community's vision and action'.

Case-study 13.4:   Introducing SWAT teams in a citywide programme

Citywide youth consultation in 2015–2016 made raising the wellbeing of Maroondah's young people top priority for the council, embodied in its new youth strategy with a vision for 'Maroondah's young people . . . flourishing as part of a healthy and thriving community'. In the council's aim to actively involve and engage its citizens, their year 10 student wellbeing action teams (SWAT) programme has been developed over the last three years, involving 20 year 10 students each year selected from across Maroondah schools. This practical leadership programme aims to upskill, empower and increase the wellbeing of other young people by inviting students to attend a one-day SWAT summit, followed by three days of leadership/wellbeing training. Supplied with wellbeing data (collected by researchers from the University of Melbourne), students are then provided with ongoing support to brain storm and develop their own student wellbeing initiatives throughout the rest of the school year. Maroondah City Council covers the cost of the programme. For more information, see www.maroondahyouth.com.au/Programs-for-Young-People/ Leadership/SWAT-2018-Project-Highlights.

Reflection questions

The following questions are suggested by Holdsworth and Blanchard:[27] [28]

- How will you involve young people in active participation in future plans following on from consultation?
- Who is allowed to speak?
- Why are you interested in encouraging and hearing the voices of your students?
- What will you do with what you hear?
- What is allowed to be said?
- Who is listening?
- What is being heard?
- What space exists for negotiating and acting upon these voices?

Other recommended questions:

- What is the student-led vision across your school?
- In what ways have you asked them, and how do you know that the insights you gained represent diverse voices in your school community?
- What do students see as the wellbeing strengths of your school?
- What does it feel like to be a student in this school?
- What do your students wish your teachers/school leaders knew about wellbeing?
- What do your students see as the wellbeing needs of their school?

- Who feels they belong at your school? Who doesn't?
- What help do your students need so they can better support other students?

Questions to ask students:

- What makes you feel good at your school?
- What makes you feel good in your classroom?
- What do your teachers do to make you feel good?
- What does wellbeing mean to you?
- Who belongs at your school? Who doesn't?

Notes

1   United Nations. (1989). *United Nations convention on the rights of the child.* Retrieved from www.ohchr.org/en/professionalinterest/pages/crc.aspx

2   Kern, M. L., Williams, P., Spong, C., Colla, R., Sharma, K., Downie, A., . . . Oades, L. G. (2019). Systems informed positive psychology. *The Journal of Positive Psychology, 3.* doi:10.1080/17439760.2019.1639799

3   Nelson, E. (2014). Enacting student voice through governance partnerships in the classroom: Rupture of the ordinary for radical practice. *Forum for Promoting 3–19 Comprehensive Education, 56*(1), 91–104.

4   Hall, V. (2017). A tale of two narratives: Student voice – what lies before us? *Oxford Review of Education, 43*(2), 180–193.

5   Bron, J., & Veugelers, W. (2014). Why we need to involve our students in curriculum design: Five arguments for student voice. *Curriculum & Teaching Dialogue, 16*(1–2), 125–140.

6   Bishop, R., Berryman, M., Cavanagh, T., & Teddy, L. (2007). *Te Kōtahitanga Phase 3 Whānaungatanga: Establishing a culturally responsive pedagogy of relations in mainstream secondary school classrooms.* Wellington, New Zealand: Ministry of Education.

7   Cook-Sather, A. (2014). The trajectory of student voice in educational research [online]. *New Zealand Journal of Educational Studies, 49*(2), 131–148. Retrieved August 24, 2019, from https://search-informit-com-au.ezproxy.aut.ac.nz/documentSummary;dn=842480978608459;res=IELNZC ISSN: 0028-8276

8   Hall, S. (2010). Supporting mental health and wellbeing at a whole-school level: Listening to and acting upon children's views. *Emotional and Behavioural Difficulties, 15*(4), 323–339. doi:10.1080/13632752. 2010.523234

9   Busher, H. (2012). Students as expert witnesses of teaching and learning. *Management in Education, 26*(3), 113–119.

10 Cook-Sather, A. (2014). The trajectory of student voice in educational research [online]. *New Zealand Journal of Educational Studies, 49*(2), 131–148. Retrieved August 24, 2019, from https://search-informit-com-au.ezproxy.aut.ac.nz/documentSummary;dn=84248097 8608459;res=IELNZC ISSN: 0028-8276

11 Bharara, G., Duncan, S., Jarden, A., & Hinckson, E. (in press). A prototype analysis of New Zealand adolescents' conceptualizations of wellbeing. *International Journal of Wellbeing.*

12 Hall, S. (2010). Supporting mental health and wellbeing at a whole-school level: Listening to and acting upon children's views. *Emotional and Behavioural Difficulties, 15*(4), 323–339. doi:10.1080/13632752. 2010.523234

13 Thomson, P. (2011). Coming to terms with 'Voice'. In G. Czerniawski & W. Kidd (Eds.), *The student voice handbook: Bridging the academic/practitioner divide* (pp. 19–30). Emerald Group Publishing Limited.

14 National Union of Teachers. (2005). *Learning to behave: A charter for schools.* London: National Union of Teachers.

15 Holdsworth, R., & Blanchard, M. (2006). Unheard voices: Themes emerging from studies of the views about school engagement of young people with high support needs in the area of mental health. *Australian Journal of Guidance and Counselling, 16*(1), 14–28. doi:10.1375/ ajgc.16.1.14

16 Hart, R. A. (1992). Children's participation: From tokenism to citizenship. *Unicef: Innocenti Essays, 4.*

17 Mitra, D. L. (2006, February). Increasing student voice and moving toward youth leadership. *The Prevention Researcher, 13,* 7–10.

18 Fielding, M. (2011). Student voice and the possibility of radical democratic education: Re-narrating forgotten histories, developing alternative futures. In G. Czerniawski & W. Kidd (Eds.), *The student voice*

handbook: Bridging the academic/practitioner divide (pp. 3–17). Emerald Group Publishing Limited.

19   Bernstein, B. (2000). *Pedagogy, symbolic control, and identity.* Lanham, MD: Rowman & Littlefield Publishers, Inc.

20   Holdsworth, R., & Blanchard, M. (2006). Unheard voices: Themes emerging from studies of the views about school engagement of young people with high support needs in the area of mental health. *Australian Journal of Guidance and Counselling, 16*(1), 14–28. doi:10.1375/ajgc.16.1.14

21   Holdsworth, R. (2006b). *Student action teams: Implementing productive practices in primary and secondary school classrooms.* Northcote: Connect.

22   Holdsworth, R., & Blanchard, M. (2006). Unheard voices: Themes emerging from studies of the views about school engagement of young people with high support needs in the area of mental health. *Australian Journal of Guidance and Counselling, 16*(1), 14–28. doi:10.1375/ajgc.16.1.14

23   Education Review Office. (2016). *Wellbeing for success: Effective practice.* Wellington, NZ. Retrieved from www.ero.govt.nz/publications/wellbeing-for-success-effective-practice/

24   Scudamore, C. (2019, April 7). *10 lessons learned in 10 years.* Key Note Presentation at the Positive Education New Zealand conference, Christchurch, NZ.

25   Vella-Brodrick, D. A., Rickard, N. S., & Chin, T. C. (2014). *An evaluation of positive education at Geelong grammar school: A snapshot of 2013.* Melbourne, Australia: The University of Melbourne.

26   Larson, E. (Ed.). (2017, February 12–14). *The state of positive education.* A Report Prepared in Collaboration with the International Positive Education Network for the World Government Summit, Held in Dubai.

27   Holdsworth, R., & Blanchard, M. (2006). Unheard voices: Themes emerging from studies of the views about school engagement of young people with high support needs in the area of mental health. *Australian Journal of Guidance and Counselling, 16*(1), 14–28. doi:10.1375/ajgc.16.1.14

28   Holdsworth, R. (2006b). *Student action teams: Implementing productive practices in primary and secondary school classrooms.* Northcote: Connect.

Watch

Anti-Bullying Learning and Teaching Resource (ALTER) Catholic Education Office, Wollongong. Retrieved from www.youtube.com/watch?v=EA5C-1N_r1w

A Chance to be Heard (Vimeo) by John Ross – stories of change through art – "their giving me a chance to be heard". https://vimeo.com/273797766

Christchurch schools promote wellbeing through student-led strengths community initiative. Retrieved from www.stuff.co.nz/national/health/84536024/christchurch-schools-promote-wellbeing-through-character-strength

Haeata Community Campus' video for Pink Shirt Day. Retrieved from www.youtube.com/watch?v=xwb_mtk2SJQ&feature=youtu.be&fbclid=IwAR346nShrMoT1LedwvE30iHD1fBwhVfvMnxVrmqB9F_G0uwBwYFkFGTzMfU

Student voice at Avonside Girls' High School Christchurch. Retrieved from https://vimeo.com/325356049

Student voice at Shirley Boys' High School, Christchurch. Retrieved from https://vimeo.com/325355845

Student wellbeing committee at Darfield High School, Christchurch. Retrieved from https://vimeo.com/325355613

Students from Newcastle Grammar School, NSW, Australia who, off their own back, created this video for Christchurch students in response to the 15.3.19 massacre at the Al Noor mosque. Retrieved from www.facebook.com/watch/?v=420806605163114

Why is Student Voice Important? Retrieved from www.youtube.com/watch?v=EMEq9EmQJks

Why should students have a voice in their learning. Retrieved from www.youtube.com/watch?time_continue=4&v=sGsXFdzvQ_s

Read

Download the Youth Development Strategy Aotearoa summary sheet, which outlines the vision and principles of youth development (from the Ministry of Youth Development). Retrieved from www.myd.govt.nz/documents/resources-and-reports/publications/ydsa-leaflet-04.pdf

For a great (and easy to read) summary of the research on student voice, see Why Student Voice? A research summary. Retrieved from https:// soundout.org/why-student-voice-a-research-summary/

InspirED, backed by the Yale Center for Emotional Intelligence, is a programme designed by young people, educators and SEL experts to empower students to work together to create more positive school climates and foster greater wellbeing. Retrieved from https://inspired. fb.com/

NSW Department of Education student voice, participation and leadership web page. Retrieved from https://education.nsw.gov.au/ student-wellbeing/attendance-behaviour-and-engagement/student-voice-and-leadership

Positive Youth Development (PYD) has been described as an 'approach that guides communities in the way they organise programmes, people and supports so that young people can develop to their full potential' (Pittman). Positive Youth Development in Aotearoa is a fantastic resource exploring the various approaches to PYD documented in local and international literature with the grassroots experiences of young people. Retrieved from https://ir.canterbury.ac.nz/bitstream/handle/10092/ w20Aotearoa.pdf;sequence=1

Listen

NZIWR podcasts are available from https://nziwr.co.nz/category/podcast/

NZIWR podcast: Clare Erasmus (Engaging Student Voice)

NZIWR podcast: Adrienne Buckingham (On creating the MenFit programme for secondary boys)

How students got involved with leading wellbeing initiaives on the Maroondah Project. Retrieved from https://2ser.com/teaching-positive-psychology-in-the-classroom/?fbclid=IwAR1z1BRvkJa8-A13_ RH43xbvf8_PSN_EolDzvyN4HC-nPdnlVfqhZVrV1hY

Connecting with parents, caregivers and the wider community

Introduction

The family environment is a major influence on young people's wellbeing, but for our efforts to be truly effective and sustainable, we also need to consider the wider community. Building wellbeing at the wider community level allows diverse contributors to add their knowledge, resources, perspectives, strengths, skills and experience toward a shared goal, thereby growing collective impact. In this chapter, we review some of the ways schools are engaging with their parent and caregiver communities as well as some new and ambitious projects aiming to take wellbeing to scale involving multi-stakeholder collaborations across large regions.

What the research says

Ecological theory[1] suggests student development and behaviour are influenced by factors from the *microsystem* (immediate surroundings and relationships with friends, colleagues and family) and the *mesosystem* (interactions between the characters in the microsystem) through the *exosystem* (things that have an indirect effect on the child) to the *macrosystem* (cultural and societal beliefs). How these factors influence wellbeing plays out through events and over time.

While the field of wellbeing in education has, for many years, remained focused on building wellbeing among individuals, more recently, researchers, educators, school leaders and practitioners have started to take a systems approach to wellbeing intervention, targeting other levels of Bronfenbrenner's socio-ecological model, including family life, parenting styles, the wider community environment and educational policy and practice.[2]

Most parents and caregivers are keen to learn how they can best support their children's wellbeing, engagement and success, and the substantial influence parents have is supported by empirical research. For example, Waters, Loton and Jach emphasise that parental influence moves across the different levels of young people's lives with daily involvement and interaction, broader influences like choosing the child's school and the longer-term influence that their support and attitudes have on student academic achievement.[3] One study, involving 741 students at an Australian public school, demonstrated strength-based parenting predicted higher student wellbeing and academic performance. Similarly, research testing the effectiveness of a three-day intensive programme for parents about wellbeing in education demonstrated significant increases in parental wellbeing and parent-school connection.[4]

While these studies demonstrate the importance of engaging with the parent community for young people's wellbeing, schools and education departments are beginning to explore opportunities to collaborate with other stakeholders, using Collective Impact as a theoretical framework informing how wellbeing can be taken to scale.

There has been much talk about the Collective Impact (CI) model of social change over the past nine years as communities come to better appreciate the potential for collective change and the intricacies involved in change dynamics when grappling with complex systems. Two seminal articles have addressed this topic, both game changers for the field of community change. The first, an article called 'Channelling Change: Making Collective Impact Work', published in the Stanford Social Innovation Review in 2012, introduced the CI framework, suggesting that if agencies, organisations and communities worked together around five conditions (agreement on a common agenda, the development of a shared measurement approach, leveraging resources through mutually reinforcing activities, building continuous communications and a backbone structure to mobilise the collective effort), they could move from fragmented action and isolated impact to 'collective action and deep and durable impact'.[5] Four years later, these ideas were critiqued and expanded upon in another article by Mark Cabaj and Liz Weaver.[6] Cabaj and Weaver suggested a change to each of the original five conditions: common agenda shifted to community aspiration, shared measurement shifted to strategic learning, mutually reinforcing activities shifted to high-leverage activities, continuous communication shifted to inclusive community engagement and backbone organisation shifted to containers for change. The main thrust of their recommendation is that taking a 'movement' approach is far more powerful than traditional 'management' approaches.

This reflects an understanding that deep and complex problems are rarely solved by focusing on any one part of the system,[7] but instead, diverse organisations should co-create shared solutions not evident to any of them individually, working together for the benefit of the whole system.[8]

Putting it into practice

Connecting with parents and caregivers

In practice, the majority of schools' endeavours to connect with their communities still focus primarily on parents. Many acknowledge the challenges in doing so, particularly for secondary schools. While establishing wellbeing committees (including parents, governors, students and teachers) is an obvious first step, we've enjoyed hearing about the multitude of unique ways schools are building community connections. Among these are offering PosEd training at Grandparent day; inviting students to select six significant people to attend a roundtable presentation and discussion of their strengths portfolio; parents running workshops for young people on specialist topics of their choice (as advertised on notice boards where students can sign up); involving parents and caregivers in discussions of individual wellbeing plans for students; parent-led training for parents in character strengths, growth mindset and mindfulness; and a librarian who created a VIA strengths Pinterest board so that anyone in the community could easily find strengths-based stories appropriate for their child's age. We've seen board chairs manning barista coffee machines in school playgrounds and sunflower seed packs provided to children to plant in their gardens, brightening up the community in the tough post-quake period in Christchurch, and talked to numerous educators who have leapt on the opportunity provided by the VIA character strengths survey to use strengths to 'build bridges' with parents.

Unfortunately, in their desire to protect their children from failure, many parents and caregivers (often referred to as 'helicopter' or 'lawnmower') have deprived their children of valuable learning opportunities that only come through failure, disappointment and setback. Introducing the importance of failure and struggle as part of education and human development can help here, and we've certainly seen many engaging forms of 'parent ed' programmes run through schools aimed at increasing wellbeing literacy among the parent and local communities.

Practical alternatives to running in-school programmes include Lea Waters's strengths switch parenting programme – a practical five-session, five-week online course: www.strengthsswitch.com/learning/?_s2member_vars=sys.. level..0..page..8496..L2NvdXJzZS8=&_s2member_sig=1567130721-06ed 2b74a31c7f6179a021bc027d56c0. Lea's strengths-based parenting survey is also a good way to get parents thinking about their parenting style. It can be found here: www.strengthswitch.com/wp-content/uploads/2017/05/12.-Quiz_How-Strength-Based-Are-You.pdf.

Other practical ideas for connecting parents to your wellbeing mission are featured next.

Case study 14.1:   St Peter's School Adelaide: Engaging with parents

St Peter's College has engaged with its parent community to rein-force its message to students about, for example, growth mindsets and mistakes:

- The school empasises that they don't expect parents to be per-fect, and teachers aren't either. This is an ongoing effort to help parents and teachers feel able to share and discuss mistakes with students so they learn to accept mistakes in themselves.
- Information evenings for parents focus on what parents can do to support their child's wellbeing and on developing a shared language of wellbeing between school and home.
- St Peter's has very clearly communicated to parents that wellbeing is at the heart of the way it works with students. When parents send their child to the school, they are buying in to this commitment.

Box 14.1: Running a successful *Whānau Hui* (family meeting for Māori)

Nathan Riki leads culturally responsive practice at Breens Intermedi-ate, Christchurch, NZ.

'Having run some unsuccessful meetings I have now learned how to make these work at my school. First, we have to understand that many of our parents, Māori and Pasifika, don't always feel confident, or welcome, coming in to school. It's the equivalent of a European person being invited to a formal event on a marae and being told they will have to speak and participate. Most Europeans would feel nervous and concerned about their dress and if they will say the right thing.

How can we make where we hold our meetings at our schools as comfortable for Māori as the marae? The recipe for success is about removing the barriers for our whānau so they can more easily and comfortably attend. This involves working out:

- Timing: Hold it at a time where whānau have finished work but it's not too late for them to bring small children. In my experience, 5.45 pm seems to work.
- Place: Hold your whānau meeting somewhere that has space for small children to play. This makes it easier for families that need to bring other children along. I hold my whānau meetings at our pre-school onsite that has lots of play equipment and toys for small children.
- Kai (food): Our ancestors based their lives around food. It's welcoming and sets a welcoming tone.
- No performance expectations: Let people know they will not be expected to perform. Many urban Māori don't know their pepeha (family lineage in Māori), so don't ask people to do that; just welcome everyone in.
- Invite their contributions: Once you have got people feeling comfortable, invite them to contribute in a low pressure way. I say to people that if they have ideas about what we could be doing for their tamariki Māori (Māori children), they could stick them on a Post-it note and put them on the window as they leave. That way it's informal and brief.
- Give them a purpose to visit. My whānau class provided the purpose for many meetings. At each hui (meeting) they would be delivering a karakia (prayer) they had learned, singing a waiata (song), or talking about a new kaupapa (ideas or topic) they were working on.
- *Limit the number of teachers: three or four is max so they don't overwhelm families. I always ask teachers to be informally dressed – "come as yourself" – and remove your principal hat'.*

Case study 14.2:   Taipei European School (TES): Engaging parents in whole-school wellbeing

In the third year of its wellbeing agenda, TES focused on the parent community, using a variety of approaches:

- Information sessions using a roundtable format where parents have a discussion circle with engaging activities that teach the topic in the same way it would be taught to students.
- This format invited parents as equals to a wellbeing conversation and was powerful for all concerned – although the school noted that these sessions are typically attended by the same small group of parents.
- From the parent body, a number of wellbeing champions emerged, who have led coaching training with the parent group.
- Where a student is struggling with wellbeing challenges, parents have appreciated being brought in to be part of the school's plan to support the student.

Connecting with the wider community

Efforts to take a regional approach to building wellbeing are now being explored in various parts of the world as diverse stakeholders seek new models for tackling entrenched cross-sector challenges. While existing efforts in wellbeing in education have almost exclusively focused on individual schools, we are committed advocates of communities of practice (COPs) around wellbeing, which foster shared understanding, language, learning, resources, support, ideas and commitment. A New Zealand government initiative in the past decade saw the establishment of *Kāhui Ako* or communities of learning, and by early 2018, 70% of schools had formed communities of learning across the country. Despite initial (and sometimes ongoing) school concerns about required collaboration and additional layers of administration, many *Kāhui Ako* have realised the potential of these communities of learning to support wellbeing initiatives and that the sharing they involve can accelerate learning.

We've been lucky enough to be involved in initiatives taking a collective impact approach – working both as part of the Grow Waitaha project and with several wellbeing communities of practice in New Zealand – and have talked to colleagues involved in others across the globe including the Maroondah Project outside Melbourne. In doing so, we've begun to see the potential for taking schools' wellbeing goals and ambitions beyond the school gates into, and across, the community much more broadly than we ever believed possible. We agree with Adam Cooper, team leader, youth and children's services at the Maroondah Project, whose own research recommends that members of the system 'need to feel part of something beyond their individual school' if we want to truly take wellbeing to scale.[9] We also believe that those community members beyond the school may benefit from contributing to school wellbeing in their communities – both in terms of being involved in meaningful work and in terms of the longer-term benefits for the whole community.

Case study 14.3:   Maroondah's communities of wellbeing

A belief in interventions across a network of schools and embracing the benefits of multi-stakeholder collaboration are at the heart of the Maroondah Positive Education Project. This is an ambitious community-wide collaboration between public primary and secondary schools, the Department of Education and Training (Victoria), Maroondah City Council, University of Melbourne, Institute of Positive Education and local community groups, all endeavouring to boost local student wellbeing. (See Figure 14.1.) Adam Cooper (team leader, youth and children's services at Maroondah City Council)

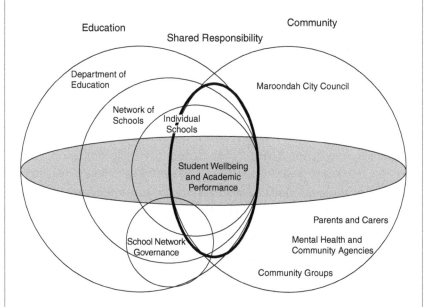

Figure 14.1 The city of Maroondah's education and community wellbeing model

believes that to improve student wellbeing and academic outcomes, influencing the language, behaviours, knowledge, processes, relationships and environments within and across education and community systems is critical. This includes students, teachers, families, mental health and community service providers, local government and other community groups.

Maroondah resident Edwina Ricci, former president of the Chamber of Commerce, a teacher at Melba College and now project manager, Maroondah Positive Education Network, describes the genesis and importance of the project from her perspective.

'In 2014, the Australian City of Maroondah, in Victoria, invited its citizens to help develop the 2040 vision. They asked two seemingly simple questions: What do you love about Maroondah? What would you change? Thousands of people responded. Maroondah, they agreed, should be vibrant and culturally rich; safe, healthy and active; attractive and well built; accessible and connected. It should be clean, green and sustainable; inclusive and diverse. Citizens should be well governed and empowered; prosperous and learning. In short, the city and its citizens would be flourishing.[10] Instead, data indicators showed citizens reporting psychological distress (anxiety and depression) well above the statewide level. Hospital admission rates for mental health-related causes were higher than in Melbourne or Victoria. Maroondah's suicide rate was one of the highest in its region and above Greater Melbourne's. This led the council to consider what they could do to prevent, as well as treat, mental illness.[11]

I was inspired by the 2040 goal for community-wide wellbeing. I knew that some positive psychology research had shown teaching groups of students' skills for resilience could prevent depression.[12] However, the programme was costly and not easy to access.

A group of interested city councilors, the directors of youth and mental health services, school administrators and business leaders began to meet monthly. We knew of South Australia's initiative for a "state" of wellbeing. Geelong Grammar School in Victoria was the international positive education pioneer in the area. Also close to home, Melbourne University was developing a wellbeing measure for use in schools.[13]

I talked to everyone I could about their ideas and experiences. I gave away copies of Martin Seligman's Flourish[14] which suggested wellbeing came from PERMA (Positivity, Engagement, Relationships, Meaning and Accomplishment) and described how PERMA had been implemented across bigger settings, like the US Army, schools and businesses.

By autumn 2014, I was fully committed to bringing positive psychology to the masses, so I contacted Sherri Fisher. Sherri had studied with Martin Seligman and Chris Peterson and earned her Master of Applied Positive Psychology (MAPP) degree in 2006 from the University of Pennsylvania. Her experience included applying Positive Psychology research in education and coaching. We've met together over Skype every week for the last five years.

Sherri had extensive professional contacts and has helped us underpin the vision with scientifically validated research.

Today the Maroondah Project is in 27 primary and secondary schools across the city[15] and I have a new position as Head of Positive Engagement (HOPE) Network Leader. The HOPE leaders in each school work with the principal and staff to bring wellbeing directly to the adults first, co-creating a school climate that supports wellbeing for all. The city has partnered with Geelong Grammar School and Melbourne University for staff leader training and measurement and the Victorian Education Department have supported the initiative with funding and will expand more broadly if successful.[16] Guided by the Appreciative Inquiry process,[17] Maroondah City Council and Communities of Wellbeing are exploring cross-sector positive engagement, asking, "What does it take to bring wellbeing to an entire city?"'

Edwina advises other regions wishing to do the same, to consider the following:

- Lower barriers for your future supporters. Make it easy for them to learn and be part of the team. Give high-quality, on-topic books. Plan lots of small events and hand out invitations generously.
- Share stories of transformation. Be very visible in the community, on a website and social media pages to showcase what's working. Be vulnerable and help others want what you have.
- Treat people who help you with genuine appreciation. Let people know they matter. Spot how they helped, not just what they

did. Express gratitude and offer personal invitations to your
next event. Be honest with each other to build trust.

- Try things out even when you are not sure if they will work.
  Put something aside while it's not working (yet). Instead, focus
  on what is working and how to get more of that.
- Know that the path is not linear. You are cultivating patience,
  perseverance, trust and resilience that will transform you and
  the communities you serve.

Expert Practitioner Insight 14.1: *Garry Williams, Ministry
of Education, Christchurch, New Zealand. Collaborating for
transformational/citywide change*

Garry Williams has more than 30 years' private- and public-sector
leadership and governance experience, with a track record of establishing and shepherding large, multi-organisation collaborative
projects that challenge traditional thinking in service delivery. Here,
in his own words, he describes the Grow Waitaha project.

'The New Zealand Government's strategic response to the
2010/11 Canterbury earthquakes was to establish a programme of
work to "position greater Christchurch as a future leader in teaching and learning practice". The Ministry of Education's work since
has been focused on developing a bold new model of support for
schools and kura founded on collaboration between iwi (indigenous tribes), providers and schools through a partnership called
Grow Waitaha that puts the needs of all our learners at the centre.

Through this more collaborative interest in what's best for
learners across a collective of schools we are, in effect, fostering a
network of learning rather than targeting individual schools. What
we've learned through an emerging evidence base is that, while
both approaches are important, a collaborative and networked
approach to developing solutions to often complex problems has
greater collective impact than doing it on your own, or simply rep-
licating what others are already doing.

A good example of this collaboration is the Grow Waitaha
Secondary Community of Practice focusing on wellbeing for
ākonga (students) and Kaiako (educational leaders). Our intention

lay around supporting secondary schools to develop systematic wellbeing strategies and initiatives to enhance the wellbeing of their whole school community. In mid-2017, a few secondary schools indicated an interest in working collaboratively with other Christchurch secondary schools to address student wellbeing in a more systemic cross-city approach. Together, we developed an approach that provided both focused time for key leaders in each school to develop a strategic wellbeing project, and opportunities for cross-pollination of ideas and collaboration to occur between schools. Over 2017, the interest from other secondary schools to be involved increased and by 2018 the Community of Practice included all secondary schools in Christchurch.

The early phases of collaboration at such scale can be challenging for all concerned. It seems like not much is happening, and usually at quite some expense. In hindsight, this is the most important time as we formed the relationships which the programme was built on and allowed the later stages to move more quickly and be agile, innovative and responsive. My advice, particularly to those funding such initiatives, is to persevere with the early stages, the investment is worth it.

One of the characteristics driving the success of Grow Waitaha in supporting wellbeing in schools is a rich, culturally responsive approach guided by our foundational partnership with Mātauraka Mahaanui. Mātauraka Mahaanui is an advisory board appointed by the Minister of Education to guide education renewal in greater Christchurch and represent collective mana whenua (people who have rights to the land), Papatipu Rūnanga, the Māori Community Leaders Forum and other Māori interests. Te Rūnanga o Ngāi Tahu, as the "Treaty partner", mandated this group to act on their behalf in the greater Christchurch area. This relationship is important in part because of Te Tiriti o Waitangi obligations but, more importantly, to ensure that Grow Waitaha initiatives, including those in the wellbeing space, meet the needs of Māori learners in a culturally responsive way.

We've also learned how important authentic engagement processes are in our work. Grow Waitaha always had a commitment to be sector-led from its inception, although there was some initial scepticism in the sector about whether this aspiration could be met. Once schools started seeing how their feedback was influencing the programme's design, and what it was offering, a higher level of engagement was reached, and more ongoing feedback and suggestions were offered.

Not only did this authentic, sector-led approach lead to further feed-back, there was also a snowball effect in relation to engagement with or uptake of other opportunities on offer by Grow Waitaha.

Other things we've learned on our journey:

- Local solutions best meet local needs.
- Building authentic partnerships and establishing the conditions for a programme such as Grow Waitaha to be successful isn't a fast process. Time needs to be allowed for thinking, planning and collaborating.
- As we are asking teaching professionals, Boards of Trustees and communities to change the way they work and scale up their efforts in raising student achievement, then we must model the values and practices we believe will lead to raised outcomes for learners. Demonstrating commitment and a strong and effective working relationship with all stakeholders is required if others are to buy into a programme of this nature and its outcomes.
- Great things can happen if the Ministry listens, rather than taking the lead all the time.
- We fundamentally believe in the capability of our Education Community to lead transformation change for themselves. The answers and the best practice already exist within. This has led to an approach where the Ministry of Education, through initia-tives such as Grow Waitaha, is supporting senior leaders to lead these changes within their schools and identifies and shines the light on great practice'.

Reflection questions

- What sort of support around wellbeing knowledge is likely to be useful to your community?
- Are there issues affecting wellbeing in your school that can only be solved 'outside the school gates'?
- How can you draw upon the wisdom and resources that exist within your wider community to support you in this work and broaden/challenge your perspective?
- Which organisations could you gather together to co-create a movement for change that would harness the potential for collective impact?

- Who is best to approach them?
- Who might support your 'compelling vision of future reality' with funds, access, resources?

Notes

1   Bronfenbrenner, U. (1977). Toward an experimental ecology of human development. *American Psychologist, 32*(7), 513–531.

2   Waters, L. E., Loton, D., & Jach, H. K. (2019). Does strength-based parenting predict academic achievement? The mediating effects of perseverance and engagement. *Journal of Happiness Studies, 20*(4), 1121–1140.

3   Waters, L. E., Loton, D., & Jach, H. K. (2019). Does strength-based parenting predict academic achievement? The mediating effects of perseverance and engagement. *Journal of Happiness Studies, 20*(4), 1121–1140.

4   Dubroja, K., O'Connor, M., & Mckenzie, V. (2016). Engaging parents in positive education: Results from a pilot program. *International Journal of Wellbeing, 6*(3), 150–168. doi:10.5502/ijw.v6i3.443

5   Hanleybrown, F., Kania, J., & Kramer, M. (2012). Channeling change: Making collective impact work. Stanford Social Innovation Review. Retrieved from http://g21hwbpillar.com.au/sites/default/files/resources/3.2_ssir_channeling_change_2012.pdf2_.pdf

6   Cabaj, M., & Weaver, L. (2016). Collective impact 3.0: An evolving framework for community change. *Tamarack Institute*, 1–14.

7   Senge, P. M., & Sterman, J. D. (1992). Systems thinking and organizational learning: Acting locally and globally in the organization of the future. *European Journal of Operational Research, 1*, 137.

8   Senge, P., Hamilton, H. A. L., & Kania, J. (2015). The dawn of system leadership. *Stanford Social Innovation Review, 13*(1), 26–33.

9   Cooper, A. (2019). *Building a positive education system: A local approach to scaling positive education.* Capstone in Positive Psychology, University of Melbourne.

10 *Maroondah 2040 Community Vision.* (2014). Retrieved from www.maroondah.vic.gov.au/files/assets/public/documents/integrated-planning/strategic-planning/maroondah-2040-our-future-together.pdf

11   *National Health Survey: Mental Health and co-existing physical health conditions.* Australia, 2014–15. Retrieved from www.abs.gov.au/ausstats/abs@.nsf/0/C0A4290EF1E7E7FDCA257F1E001C0B84?Open document

12   Seligman, M. E. P. (2011). *Flourish.* New York: Simon & Schuster.

13   Even, M., producer. Teaching positive psychology in the classroom. *Weekend Breakfast. Podcast.* Retrieved from https://2ser.com/teaching-positive-psychology-in-the-classroom/?fbclid=IwAR10oy90fsk8lGCUKonM28llfrK98hM3K_s_3dNDxAI43CFTX69xYJW-uxo

14   Seligman, M. E. P. (2011). *Flourish.* New York: Simon & Schuster.

15   *Maroondah Plus 10 Schools* Maroondah City Council Youth Services Published on July 10, 2018. Retrieved from www.youtube.com/watch?v=oDXj8-D4DEw

16   Ciarrochi, J., Atkins, P. W. B., Hayes, L. L., Sahdra, B. K., & Parker, P. (2016). Contextual positive psychology: Policy recommendations for implementing positive psychology into schools. *Frontiers in Psychology, 7,* 1561. doi:10.3389/fpsyg.2016.01561

17   Cooperrider, D. L., & McQuaid, M. (2012). The positive arc of systemic strengths: How appreciative inquiry and sustainable designing can bring out the best in human systems. *The Journal of Corporate Citizenship, 46,* 71–102.

Watch

The Maroondah Project (Australia). Retrieved from www.youtube.com/watch?v=oDXj8-D4DEw

School TV, created by Australian psychologist, Michael Carr Gregg, is a dedicated resource aimed at building parents' capacity and understanding of wellbeing. Retrieved from https://schooltv.me/

Sonja McFarlane talking about how schools can make families feel they belong and are valued in our schools. Retrieved from https://vimeo.com/337668774

Read

Recommended reading for parents: *The Strength Switch: How the New Science of Strength-Based Parenting Can Help Your Child and Teen to Flourish* by Lea Waters. (Avery, 2017).

Listen

NZIWR podcasts are available from https://nziwr.co.nz/category/podcast/

NZIWR podcast: Nathan Riki (Whānau hui).

NZIWR podcast: Chris Jansen (Collective impact through the Grow Waitaha project).

Promoting wellbeing through coaching in schools

Introduction

Schools are networks of people engaged in various forms of conversation designed to progress the purpose and goals of the school.[1] Accordingly, there is growing recognition of the importance of coaching in education to enhance learning and development and also for promoting and protecting personal and collective wellbeing. The term 'coaching' is used broadly and refers to a wide range of interventions to meet these ends. While early uses focused on leaders receiving executive coaching, the field's models, skills and techniques have expanded markedly in recent years and now include leaders coaching staff, peer-to-peer staff coaching, staff-to-student coaching, peer-to-peer student coaching, parent coaching and staff-to-parent coaching. In effect, coaching can support almost any school improvement initiative, and its theoretical underpinnings make it a natural partner for wellbeing.

What the research says

Coaching is now acknowledged globally as a powerful intervention to support both educators and learners, with education regarded as a 'natural home' for coaching and a growing evidence base supporting its effectiveness.[2] According to Campbell and van Nieuwerburgh, 'Teachers and educational leaders in schools and colleges around the world are experiencing for themselves the transformative effect that coaching can have on themselves and others'.[3]

There are as many definitions of coaching as there are personal interpretations of wellbeing, so, for the purposes of this book, we are adopting the definition used by Jan Robertson, a world leader in educational coaching from the University of Waikato: a special, sometimes reciprocal, relationship between (at least) two people who work together to set personal and professional goals and achieve them. This relationship involves participants being open to new learning, engaging together and equally committed to facilitating one another's learning, development and wellbeing.[4] We also like van Nieuwerburgh's definition, describing coaching as enhancement through 'increasing self-awareness and a sense of personal responsibility, where the coach facilitates the self-directed learning of the coachee through questioning, active listening, and appropriate challenge in a supportive and encouraging climate'.[5]

Studies describe multiple benefits, including improving the quality of educational leadership and capacity building; encouraging reflective practice and self-development; maintaining energy and motivation (in oneself and others); enabling leaders to coach others; helping manage meetings, professional learning events and training days; enabling more effective feedback; building collegial culture; improving teaching practice; positively impacting student achievement; building connections across the school community and, for parents trained in coaching, improved relationships with their children and an improved ability to support their learning.[6] Benefits have also been demonstrated for students, including improved examination performance,[7] wellbeing and academic goal striving,[8] and reduced depression, anxiety and stress.[9] Furthermore, students who have been trained to coach others have reported enhanced communication skills, augmented problem-solving abilities and increased confidence in finding solutions.[10]

Coaching in schools draws upon several aspects of positive psychology for its theoretical foundation, including appreciative inquiry; self-determination theory; taking a solution-focused, strengths-based approach and positive emotion theory, making it a natural foundation for building wellbeing, strengthening purpose, personal growth and fostering supportive relationships.

Putting it into practice

A growing number of educators we've spoken to over the past year have described coaching conversations as among the most important skills we can teach young people at school. Again and again, school leaders relay the impact on emotions, motivation and relationships they've witnessed when educators and students have learned the skills to have solution-focused coaching conversations. Clive Leach describes the benefits, echoing the sentiments of multiple educators and practitioners we've spoken to and worked with: 'I once heard [University of Melbourne researcher] Lindsay Oades at a conference saying that if organisations had coaching cultures they wouldn't need to have wellbeing strategies. I couldn't agree more. Because a coaching culture allows people to feel safe to talk about their challenges, to focus on solutions, develop trust and high quality connections, then we wouldn't need to be thinking about wellbeing so much in organisations. I've seen examples where teachers have been supported to have relatively short coaching conversations with each other and have reported back to me (maybe even a year later) that they continue those conversations and now feel better equipped to deal with some of the challenges and opportunities they're facing. It's a win-win; being a coach adds to my wellbeing and we hope the person receiving the conversation also benefits'.

Coaching can be used in any conversation (group or one on one); in formal staff or student appraisals/reviews and for any informal interaction/communication between staff and students, staff and staff, staff and parents, and opportunities to give and receive feedback (again, both formal and informal).

In order to assist these conversations, many schools have adopted the global framework for coaching in education.[11] Created by van Nieuwerburgh, Campbell and Knight, the four-quadrant framework is aimed at providing a 'helpful conceptual playing field and context' for schools to base their coaching on. The playing fields (called portals) represent different ways schools can view and introduce coaching. The four portals and their individual uses are summarised here:

- **Educational leadership:** Refers to the opportunities for leaders to receive executive coaching and also to become coaches themselves;
- **Professional practice:** Refers to the opportunities for teachers to support each other and for follow-up support for educators and other school staff who have attended professional learning;
- **Wider school community:** Refers to opportunities for parents as coaches and teachers using a coaching approach in interactions with parents and caregivers; and
- **Coaching for student success and wellbeing:** Refers to opportunities to provide coaching to students.

Alongside the global framework for coaching in education, schools are basing both formal coaching and informal coaching conversations on the GROWTH model.[12] GROWTH is made up of eight steps:

G = Goals (What do you need to achieve?);

R = Reality (What is happening now?);

O = Options (What could you do?);

W = Will (What will you do?);

T = Tactics (How and when will you do it?); and

H = Habits (How will you sustain your success?)

In addition, the GROWTH coaching system encourages eight communication skills, which are:

1   Building trust;

2   Being present;

3   Listening actively;

4   Clarifying;

5   Empathising;

6   Being succinct;

7   Asking the best questions; and

8   Giving feedback.

Expert practitioner insight 15.1: *Rhiannon McGee, Geelong Grammar School. How coaching can complement positive education*

Head of positive education at Geelong Grammar School Rhiannon McGee is well known for her long-term and deep commitment to coaching. GGS uses the GROW and GROWTH coaching model in various ways across the school, with a core coaching team of around ten staff meeting fortnightly to share experiences and support each other through stumbling blocks. Here, she explains how important she believes adopting strengths-based organisational practices such as appreciative inquiry and coaching into schools is for creating a culture of wellbeing.

'I see coaching as a strengths-based approach complementing Positive Education. If we're cultivating the right culture, I think we can have greater impact than taking an explicit approach. Positive Education is a one-size fits all approach to wellbeing, while coaching gives us a way to differentiate our approach. A lot of what students and staff are learning can really be drawn on when having one-on-one coaching conversations and setting goals around wellbeing or learning – whatever is the need for that particular individual.

Understanding coaching relationships – how we can shift from the mentor role that we as teachers are so good at and move to a coaching role exercising powerful listening and powerful questions – can really change the nature of the conversations we have in a school. It complements a strengths-based approach, enhances professional relationships and professional efficacy, and teacher-student relationships. It's a lovely overlay enhancing everything we're trying to do academically, pastorally and in terms of wellbeing'.

Based on a previous experience of a top-down approach involving all middle leaders being trained as coaches and coaching their direct reports, she recommends a drip-feed approach. 'I really loved the potential for this programme, but expecting all staff to opt in was probably not the best way to go. Bringing in key practices to already existing contexts, such as annual reviews, in the pastoral programme – using the existing practices works as a better entry point for coaching.

At GGS, there's a wonderful team of staff members who have chosen to undertake the Growth Coaching training. They've taken a grass roots, bottom-up approach which has been really effective. I've learned a lot from this team about what can be achieved in an organic drip-feed way. Our staff who are trained as coaches, coach other staff members who elect to be involved in that experience. We're starting to run pilots in various boarding houses, where our tutors are being trained up in some core coaching skills and working with their tutees (students) in a coaching capacity. Further to that we're now working on a pilot this year with students having coaching conversations with other students. It's happening more slowly than I'm used to, but I'm learning that it can be very effective that way. Six girls in year 11 in one of the boarding houses have elected to be coaches and six year 10s have elected to be coached, so a handful of us in the coaching team will run some learning around coaching that they will implement. We'll see how that goes and let that evolve organically.

Imagine if we can give students the opportunity to learn these coaching skills that they can take with them into the workplace and tertiary education, to equip them for this 21st-century landscape. My great vision – best possible case scenario – would be extending our explicit Positive Education program students are exposed to up until year 10 in to a coaching model for senior students. I think that would be the best evolution of Positive Education where it becomes much more personalised and relevant to their needs'.

Case Study 15.1:   Personal reflection: Sherri Fisher and Edwina Ricci on professional coaching for community influencers

Sherri Fisher (MAPP, Med.) and Edwina Ricci (project manager, Maroondah Positive Education Network) discuss how their coaching relationship has supported Edwina through five years of professional growth.

'In the kitchen of her rustic house at the top of a hill, Edwina Ricci chops loudly into the assortment of veggies on a cutting board. Her phone on speaker, Edwina is preparing a late dinner while meeting with her coach, Sherri Fisher, on Skype. Thirty hours travel time and 17,000 kilometers away, the invention of video chat has made an unusual and influential coaching relationship possible. While both have made the 30-hour journey to work alongside each other in person, they believe the coaching relationship forged on Skype has brought them closer in ways that airplanes cannot. Here, they reflect on the evolution, purpose and benefits of a professional coaching relationship that has spanned five years and half the globe.

Edwina: Before I had a coach, I attended lectures by luminaries; read research papers and books about positive psychology and talked to everyone I could who seemed to be doing work in the positive education space. There were master's degrees and certificate programs that could teach me even more about applying the research. Instead, as a teacher and community connector, I wanted practical skills that could transform my entire city. It was important to me that my coach not have a stake in any particular outcome or be trying to sell me a solution. I wanted someone who would uncover new directions. I wanted someone who cooks every day with confidence; knew how to deviate from the cookbook; would help improve the recipe and adapt the recipe to individual circumstances and ingredients.

I had seen Sherri interviewed on video. I already had my question list ready. The questions tumbled out of me. I asked her, 'How has this field changed your life? The lives of clients and students? Do you go beyond the tools? How and when do you know how to apply research to get your outcomes? What are the ingredients of community wellbeing?' She understood the education context, the roles of different people in a school setting, and the potential challenges in implementing community-wide change. She offered me the opportunity to learn my way around the positive education kitchen and to taste and see what was good for myself.

Sherri: How did it feel to be coached?

Edwina: Part of being coached is learning the skills of resilience and reframing. In my case, the citywide vision (for Maroondah) was developing while I was, too. After a typical 90-minute coaching session, I often felt committed to specific action. Sometimes I had absolutely no confidence I would be able to put that important puzzle piece in place. Sherri was my champion and accountability partner when things went well. She kept me on the ground when the runway was foggy, and my destination was unknown. When I was headed somewhere the research did not support or made conclusions based on very little evidence, she reset my direction by asking seemingly simple questions. What *can* you do? What else? What is enough for now?

I eagerly anticipated our meetings and felt a sort of relentless enthusiasm for applying what I was learning. The pace of change in institutions, though, is frustratingly slow, and given we usually met at 9 or 10 pm my time, I was often physically as well as emo-tionally exhausted from my day. Underneath my zest, I was some-times quite discouraged. Fortunately, the coaching relationship felt honest. It was supportive and generative, productive and reflective. She'd say things like 'That sounds brave. I'm sorry it hasn't worked yet. Sounds like a win! Tell me more. What haven't you tried yet? What resources would help?'

She sent me articles and recommended reading, provided resources that were hard to argue with (even for me!), but informed my steps ahead. She even sat in on video calls I had with potential project partners. We had impromptu meetings and dialogued on Skype messaging, and chatted as if we were having a coffee. When we were working together, I felt deeply respected for my life's purpose.

Sherri: How did positive psychology coaching change you and the way you work?

Edwina: Coaching and positive psychology were multiplying factors in my life and work. Instead of trying to fix what was wrong – even though there were plenty of statistics that portrayed my community in crisis – my own coaching focused on what was going well and how I could choose, measure and share ingredients to get more of that.

In retrospect, I did not begin by trying to change the way I worked. Like most teachers, I wanted to apply research for the benefit of students. I also wanted to learn positive psychology principles and apply them with wider impact. By speaking weekly with you, a true pioneer expert in the field, I developed my language around wellbeing literacy. Every day, at school and in the community, I shared what I was learning. As my confidence and enthusiasm grew, so did my skill at communicating to my network. I was transforming my own way of cooking in the positive education kitchen.

Sherri: What did you gain from coaching?

Edwina: In my coaching, I took a personal learning journey. Though principals and networks are quick to want what research outcomes seem to promise, I believe the personal practice of positive psychology – actually applying wellbeing principles to our own lives – is the most important part of any implementation strategy. Because coaching is not didactic but nimble and open minded, it lets me fly the plane as I build it, reappraising new runways as the project and opportunities are revealed. As a result, it feels productive on different fronts, making room for fast prototyping while treating iterations of the 'recipe' as part of the work. As the Maroondah project has expanded, I've become convinced coaching is a mechanism for designing our greater implementation scheme. It builds a human foundation for positive change. We can bring curriculum to classrooms, but it is much richer and more impactful when we deliver it with ourselves.

I now have my dream job: I support the change process for other influencers of young people – teachers, students, building leaders, parents and community youth workers. I let them try things out and offer myself as a co-creator in community thriving. With the evidence from the research base, Sherri empowered me to try things out responsibly and reflect on that experience. My work now directly impacts over 100,000 people. Today, when I am faced with a seemingly impossible challenge, I can compassionately ask myself questions she taught me: What *can* you do? Who can help? What is something you have not done yet?

Sherri: What obstacles did you face, and how did you overcome them?

Edwina: Even though it may look as if it happens in an instant, cooking up community-wide change can take a long time! People who see what is now the Maroondah project don't generally know that over five years of coaching supported it. The work is hard, especially in schools. People and their contexts have their own ways to do things, and there is also the national curriculum to consider. Any change needs to prove beneficial for students and doable for educators, and it can't ignore the reality of community problems like depression, anxiety and suicide. There is no such thing as a community-wide project without politics. Together, Sherri and I have worked through times of significant political change as well as partnering realignment.

The field of positive education has also grown exponentially in places all over the world during this time. We have both needed to keep up through continuing education and international conference attendance. Other community models and solutions have been developing simultaneously.

Sherri: Because of shifting times over the seasons, we have met in the wee hours of morning and in late night darkness. Because of this relationship, I can now automatically think in Australia's East Coast time, I have hugged a baby wombat and fed kangaroos, we know where the cell phone dead zones are while the other person is driving to and from work. Edwina has connected me with the network she has spun. And together we've cooked up whole new wellbeing recipes for each other over time, which has been incredibly rewarding.'

Words supplied by Sherri Fisher.

Case Study 15.2:   Personal reflection: Julie Small, St Peter's College, Cambridge, on coaching as a way of leading and learning – growing staff and students to unlock their potential

Julie Small is Associate Principal at St Peter's Cambridge, NZ. For the past 20 years as an educator, coaching has been Julie's passion. We asked her why she values it so much, and how schools can get started.

'Early in my career, I was fortunate enough to have a Principal who believed every teacher should have a person to grow their capacity – not tell them what to do. Setting myself up with a leadership coach proved to be of great value, not just for my personal growth but for working alongside others – students, staff and parents. This experience has convinced me coaching contributes to overall wellbeing – after my weekly sessions I felt inspired, uplifted and ready to take next steps. At times coaching has been a 'grappling experience' where I came to know myself, and how my responses encouraged or dis-encouraged others. It has allowed a fresh perspective to unlock my potential.

While I have always worked with a leadership coach myself (and still do), the opportunity to develop a culture of coaching as a way of being with teams in schools has been the most rewarding thing. Our own evaluation process indicated the success of the programme – 100% of our staff moved their capability along the coaching skill set continuum. Given the opportunity, staff want to be able to learn how to use coaching to have better conversations. Many of these staff have also applied their learning to working with students. Our middle leaders have trained student coaches to work with students.

Coaching aligns well with our new Wellbeing and Pastoral Framework and has supported the Framework's introduction to the school'.

Expert practitioner insight 15.2: *Clive Leach. Coaching in schools*

Clive Leach has worked with schools around the world for the past decade to support wellbeing. As well as being an experienced executive coach and facilitator, Clive is a former teacher and youth worker with over two decades' experience in inner-city schools in the UK.

Insights into coaching in schools:

- 'It's challenging to embed a coaching culture in a school, but the benefits are significant and include:

  - Marked improvements in relationships around the school;
  - Students engaging and looking for pastoral care support before they reach crisis point; and
  - Higher trust and openness.

- Using coaching models for coaching conversations between teachers and students enables students to more easily share when they are feeling stressed or anxious, thereby supporting early intervention.
- Creating a coaching culture can support wellbeing.
- Where teachers have been supported to have brief coaching conversations with each other, they report, even a year later, that they feel better able and equipped to deal with the challenges they are facing.
- This is not just about coaching; it's about having solution-focused conversations. Where individual educators are being encouraged to do that for each other (and for their students), this can add up to change over time.
- Coaching is good for both parties. To coach adds to my wellbeing, and, if we're working appropriately, the coachee will also benefit.

One school's coaching journey:

- The school started with SLT being coached – so they experienced it – on their strengths use and wellbeing.
- Staff were then introduced to coaching conversations and given a model they could use to bring into conversations when they thought it was appropriate.
- Staff who chose to attended a two-day programme on coaching to support their skills. They've used it to coach students on the results of their wellbeing and mental toughness assessment. These coaches can work with young people who have potential concerns and then engage with the school to provide suitable interventions for individual or groups.'

Box 15.1: Questions for coaching students (supplied by Rhiannon McGee, head of positive education at Geelong Grammar School)

'This is the format we use with students and staff as the basis of our Tutorial Program (adapted from materials developed by a Growth Coaching International resource, The Leadership Coaching Guide). This is the "bare bones" of a coaching approach for those staff who have not been trained as coaches' but want to take a coaching approach to conversations with students.

   Students should begin by reflecting on the previous term (or year).

What did they achieve?
How did they engage with their academic or cocurricular responsibilities?
How well did they look after themselves?
What are some of the strengths and success stories they can identify?

Students can reflect on this either individually, in pairs or with the broader group.

If they could envisage the most successful term possible in relation to their academic and cocurricular involvements, as well as their personal wellbeing, what would this look like?

Reflecting on this vision of the best possible term, what should they prioritise to ensure this comes to fruition? Academics? Cocurricular? Wellbeing?

   Ask students to set a goal in relation to this priority. Suggest they make it inspiring, specific, measureable, achieveable, realistic and timebound (ISMART).

Does this goal make you feel happier, confident, in control or motivated? Can you see the personal payoff?

By the end of this first session, students should have identified an ISMART goal. In the first check-in on progress when you next meet, ask:

What is happening now in relation to your goal?
What successes have you had?
What obstacles have you encountered?

(continued)

What can you do to capitalise on this success? Overcome these obstacles?
What will you do next?
How and when will you do this?
What support do you need?

Later, in reflection, ask:

What did you achieve this term/semester?
What are you proud of?
What strengths did you engage in order to accomplish this goal?
What challenges did you experience?
How did you overcome these?
What will you do differently next term?
What have you learned that you will apply next term?
What is your next priority? Next step?

Setting a goal for the next term, ask them to reflect on the previous term (or year) and repeat the process.'

Reflection questions

- What is your current view of coaching?
- What type of leader are you striving to be?
- What type of leaders would you like the young people in your school to be?
- Which of the four ways of coaching already occurs in your school?
  - Where, when, who by and in what formats?
- Which areas of your school could benefit from adopting a coaching approach?
- Do your performance reviews use a coaching approach?
- Does your school use a coaching approach when engaging with parents and caregivers?
- What could a formal approach to coaching look like in your school?
- What could an informal approach to coaching look like in your school?
- Who might lead these changes?
- What types of professional learning in coaching could you introduce in your school? Where would you start?

Notes

1   Campbell, J. (2016). Coaching in schools. In C. van Nieuwerburgh (Ed.), *Coaching in professional contexts* (pp. 131–143). London: Sage.

2   van Nieuwerburgh, C., & Barr, M. (2017). Coaching in education. In T. Bachkirova, G. Spence, & D. Drake (Eds.), *The SAGE handbook of coaching* (pp. 505–520). Thousand Oaks, CA: Sage.

3   Campbell, J., & van Nieuwerburgh, C. (2018). *The leader's guide to coaching in schools: Creating conditions for effective learning.* Thousand Oaks, CA: Corwin.

4   Robertson, J. (2016). *Coaching leadership: Building educational leadership capacity through partnership.* Wellington, NZ: NZCER Press.

5   van Nieuwerburgh, C. (Ed.). (2012). *Coaching in education: Getting better results for students, educators and parents.* London: Karnac.

6   van Nieuwerburgh, C. (Ed.). (2012). *Coaching in education: Getting better results for students, educators and parents.* London: Karnac.

7   Passmore, J., & Brown, A. (2009). Coaching non-adult students for enhanced examination performance: A longitudinal study. *Coaching: An International Journal of Theory, Research and Practice, 2*(1), 54–64.

8   Green, L. S., Norrish, J. M., Vella-Brodrick, D. A., & Grant, A. M. (2013). Enhancing well-being and goal striving in senior high school students: Comparing evidence-based coaching and positive psychology interventions. *Institute of coaching, breaking research, scientific findings from Harnisch grant recipients.*

9   Dulagil, A., Green, S., & Ahern, M. (2016). Evidence-based coaching to enhance senior students' wellbeing and academic striving. *International Journal of Wellbeing 6*(3), 131–149.

10 van Nieuwerburgh, C., Zacharia, C., Luckham, E., Prebble, G., & Browne, L. (2012). Coaching students in a secondary school: A case study. In C. van Nieuwerburgh (Ed.), *Coaching in education: Getting better results for students, educators, and parents* (pp. 191–198). London: Karnac.

11 van Nieuwerburgh, C., Knight, J., & Campbell, J. (2019). Coaching in education. In S. English, J. Manzi Sabatine, & P. Brownell (Eds.), *Professional coaching: Principles and practice* (pp. 411–426). New York: Springer.

12   Campbell, J. (2016). Coaching in schools. In C. van Nieuwerburgh (Ed.), *Coaching in professional contexts* (pp. 131–143). London: Sage.

Watch

Campbell & van Nieuwerburgh: Growth Coaching as a Vehicle for Transforming School Culture Webinar. Retrieved from www.youtube.com/watch?time_continue=1&v=zUlmnu76F08

Dr Christian van Nieuwerburgh, University of East London, on why coaching is being used in education. Retrieved from www.youtube.com/watch?v=IqNS6GstNKw

Growth Coaching International: how schools are using coaching in NZ and Australia. Retrieved from www.youtube.com/watch?v=8f4S4ncY5ck

Robert Biswas-Diener on positive psychology and coaching. Retrieved from www.youtube.com/watch?v=TYFBRa1N0_U

Suzy Green Positive Psychology Coaching – Optimising your potential. Retrieved from www.youtube.com/watch?v=1y0TZcKlrTk

Read

Campbell, J., & van Nieuwerburgh, C. (2017). *The leaders' guide to coaching in schools: Creating conditions for effective learning.* Corwin: Sage.

Green, S., & Palmer, S. (2019). *Positive psychology coaching in practice.* Abingdon, Oxon: Routledge.

Robertson, J. *Coaching leadership.* Wellington, NZ: NZCER Press. Retrieved from www.nzcer.org.nz/nzcerpress/coachingleadership

Robertson, J. (2016). *Coaching leadership: Building educational leadership capacity through partnership.* Wellington, NZ: NZCER Press.

Tschannen-Moran, B., & Tschannen-Moran, M. (2010). *Evocative coaching: Transforming schools one conversation at a time.* John Wiley & Sons.

Using Coaching to Support a Positive School Culture, Rhiannon McGee, Geelong Grammar School. Retrieved from www.ggs.vic.edu.au/institute/blog/blog-posts/using-coaching-to-support-a-positive-school-culture

Listen

NZIWR podcasts are available from https://nziwr.co.nz/category/podcast/

NZIWR podcast: Clive Leach (Coaching)

NZIWR podcast: Christian van Niewerburgh (Coaching)

NZIWR podcast: Rhiannon McGee (Coaching)

The Positive Education Podcast: Suzy Green (Coaching)

CHAPTER 16

Lessons learned from a decade of wellbeing in education

Introduction

A decade of growth and learning in wellbeing in education

In considering the lessons learned over the past ten years, we take a moment to reflect on our journey and how both our work and the field have evolved during this period. Our commitment to the science of wellbeing began with many long treks to the University of Pennsylvania, where we both completed our master's degrees in applied positive psychology. Denise's year group (2007–2008) were present for the genesis of Martin Seligman's four pillar model of wellbeing, and Lucy's time in Philadelphia (2009–2010) saw Seligman and colleagues coin the term *positive education*. Denise visited Marty during his residence at Geelong Grammar School and went on to work with the University of Pennsylvania as a facilitator and senior trainer, delivering their wellbeing and resilience training to schools and local authorities in Australia and the UK.

The focus of UPenn's training was on sharing research from the field of positive psychology with educators. Dr Karen Reivich, lead trainer with the UPenn team, was clear from the outset that it was our job to share the research but the educators' task to work out how best to implement and teach the science. As the field of positive education has evolved over the intervening years, the wisdom of this approach has become clear. What was initially called positive education has enabled educators to use their skills and knowledge of pedagogy and school systems to apply research findings to real-world practice.

It has been a steep learning curve. Initially, schools focused on learning the research and passing that on to students, sometimes in a less than totally engaging way. The focus for many schools was on finding programmes they could teach to students. Many wellbeing programmes came and went, causing wellbeing to be dismissed by some as another passing fad. Off-the-shelf wellbeing curricula were purchased and dumped on unsuspecting teachers, who then became the sole focus of wellbeing in the school, often precipitating burnout. The problems arising from these approaches were quickly apparent, prompting schools to seek a more sustainable approach.

This awareness resulted in increased attention on professional development in wellbeing and recognition of the importance of teacher wellbeing – for the individuals, for the profession and for quality of teaching and learning. More schools now recognise the importance of building capacity among staff and sharing responsibility for wellbeing more broadly. In parallel with growing awareness of the importance of professional learning for sustainable wellbeing change, schools have also identified the many opportunities to support (or hinder) wellbeing beyond explicit teaching. Teachers who were well versed in wellbeing research brought wellbeing learning into a range of other areas of school life, from English literature to pastoral care and sports team coaching.

Over the past decade, we have gone a step further, becoming aware of the influence of the school environment – policies, systems and processes – on wellbeing. Whole-school wellbeing also includes the recruitment and review processes for staff, assessment schedules and processes, behaviour management and communication with caregivers and families.

In our work, we now prefer to speak of whole-school wellbeing or wellbeing in education, rather than positive education, because this field has grown far beyond its roots in positive psychology. Some of the most important contributions to wellbeing in education over the past decade come from fields outside (and sometimes before) positive psychology but have been embraced within schools. Mindfulness training and practice in schools are helping address self-regulation, focus and anxiety issues, while coaching and restorative practices (which pre-date positive psychology) are increasingly recognised as an integral part of whole-school wellbeing.

In the early days of this field, we tended to rely on research and strategies from the USA or the UK. As research grew in New Zealand, Australia, Africa and Asia, it became clear that the dictum of 'one size does not fit all' – which had been applied to different individuals within a school – also applies to different cultural groups. The growing call for cultural responsiveness in education has perhaps been heard most keenly by those working in the field of wellbeing. It is not possible to support wellbeing without seeing and valuing people for who they are, where they come from and what they stand for. Cultural identity is an important part of who we are, how we feel and how we function. We are proud to include a strong chapter in this work that shares the significant body of research on cultural responsiveness and are resolute that this is an integral part of building whole-school wellbeing.

Most recently, we are witnessing a realisation that the challenges arising within our schools will not be solved within the school gates. Many of these issues have their roots in the way our communities and national societies evolve and include problems of drug and alcohol abuse and violence in the home and community, as well as growing inequality and poverty. Some pioneering schools are now starting to work more closely both with their school community and across the wider community. Our work co-designing prototype models for communities of practice around wellbeing in post-quake Christchurch is teaching us the transformational potential of 'collective impact', which comes from working with diverse stakeholders who have previously not collaborated. We look forward to seeing what exciting new developments may unfold in this area as we seek to replicate the wellbeing community of practice model across other regions.

Over the past five years, we have encouraged and witnessed a sea change in wellbeing in education. Whereas previously wellbeing was seen as a problem that smart educators would fix for students, schools are now starting to work closely with students. Doing so enables us to better understand their challenges and concerns; respect their knowledge, insight and ideas and co-design responses. The leading role of students in climate activism also serves as a reminder to schools of the contribution students can, and should, be making to the future of whole-school wellbeing.

Learning from those who have walked the path

Some of the most valuable learnings come from those who have gone before us, led the way, learn through their mistakes and are willing to share them. This final chapter explores the process and impact of building whole-school wellbeing from multiple and diverse perspectives – educators, wellbeing practitioners, psychologists and other researchers.

We have chosen contributors who have been active in the field for more than a decade, who have in some way shaped its direction through research, practice or both.

Justin Robinson and David Bott are part of the team which has done the hard yards at Geelong Grammar School, turning Marty Seligman's positive education vision into whole-school wellbeing reality over the last decade. They share their learning with us. Dr Mathew White who served as head of positive education at St Peter's Adelaide and previously at Geelong Grammar School is now at the University of Adelaide, where he has developed bachelor's and master's programmes integrating wellbeing as part of teacher training. Dr Tayyab Rashid has studied, worked and published with Professor Martin Seligman for over a decade, working as a trainer with the University of Pennsylvania, developing programmes for high school and tertiary students and contributing to the field through his strengths-based clinical work and development of the field of positive psychotherapy. Dr Toni Noble and Dr Helen McGrath's work on resilience pre-dates positive psychology and has been embraced by schools for its practical and useful approach, reflecting a deep understanding of the needs of educators and schools when working in this area. Dr Paula Robinson has supported wellbeing change in schools for over a decade, bringing useful tools and approaches from beyond positive psychology into the school toolkit, and has supported and encouraged rigorous measurement and evaluation of wellbeing work for greater learning and to progress the field. Dr Sue Roffey has worked for over three decades furthering her view of 'learning to be' and 'learning to live together' as integral to education. Her strongly relational approach to managing classroom behaviour informs teachers around the world, supporting educator and student relationships and wellbeing. Dr Helen Street has worked for over two decades in the field of wellbeing, exploring the impact of motivation and goal setting on wellbeing. She has created a Contextual Wellbeing model emphasising the important role schools as social systems and contexts have on student and staff wellbeing. Dr Tom Brunzell (the Berry Street education model) works with trauma-affected students and sadly has witnessed the growth in need for this knowledge in non-specialist schools. Many schools serve students and communities where trauma is part of daily life (some fuelled by the opioid and methamphetamine crises) or where students and their families are refugees who have fled violent situations. Nathan Wallis is an experienced neuroscience educator and child advocate, whose insights into brain development are something every educator (and parent) needs to hear. Dr Jillian Coppley Darwish leads the work of Mayerson Academy to bring wellbeing to schools and their communities, weaving strategies and practices through these structures to build sustainable wellbeing change.

Reading these educators' insights and viewing wellbeing promotion from diverse perspectives underscores the importance of gaining input from across the entire school system. Expertise and good ideas are never exclusively the domain of school leaders, and the more we view challenges from across the ecosystem, rather than through our own egotistical lens, the better. We always return to Richard Zare from Stanford University's wisdom that 'real problems are rarely solved by a single department', a reminder that sits on our office wall.

Challenges and opportunities for positive education

Mathew White PhD, is Associate Professor in the School of Education at the University of Adelaide. We are always particularly interested in Mathew's insights because of his dual perspective as an academic researcher who has over 20 years' experience as a teacher. Mathew also led wellbeing change as head of positive education at St Peter's Adelaide and previously at Geelong Grammar School. We asked Mathew to review the field's challenges and opportunities in the decade ahead.

'One of the biggest challenges in the implementation of positive education over the last decade has been an over-reliance on science and under reliance on educational philosophy. One of the major aspects holding positive education back is that many people equate activity in positive education with impact. They haven't engaged with big questions facing professional practice and the implications of pedagogy.

The growth of positive education is hampered by a paradox: there is universal agreement that wellbeing education matters, but no agreement on what wellbeing education is and what it is not. Recently I surveyed a number of wellbeing frameworks in Australian schools. I stopped counting at around 15 different models. A handful of these are scientifically informed, the majority are values based, but hardly any are empirically driven. A notable exception to this is the development of the SEARCH approach by Prof Lea Waters. Professor Lea Waters and Dan Loton's recent meta-analysis is a game changer for the next wave of positive education. It may also act as an important framework for future educational research and exploration of the philosophical implications of the field.

I've argued for a caught and taught positive education curriculum. The most effective whole-of-school strategies adopt both. These are inquiry based, descriptive and not prescriptive in their approach. Where many schools find initial positive education approaches stall, or completely collapse, is the disconnection between the two.

In the 2016 article Why Won't it Stick? I identified a number of challenges many schools face, including: financial implications of incorporating positive education into the taught and caught curriculum (early investment is often needed, with the return on investment not apparent until years later); the tendency for education leaders to focus on binary thinking when considering wellbeing (regarding it as a marginal topic when compared with other areas such as numeracy and literacy); the growth of maverick providers (questionable programmes with very limited evidence); the over-reliance on science and the under-reliance on educational philosophy and educational best-practice; traditional deficit-oriented forms of governance, leadership and management in many schools that prevents adopting a whole-of-school wellbeing approach to wellbeing and learning; enthusiasm running ahead of the challenging questions around professional practice; and the substantial socio-economic and cultural challenges between and across schools.

A decade later, where I would advise people to begin? First, alignment between governance, leadership and management is critical. For positive education to flourish, in individual schools and sectors, the relationship between governance, leadership and management, the alignment of individual vision, missions, objectives, and measurable goals is critical. Without this approach profound institutional growth is challenging to achieve within five years. This, combined with adopting positive approaches to the change process so that it is aligned with the end goal of a flourishing educational community, is foundational.

Next, focusing on collective teacher efficacy and inviting staff to engage in critical self-reflection aligned with institutional goals, is key. Creating the institutional mindsets required in order to undertake this important work is a major hurdle. Discussion needs to be relentlessly focused upon improving the quality of learning (and teaching) for every child within the school and thereby focusing upon instructional leadership as one of the dominant vehicles to be able to enhance a whole-school strategy. Unless the principal is deeply involved – and models the learning required in order to enable others to take risks both professionally and also personally in their pedagogy – wellbeing education will stall in many institutions.

Finally, regardless of the circumstances of the school implementing positive education in small and large ways, institutions need to build a commitment to give away the best of professional practice to others. This is a critical part in the ability for institutions to be able to internalise the major challenges of wellbeing and the integration of student voice throughout the process'.

Positive education –Ten years – Ten lessons learned . . .

No book on positive education would be complete without reflections from the leadership team at Geelong Grammar School – the first school in the world to embrace positive education as a whole-school approach to wellbeing. It is now 11 years since Denise visited Geelong as part of the University of Pennsylvania's training team, delivering the Strath Haven and Penn Resilience Program to the Geelong staff and then educators from around Australia. We have huge respect for all Geelong Grammar has done as a pioneer in the field and the way they have shared their learning with other schools. We asked Justin Robinson and David Bott, both former directors of positive education at GGS, and now director and associate director of Geelong Grammar School's Institute of Positive Education, respectively, to reflect on some of the challenges, successes and mistakes along the way.

Lesson #1 – Measure Purposefully

The value of collecting baseline wellbeing data and ongoing comparative data is an important element of any whole-school approach to wellbeing. Sustained, effective implementation of Positive Education requires schools to be responsive to changes in environment, context, and culture.

When designed well, a school's evaluation strategy allows for efficient collection, effective analysis, and impactful response to wellbeing data. Whilst the dynamic nature of wellbeing and inherent challenges in accurately measuring wellbeing mean data typically tells a complex story, there are often clues provided that may otherwise go unnoticed. Effective data helps a school be more refined and targeted with its wellbeing strategy.

Lesson #2 – Do PosEd with students not to them

Unfortunately, in some schools around the world, evidence-informed wellbeing programmes are being implemented by well-meaning, passionate and highly capable educators – who fail to embrace fully the wisdom, voice and perspective of their students. When schools fail to view students as partners in their wellbeing approach, there is a risk that students will perceive Positive Education as just 'another programme' imposed upon them. When schools genuinely partner with their students, not only is there likely to be greater buy-in, but the authentic experience of the youngest members of the school community directly informs the approach itself. Ideally, students should have more than just a 'voice' – they should be directly involved in the design and implementation of Positive Education. Student partnership can involve: Strategic planning discussions; Student-representative wellbeing committees; Students designing, introducing, leading, promoting wellbeing initiatives; Student contribution to assemblies, newsletters, parent forums; Peer mentoring and teaching of wellbeing skills and knowledge.

Lesson #3 – Less is more

In any school, new initiatives, new programmes, and new approaches can be exciting and energizing. At the same time, change can be stressful.

As the science that informs Positive Education continues to evolve, new practices are emerging together with new and improved ways of learning, teaching, and structuring schools. However, schools are already busy with full schedules. Positive Education is an approach that needs space; space to learn and to live and to teach and to embed. If a school is really committed to implementing Positive Education in a sustainable way, it must be prepared to ask hard questions, "what goes, what do we do less, or possibly what do we even stop doing?" Without courageously addressing these questions, there is a risk that Positive Education is viewed as an add-on, another "thing to do" rather than a key strategic and philosophical priority. That said, when implemented effectively, Positive Education can create efficiencies in the school system. When people are at their best, they perform better.

The "less is more" maxim should also inform the way Positive Education is implemented. Positive Education should not be rushed. It requires prudent, systematic upskilling of educators and carefully considered adaptation of processes and procedures. An overly accelerated learning, living, teaching, or embedding process can lead to avoidable resistance and unnecessary strain on the system. We over-did the VIA Character Strengths survey. Although the introduction of a strengths framework was welcomed, asking students to complete their VIA Character Strengths twice a year lead to students disengaging with the concept.

Lesson #4 – The teacher matters a lot

As we have always known, the personal attributes and professional skills of a teacher play a significant role in student learning. High quality teaching relies on strong relationships, a safe and cohesive environment, authentic delivery, and an ability to motivate and inspire young minds.

Whilst this is true of teaching Science or Grade 3, the impact of the teacher seems to be amplified in the teaching of wellbeing skills. Successfully teaching "soft skills" requires refined pedagogy, genuine authenticity, and consistent role-modelling. It is very difficult to teach 16-year-old boys or 6-year-old girls about the value of forgiveness if the teacher is perceived as disconnected, disingenuous or unforgiving! In order to enable real buy-in from students, schools need to think very carefully about the skills and attributes of the people leading and teaching Positive Education.

Lesson #5 – Often, parents matter even more

Although it is not always the case, many students are fortunate to have parents or other caregiving adults at home to support them when they are not at school. These adults play a very significant role in shaping the foundation of a child's wellbeing and they can directly moderate the impact and success of Positive Education.

It may be helpful to think of parents, ideally, as a force-multiplier. When a student is exposed to a well-designed Positive Education at school, and then comes home to a parent who reinforces the same messages, we are likely to see much greater positive impact on the child. The parent significantly amplifies the work being done at school. However, if that same child returns home to a parent who provides conflicting messages, the Positive Education work at school is impeded.

Almost always, the problem is not that a parent is critical of Positive Education itself. What parent doesn't want their child to be well and performing optimally? Problems arise when schools fail to communicate effectively with parents or fail to include them as partners in the Positive Education process. Providing opportunities for parents to be educated in the science and philosophy underpinning Positive Education and offering forums for them to provide input into the approach itself, are pivotal. Positive Education is at its best when we have the school, the student, and the parents working together to nurture the wellbeing of the child.

Lesson #6 – The importance of language

Humans think in language. The words we have, and use, shape our perception of the world. It is, therefore, important for all schools to consider carefully the language they use in introducing a whole-school approach to wellbeing.

What are the preconceptions the community bring to the words "Positive Education"? We have found the term to be incredibly powerful and it draws people to the experience they want their child or children to have in education. It is also regularly misunderstood, with some people wrongly dismissing it as a "happyology" or as an approach that deemphasizes academic learning. Alternatively, it can be dismissed as just a modern term for traditional values and approaches. This is an ongoing challenge for the field which lacks a unified definition of Positive Education. However, despite some of the challenges associated with language, Positive Education provides a school-wide lexicon for a strengths-based approach to wellbeing that, in itself, can have a powerful impact on the community.

Lesson #7 – "Interventions" are never permanent

The field of Positive Psychology is continuing to develop empirically validated interventions; changes we can make to positively impact wellbeing. Concurrently, schools are becoming increasingly sophisticated at integrating these interventions into their unique school culture.

When a Positive Education intervention works really effectively over an extended period, it may eventually become part of the 'way things are done'. One campus at Geelong Grammar School begins all of its meetings with a "What Went Well" sharing of good news. This is no longer an "intervention", it is has transitioned instead into a habitual, engrained cultural practice.

Some interventions, however, are more effective when presented occasionally or utilised for a short time period only. For example, creating a gratitude-wall in the teacher lounge or staff room might create excitement and elevated awareness of the positive impact of others for a week as it becomes populated with little sticky notes. Reduced levels of engagement with the wall two weeks later do not mean the intervention has been unsuccessful.

Lesson #8 – Wellbeing is caught and taught – Positive Education is not a curriculum

From the moment we are born, our genetic programming compels us to learn from both our own experience and the behaviour we witness in others. When a student is exposed to a school culture and repeated interactions grounded in integrity, trust, compassion, hope and forgiveness, it is impossible not be influenced by these values.

There are various Positive Education curricula available, some of which are carefully sequenced across the 15 years of schooling, providing opportunities for schools to explicitly teach evidence-informed skills and knowledge. These lessons can be very powerful in allowing students time and space to practise their skills. However, they are just part of the way Positive Education influences the development of students.

The most sophisticated Positive Education implementations expose students to wellbeing science via explicit teaching, implicit teaching (integration of wellbeing skills and knowledge into traditional, existing curriculum opportunities), and via pedagogy – the way teachers teach.

Lesson #9 – Positive Education must be tailored to fit each school and each student

Every school environment is unique, with unique individuals, unique needs, unique strengths, a unique history and a yet-to-be-determined unique future.

Although the foundations of wellbeing science are universal and have been successfully implemented in a range of cultural settings around the world, Positive Education must be brought to life in harmony with (and ultimately enmeshed with) the existing culture of each school. Positive Education is not seeking to change culture, but rather to enable each culture to be at its best.

The four key processes of learn, live, teach, embed appear to be the simplest and most universal way to distil the systems-thinking that underpins successful Positive Education implementation. However, the way these four processes are orchestrated and integrated into existing culture allows for vastly different operationalisation of the constructs.

Similarly, while we all share a common humanity, we are all at different stages of our wellbeing journey. Ideally, Positive Education strategies and interventions should be flexible enough that they can be adapted to enhance the individual lives of each member of the community. Positive Education will have limited impact if it is viewed as a 'one-size-fits-all' approach.

Lesson #10 – Beekeepers don't just make honey

The primary outcome of beekeeping is the production of delicious honey. One side effect of beekeeping is that surrounding crops get pollinated which increases the yield for crop farmers. The beekeeper receives no direct income from the healthier, higher value crops but the whole community is better off because of the bees. In economic terms, this phenomenon is referred to as a positive externality. We see externalities occur in almost all interconnected systems. In schools, a student's experience in Lesson 1 with Teacher A can have a huge impact on that student's approach to Lesson 2 with Teacher B. When Lesson 1 is full of positive emotion, engagement, meaningful connection, achievement and purpose, students walk into Lesson 2 with an optimised psychology and a neurology primed for learning.

There are also negative externalities – such as when pollution emitted by a factory spoils the surrounding environment or when Teacher A allows negativity, disengagement, or disempowerment to fester in Lesson 1. In this case, Lesson 2 feels very different for Teacher B and the students. This is a big part of the reason why wellbeing needs to be placed at the heart of a school for it to really transform a culture. The more of the community who embrace and "live" wellbeing, the more likely we are to experience the dynamic upward spiral of wellbeing that positive externalities can empower.

While the above list is not exhaustive (there are many more lessons we have learned!) and we continue to learn as the field evolves, we hope that in sharing some of our lessons, we can assist you to enhance the wellbeing of your own community. Positive Education is not easy to do well but it does have the potential to transform the life of a school'.

Lessons learned from three decades of working with schools

Dr Sue Roffey is an honorary associate professor at Exeter and Western Sydney Universities and director of Growing Great Schools Worldwide, as well as the author of many books relating to wellbeing in education, our favourites of which are *Changing Behaviour in Schools* and her *Primary Behaviour Cookbook* and *Secondary Behaviour Cookbook*. Her longstanding focus on the 'whole child' and relational approaches to behaviour and wellbeing are borne out by neuroscience.

'I have worked in the field of school and student wellbeing for over three decades, primarily in Australia and the UK but also with schools across the world. My experience has included teaching, educational psychology, research and consultancy so I have been privileged to see things from a range of perspectives. This is what I have learned.

It begins with what people believe education is for. If schooling is focused almost exclusively on students being filled with knowledge and skills that are the subject of high stakes testing then wellbeing will be barely on the agenda. If, on the other hand education includes "learning to be" and "learning to live together" (Delors 1996) there is a chance that issues such as relationships, resilience, critical thinking and pro-social behaviour will be part of student learning. Much of the time the purpose of education is determined by government policies – it may take a brave school leader to say that excellence is beyond a score and an outstanding school may be one that enables everyone to believe they have something to offer and empowers them to do so. Although state schools operating within a curricular straight-jacket and with smaller budgets are often less able to focus on wellbeing than independent schools, these more privileged institutions still have to persuade aspirational fee-paying parents that their approach is in the best interests of all students. In our competitive world it may be hard to convince people that wellbeing begins with "we" not "me". The increased concern about young people's mental health is however, refocusing everyone.

Leadership is vital to the development of whole school wellbeing. If the vision of school leaders is to honour the whole child and every child so that each feel accepted and see themselves as a valued member of the school community, they will be promoting wellbeing from the ground up. Many schools, however, appear to confuse wellbeing with welfare or pastoral care. The latter is what happens when individuals come to the attention of teachers, usually on account of deteriorating attainments, challenging behaviour or poor mental health. They are invariably referred onto senior or specialist staff. Although there is a place for this extra support it is not wellbeing. Wellbeing is the province of everyone, all the time. It includes every interaction, every policy and how time is prioritised. Wellbeing is not just whole child but whole school.

So, school leaders need everyone signing up to their vision – being a hero-innovator simply doesn't work. Wellbeing, and what it means, needs to be communicated clearly and consistently throughout the school, with students, staff and community – and modelled with an expectation that people will "walk the talk". School leaders lose credibility fast if they are unable to do this. Carefully planned professional development can be critical.

Many schools begin their wellbeing journey with the needs of teachers to ensure that staff mental health is supported so they can give of their best in the classroom. Although this is undeniably valuable, there have been times when there has been conflict between the needs of staff and the needs of vulnerable, challenging students. This is probably the trickiest element of whole-school wellbeing and requires relationships to be high on the agenda. Firstly, ensure that a positive culture exists across the entire school so that no individual feels they have to deal with difficult issues alone and, secondly, school behaviour policies must to be relational rather than based in rewards and sanctions – sometimes leading to the marginalisation of the most needy.

Social and emotional learning (SEL) on the curriculum provides a space for students to learn pro-social behaviour "from the inside out" as well as strategies that promote wellbeing. To be effective this requires a safe pedagogy, must happen regularly, and the learning embedded in everyday interactions. Circle Solutions is a framework I have developed for this and where it is happening both pupils and teachers have reported higher confidence, stronger relationships, better conflict resolution and a more positive classroom ethos.

Wellbeing is not exactly the same in each school, but these are overarching fundamentals – a vision for the whole child, a whole school strengths and solution-focused approach, and an emphasis on relationships across the school. It is not always easy but always worthwhile'.

Lessons learned implementing positive education initiatives

As educational psychologists and teachers, Toni Noble and Helen McGrath saw the need almost 20 years ago to develop a teacher-friendly wellbeing and resilience programme for children and young people that was underpinned by rigorous science. That programme, Bounce Back, is now in its third edition and has been joined by 11 other highly regarded teacher resource books.

Their work is respected by academic colleagues and educators alike, so we asked them to share their insights as to what makes wellbeing and resilience training work in schools.

'As teacher educators we saw that any educational programme must incorporate evidence-based effective pedagogy and ideally be taught in all classrooms across a whole school, so all students learn the key skills for happiness and wellbeing. We also understood that a whole school programme offers greater opportunities to develop a safe, supportive and respectful school culture than a programme implemented only in one, or two, year levels.[1]

Over the years we have learned many lessons about the school, school system and programme factors that contribute to the successful implementation and sustainability of initiatives in positive education.[2] We describe these below:

School-based factors:

- Making student wellbeing and social-emotional learning a top school priority;
- Staff recognising that student wellbeing underpins academic learning;
- Providing high level leadership support for the programme;
- Adopting a whole school approach that recognises that all aspects of the school community impact on students' health and wellbeing;
- Focusing on both explicit teaching of the skills and understandings to improve wellbeing and resilience and embedding the understandings and concepts across the whole school environment (e.g. the programme is aligned with classroom and school norms, the school's values, the school's approach to behaviour management and to student support structures such as peer support);
- Teaching the programme across all year levels;
- Offering professional learning to teachers to build their expertise;
- Teachers acting as role models for the social-emotional learning (SEL) skills and understandings taught in the programme;
- Keeping school families informed about the implementation of the programme and seeing them as partners in teaching the social-emotional learning skills; and
- Integrating the programme's content across different curriculum areas where appropriate.

School-system factors:

- The programme must meet their school system's priority for student wellbeing and social-emotional learning;

- The programme must align with the system's educational policy and recommendations for student wellbeing; and
- The programme must be underpinned by research outcomes deemed important;

Programme-specific factors:

- Acceptability of the programme to the schools and their teachers. Teachers' evaluation of any programme significantly influences not only their preparedness to implement it but also the extent to which they implement it accurately (Durlak et al. 2011; Han and Weiss 1995). This is influenced by: i) teachers perception that it was important to teach resilience for social-emotional learning and engagement in learning; ii) the programme being perceived as teacher-friendly and easy to teach; iii) programmes having a sequenced structure; and iv) the use of children's literature with follow up literacy and language activities to teach key messages;
- Programme Effectiveness: One of the most significant factors contributing to a programme's sustainability is teachers' perception that the learning and behaviour of their students has changed as a result of their implementation of the programme (Han and Weiss 2005; Datnow and Castellano 2000);
- Feasibility: schools look for a programme that can be implemented on an on-going basis with minimal but sufficient resources. One of the success of our Bounce Back programme is that it is seen as practical and feasible for teachers to implement in their classrooms. This was important given many schools don't receive funding or external support to run their programmes; and
- Flexibility and Adaptability: Programmes must be flexible and adaptable'.

A journey to trauma-informed positive education

Dr Tom Brunzell, Director of education and co-founder of the Berry Street education model at Berry Street, Victoria, has worked as a teacher, school leader, researcher and education advisor in New York City and Melbourne. As many schools struggle to support an increasing number of trauma-affected students, demand for the Berry Street education model is growing across Australia and New Zealand. We asked him to share his journey to trauma-informed positive education, what it has taught him and the lessons it offers for all educators and schools.

'I love being an educator because teaching offers the possibility of lifelong learning for students and the professionals that care for and educate them. Learning about and implementing whole-school wellbeing is the next step for many of us. Wellbeing is now considered an integral part within many schools; however, it was not always this way. In my years as an educator and education researcher, I have learned lessons that have marked my own journey towards healing and growth through the classroom.

Lesson #1: Yelling makes things worse

Nobody ever told me this. I started teaching in the central Bronx, NY, and I taught many students whose behaviours were dysregulated, resistant, angry, and withdrawn. At that time, we called those kids difficult, unmanageable and feral. Nobody corrected us. It was industry standard. Now, I look back and understand those children to be trauma-affected with complex un-met needs, most of them living in systemic, generational disadvantage feeling the effects of poverty, societal neglect and chronic community stressors. We can now understand trauma as the overwhelming belief that one's world no longer feels good and safe. My students felt the daily, overwhelming effects of stressors in their uncertain, unpredictable world.

My students would yell at me in the worst of times. My solution was to yell at them. They would yell back at me – and this cycle continued throughout the day. I had a mis-guided self-perpetuating theory that angry kids required angry adults to give them the motivation to change. Everyone around me yelled at the students, and I thought it was what successful teachers needed to do. The yelling infected my own body – and I came to believe teaching was about escalation and stress. I did not feel I was fully present at my job until about 9:15 am, when I, myself, felt hypervigilant and adrenalined- and cortisoled-up.

Lesson #2: Strengths-based teaching offers hope

I was first introduced to a new burgeoning science called positive psychology back in the year 2004. The integration of wellbeing in classrooms – positive education – was a new idea and at the time, I became co-founder of the KIPP Infinity Charter School in Harlem. I also put my hand up to be one of the first leaders to work closely with Martin Seligman's team from the University of Pennsylvania. I had the privilege of collaborating with Angela Duckworth, who was becoming the world's expert on grit and building classroom interventions to embed positive psychology across a network of New York City schools.[3]

This work began to change me. I was ignited by the ideas but struggled to integrate them into my own life. Over time, I felt myself becoming a new teacher, someone who saw as their professional responsibility to live the character strengths of self-regulation, curiosity, social-intelligence and kindness. We saw these strengths reflected in our students, and our school culture began to shift. Best of all, students themselves began to identify, practice, and articulate their strengths in daily ways.

A series of synchronistic meetings lead to the surprising decision to move to Australia to spend a year working at Berry Street, a Victorian child and family services organisation. Berry Street supports children and young people who have experienced violence, abuse and neglect through therapeutic, out-of-home care, and education supports. That one year has turned into nine, and what I found at Berry Street was another new science: the study of trauma and trauma's impacts on students and their learning. This bolt of lightning immediately created a new intuition – and a new way of seeing the purpose of what we can and must do in the classroom.

These two ideas – positive psychology and trauma psychology – were both holding important pieces for educators to understand the un-met needs of their struggling students. In my early excitement, I spoke to many folks on either sides of these lines and I realized the two paradigms had arisen in silos. These silos were industrial strength! My conclusion then was that the trauma-based people felt the need for healing was too great to have room for wellbeing, "He needs to regulate himself and sit still first before we can do any learning!" and the positive education people were giving up on positive psychology interventions in the classroom when students resisted, "I'll never try talking about strengths again with this class – they just don't care!".[4]

There had to be an integrated and/or developmental way to consider both camps in order to take advantage of the valuable contributions of what was becoming known as trauma-informed practice and positive education. Corey Keyes'[5] research proved pivotal to forwarding my own theorising: Mitigating illbeing is not the same thing as increasing wellbeing. In other words, we must help students contend with meeting their unmet needs in healthy ways at the same time as pushing the gas pedal on opportunities for them to discover and build upon a new identity – one that is anchored in the strengths that rest inside every one of us bolstered with the tools of having a resilient mindset and emotional intelligence.

Lesson #3: Wellbeing can be a developmental journey for schools who educate trauma-affected students

Together with my colleagues Professor Lea Waters and Associate Professor Helen Stokes, we integrated trauma-informed practices for teachers within a positive education framework by reviewing the literature and creating a new practice model for teachers: Trauma-Informed Positive Education.[6] In this new model, we advocate for a teacher practice to first build a classroom that supports increasing self-regulatory abilities (i.e., through rhythm, co-regulation, and other strategies to strengthen the body); next to fortify the classroom to create relational capacity (i.e., through attachment, attunement and unconditional positive regard); which then lays a strong foundation for the teaching of cognitively-mediated (brain-based) strategies which require self-reflection such as identifying and employing one's strengths.

Lesson #4: Everyone deserves to build wellbeing

I have found in my own research and practice that trauma-informed positive education can be a path of professional and personal refinement. Teachers are now understanding that they are mirroring and modelling humanity – and can be living examples of learning and living wellbeing strategies. For trauma-affected students who are sitting in trauma-affected schools, we can shift this identity to become trauma-aware schools. This awareness changes teachers. And questions shift from "Why is he treating me like this?" to "What unmet needs is he trying to meet?"

We'd like to see it become non-negotiable for teachers working in trauma-affected classrooms to not just apply trauma-informed positive education strategies to their students, but to first apply these same strategies to themselves. As educators doing some of the most complex work in our community, we are the ones that need to build our capacity to self-regulate, our ability to form and maintain healthy connections, and to instill a deep understanding of wellbeing practices in our daily lives. Beyond mitigating pathways to burnout, these new ways of working hold promising potential to increase the compassion, the purpose and the wellbeing required to contribute to communities every day'.

Lessons from neuroscience: Relationships matter most

Nathan Wallis has a background that includes early childhood teacher, child therapist, social service manager, university lecturer and neuroscience trainer. His ability to de-mystify neuroscience by translating it into everyday language makes him a popular presenter and parenting broadcaster in New Zealand and beyond.

'My first experience as a primary school teacher, straight from teacher training, taught me that scared kids don't do a lot of learning. At that stage I knew nothing about neuroscience or social-emotional wellbeing, but you just work out that some kids' minds are not focused on learning, so you need to do something to make them feel safe. I needed to act more like a nurturer or a dad, and then I could act like a teacher.

That made me realise the huge significance of social-emotional wellbeing. We tended to think school performance is a matter of IQ – how intelligent you are – but I realised that varies hugely according to how safe you feel and how looked after you are. So I went back to university to train as a child therapist and learn more.

Lessons for pre-schools

The three Rs are the most important – that's Relationship, Relationship and Relationship. It's not so much about reading, writing and arithmetic.

The research shows the number one factor determining kids' outcomes in the classroom is the quality of the relationship with their teacher; that's beyond the parents' qualifications, and relationships with peers. So, the more you can invest in one-on-one high-quality relationships the better the outcomes are going to be for that kid for the rest of their life. Fostering that intimacy and that partnership is key.

What changes can schools make to support optimal child development and learning?

If I could change one thing it would be to stop schools from changing the teacher all the time. I'd love to get rid of the idea of having a new entrants teacher, then a year one teacher and then a different year two teacher. A lot of children end their primary school experience having had six or seven superficial relationships and not one deep meaningful one, when their brains need deep meaningful relationships. Some of the children in our classes, when they've come from traumatic backgrounds, take longer than a year to establish relationships, to let people through the layers they've built up to protect themselves. So, if we want their brains to develop, they need to develop a dyadic relationship. Most of us get that from our mums, or aunties or grandmas – it doesn't matter who – as long as you have that one-on-one relationship that gives your brain what it needs to grow the frontal cortex (giving us empathy, control of emotions, seeing things from other people's point of view, focusing attention). This isn't new thinking. We've known this for a long time, that's what Celia Lashlie was referring to when she said she could predict who the prison population would be at 25 years, by what was going on with three year olds.

It disturbs me that we know who the prison population is going to be at 25 by looking at them as 3 year olds – not with a 100% accuracy but with a really high degree of accuracy – when we know the single thing that could save them is a dyadic relationship. Most of them don't even get to develop their frontal cortex – to access that part of the brain – because no one's given them a dyad.

Lessons for the parents of teenagers

The message for parents is to understand that adolescence is a real thing happening inside the brain. It's not just made up, it's not caused by Facebook, and it wasn't caused by too much video games. Brain number four (your frontal cortex, the last one to develop, the one that controls your emotions, sees things from other people's point of view, understands consequences) is going to shut for renovations for around about three years, somewhere in between seven years and 27. That's called adolescence. So, yes your teenager is supposed to go backwards in empathy, and not be so good at controlling their emotions, during adolescence. Yes, you'll get flashes coming through of your teenager's frontal cortex – they have moments when they're wonderfully articulate and behave like adults – but for much of the time, the part of the brain that controls this stuff is shut for renovations. The process of becoming an adult from being a teenager doesn't involve your frontal cortex getting better, just moving from only being online 10% of the time to being online 90% of the time.

Fifteen year olds, operating out of brain number three, are emotional and lack logic. Parents need to understand teenagers are supposed to be emotional, it's something we have to nurture them through. When they were two you had to be their frontal cortex for them – they could do bugger all – they couldn't calm themslves down or go to bed by themselves. When they're teenagers you have to realise you are back there again, and take back lots of that responsability. Don't try to frighten your teenager into being well behaved, nurture them into being well-behaved instead.

My advice is chill out and shut-up. You are not shaping their character or work ethic during that adolescent phase, that was done well before. You had the first three years to build their brain, until 11 years to shape their character, and now you've just got to live with them. Stop creating fights by trying to build character because that stuff happened beforehand. Let them be a bit of a sullen lazy teenager, that doesn't mean they are going to be sullen and lazy for the rest of their life. They might not get out of bed until four, but you don't find many adults doing that. Don't try to fix their problems for them, but validate their emotions first. Speak to their emotional brain – acknowledge what they're saying, what you are hearing, what's going on for them – don't go straight to logic, let them know you recognise what they're going through.

Lessons for secondary schools

The NZ education systems is very focused on preparing young people for the work force, so you're more likely to come out of school being equipped for work than emotional intelligence. Our high school is all about getting a job, getting credits. Teachers need to know the more we focus on wellbeing, and care, the better their credits will be. Again it's about fostering that dyadic relationship, only it's even more important now as their teachers are changing every hour. The naughty kids especially need to have an anchor relationship. What's good for traumatised kids is good for all children. If we anchored all our policies around wellbeing, you'd come to high school and have one important relationship – the same dean, home room or tutor teacher throughout your time at secondary school. That way that child can develop a high quality relationship with one teacher which will probably save them from going to jail. The other thing we know from the research is the importance of the connection between home and school for young people's outcomes: when those two are connected, those kids do well, when there isn't they don't. Having greater consistency around home-room teachers would also help that: the parents would have one known person to form a relationship with over time'.

Critical success factors in character strengths interventions

The Mayerson Academy (MA) offers three strengths-based programmes to 120 schools and universities and 40 non-profit organisations across the US and internationally. As a practitioner fiercely committed to taking strengths to the world, Dr Jillian Coppley Darwish, MA's president and CEO, shares her critical success factors for character strengths interventions.

'We are motivated by a shared belief that, when people are at their best, every part of the world is made that little bit better. As we evaluate, research, and reflect on our practice, we have found that for schools, neighborhoods and organisations there are several critical success factors which remain stable. Some of the most important include:

Building capacity from the Inside

There is a persistent call in the research for professional learning to be "context aware" with suggestion that social-psychological interventions are particularly context-dependent. In our practice-based experience, a nuanced understanding of environment and culture is absolutely required for success and therefore the effort is best led from the inside, by school-based leaders.

While partners have acknowledged to us the unique role external expertise plays in providing research, capacity, and authority to the work, they understand the driving force must come from within. As one of our partners has shared, "We could have ruined it if we brought an expert in house. We would have felt like we didn't have to do the work. On our own, we had to live the work ourselves".

In the work of character strengths interventions there is an interesting double meaning to building capacity "from the inside". Creating experiences to shift individual mental models and let go of existing beliefs is where the work truly begins in our experience. Therefore, capacity building can't be a matter of direct instruction, but rather it requires exploring the concepts in the context of one's own life. For robust implementation, educators must first experience for themselves what they hope students will experience.

Weaving into the structure

We are very intentional about taking a systems approach to change, to the greatest degree possible. A central axiom of systems thinking is that everything is connected, and careful attention must be paid not to optimise a part of the system at the expense of the whole system. In practical experience this means that interventions simply bolted onto the system will be rejected. To be sustained, new elements must be rooted in the system's structure and processes as an expression of internal consistency and coherence.

Beyond the instruction of strengths with staff, faculty, students, parents and citizens, our partners have embedded a strengths-based perspective in their communications, policies and practices. Character strengths are integrated into on-boarding processes, academic curriculum, performance reviews, sports and extracurricular activities, newsletters, meetings, conferences, marketing, student conferences, community councils, and more. These practical connections have a secondary effect of creating strong personal connections, invaluable for successful change efforts.

As another partner has shared, "the common language of character strengths in our meetings and across our activities connected us, got us out of our silos and created new relationships and potential".

Enjoy the ride

Change is hard, but you can have fun along the way. We have come to understand this isn't just a nicety, but it is actually a powerful support as we experience the demands of creating change efforts. We always have and will take our work (not ourselves) seriously, and at the same time we remain committed to infusing positive emotions at every step along the way.

Our partners frequently refer to the resiliency, lightness, collaborative and even energising experience of doing difficult work when a sense of fun and joy are infused in the experience. Research supports their experience. When people experience playful and social activities intended to arouse amusement and enjoyment, studies suggest they are more likely to help one another, be more motivated and productive, and experience less stress. Each of these outcomes goes a long way toward supporting character strengths (or any!) change effort'.

Positive psychology and positive education over the last decade: Key threats and opportunities

Dr Paula Robinson has over 25 years of experience in traditional and positive psychology science and practice. A registered psychologist and managing director of the Positive Psychology Institute, she is the author of numerous books and journal articles including Practising Positive Education: A Guide to Improving Wellbeing in Schools and a staunch advocate for rigorous practice and measurement in wellbeing. As she launches her own practice into a new phase, with the creation of Appli (delivering and measuring wellbeing initiatives to improve wellbeing across the lifespan – at home, at school, at work, during the ageing years and in society), we asked her to reflect on how positive psychology and positive education have changed over the last decade and to consider the field's key threats and opportunities.

'The burgeoning science and practice of Positive Psychology (PP) was, from its inception, intended to complement, not to replace traditional psychology. Today, PP is still grounded in the belief that people want to lead meaningful and fulfilling lives, to cultivate what is best within them and others, and to enhance their work, school and life experiences.

Since the early 2000s PP has gone through a number of stages of growth and evolution. The USA has been prolific with both the scientific study of wellbeing and its application, with universities such as Harvard, Yale, Claremont and Berkeley embedding PP into their subjects, courses and/or degree programmes. The study of wellbeing science and practice continued to grow through the next decade and beyond, taking its place in Australia, Europe, Canada, China, Africa, Russia and many other parts of the world.

As should be the case with all burgeoning scientific endeavours, there were critiques of PP including the cautionary message that the pressure to be "happy" may actually cause people harm (e.g., Ehrenreich, 2010). Dr Paul Wong has regularly commented with insight and clarity the benefits and pitfalls of simplifying the complex nature of wellbeing, pointing out the importance of (a) developing culturally appropriate research, (b) emphasising a sense of personal and social responsibility, and (c) ensuring that PP is given a voice for the suffering masses (e.g., Wong & Tweed, 2016). Research and funding must be placed where it is needed the most and not just in wealthy countries and populations.

While wellbeing is a hot topic everywhere, now, more than ever, we need to ensure best practice is adhered to, and that wellbeing is explored and applied through the lens of scientific research methods, not pseudoscience. PP is definitely not a self-help movement or a re-packaging of "the power of positive thinking". PP is definitely not American-style "happy-ology" either. Nor has it proved to be a passing fad. PP must be protected as a science that utilises the many virtues of science, for example, replication, controlled causal studies, rigorous peer review and representative sampling.

It is becoming increasingly difficult for the layperson to distinguish between valid scientific research, self-help and commercialisation. This risks the complex nature of wellbeing science and application being "dumbed down" and diluting the valuable body of evidence-based work accumulated so far. This is especially important for schools.

Students and children are one of PP's most vulnerable populations, so PP in schools must be very careful not to move from scientific to "self-help" measurement and practices. There are now many so called 'experts' in Positive Education promoting measures and interventions in their marketing materials and websites that are so far untested and not peer reviewed. For example, students are sometimes being tested with measures not scientifically proven to be reliable and valid, nor peer-reviewed. These measures can produce "individual wellbeing reports" (IWRs) for students with their 'grade' in wellbeing and suggestions on how to improve it. Should these tests on our youth and resulting IWRs undergo published peer review, be selected ethically and administered, scored, interpreted, and communicated to the student (and parents) in line with accepted scientific standards? Are the results taking into account the cultural diversity and age appropriateness of the students? What does "grading" wellbeing do to the wellbeing of the student?

Have these students been screened for mental illness, are they languishing? How do students interpret and compare their reports? Moreover, are there legal and ethical risks for schools administering IWRs and can parents be reassured that schools entering their child's psychological space are doing no harm? These are crucial questions for schools – and indeed organisations and communities – as wellbeing science and practices gain more momentum.

To achieve scientific best practice and real, measurable and sustainable improvements in wellbeing requires scientific literature reviews, thoughtful leadership, a compelling "business" case, reliable and valid measurement, a systematic, long term plan and an effective implementation strategy. Improving and sustaining the wellbeing of young people requires a layered approach, for example, the involvement of local preschools and schools, parenting awareness and support, grandparents and retirees' involvement, local business buy-in, and public health advocates. These are all crucial stakeholders in the process. It takes a village to raise a child.

We must continue to study, teach, practice and promote the science of wellbeing for individuals, families, communities, governments, private sector organisations, not for profit groups, and educational institutions. But we must be determined to ensure wellbeing promotion is backed by rigorous studies and implemented in ways more likely to lead to sustained, meaningful change. We must ensure those who buy-in to the practice of PP and Positive Education understand the importance of formal qualifications, as well as valuing the knowledge and experience of the leaders, trainers, lecturers, advisors, coaches and consultants they work with. Wellbeing takes time, commitment, motivation and evidence-based practices to achieve the benefits of creating regular, positive habits of thinking and behaviours. We all have a responsibility to be scientifically driven rather than making commercial, short-term promises that may do harm'.

Lessons from research, practice and student health

Dr Tayyab Rashid is a licensed clinical psychologist at the Health & Wellness Centre, University of Toronto Scarborough. He has worked as a clinician, researcher and teacher in positive psychology for more than a decade. His book Positive Psychotherapy, co-authored with Prof Martin Seligman, is considered the most comprehensive in the field and has been translated into five languages since its publication in late 2018. He has also contributed extensive programme development and research in schools and universities, developing the Strengths-Based Resilience programme with Dr Jane Gilham and Dr Afroze Anjum and the inventory of campus mental health for Canadian universities. He emphasises the need for wellbeing in education to focus on context, equity and addressing disadvantage. As a clinician, he encourages us to become comfortable with negative emotions – our own and others'.

'**Lesson #1:** We need to be more mindful of the circumstances from which students come. We need to look at them as a whole, not just as individuals. We must consider where they come from, which neigbhourhood, what their previous experiences have been. At the beginning with Strengths-Based Resilience we didn't do enough of that but have made changes since then.

Lesson #2: We talk about growth and wellbeing, which is all very well and they are nice sounding, worthy goals. However, the challenge is that positive psychology has fallen into the Western trap of selling the idea that "if you work hard you can do almost anything". Sadly we are not living an equal opportunity world. I have seen many people who work hard and have not been successful, especially immigrants and historically marginalised groups. I have a number of students whose parents were an engineer or dentist in their native country, but they cannot qualify here in Canada. I have seen how this can directly impact students and their wellbeing. We need to acknowledge and address the real issue that disadvantage plays when it comes to wellbeing.

Lesson #3: We have to understand that when we bring our work to schools, many of those present welcome this kind of paradigm shift, but what we still often have to learn is that it's alright if everyone is not on board at some level. Not that everyone has to be on board by prescription but conceptual consensus that wellbeing is the right thing to do. That also means that we we need to be inclusive; that we are committed to including those people who do not agree with us – even if this makes us uncomfortable. In time your actions will speak louder than any words can.

Lesson #4: The culturally relevant adaptive use of strengths is extremely important. When working to build wellbeing in schools, it is vital that educators understand cultural nuances – that strengths have different connotations in different cultures and that we need to respect this. A strength may have a strongly positive connotation in one culture, but in fact be used as a pejorative in another culture. Independent in one culture can be regarded as selfish and not community-minded in another.

Lesson #5: We must take a more comprehensive approach to the assessment of strengths. Self-report is not sufficient because it cannot give us the whole picture. We must always remember that strengths are driven by context; different people use strengths, exhibit them and see them in different ways, at different times. The assessment that others can make, of our strengths, and insights they have regarding our strengths, can be equally important and valuable. These applies, I believe, in all cultures, and not just more inter-dependent or collectivist cultures.

Lesson #6: When we are tackling negative emotions and experiences in our work in schools, we should not try to switch people away from holding on to negative memories- asking them to pivot quickly towards positive and strengths. We need to ackknowledge that this is going to take some time. Sometimes holding on to feelings of negative memories – I call them grudges in my work – is adaptive. This is because the grudge has two parts – affective (emotional) and intellectual – so you can have an intellectual grudge because you were transgressed, that is, someone really offended you and you were harmed. Then looking from an affective (emotional) perspective, we can ask the grudge holder, "What is the impact of thinking that way on you?" We can then encourage them to see how the intellectual grudge is affecting them emotionally, in a way that honours them and their process. It's not fair of us to ask or force people too quickly through these emotions. We need to give them enough freedom and time to make their way, but clearly, we are also gently nudging them along over time.

Lesson #7: Research on wellbeing in education can really benefit from using a mixed methods approach (i.e. quantitative and qualitative) when it comes to student assessment. We can ask students to write about their experiences of being resilient and what has helped them cope with adversity to capture the richness of their experience. We can also use a wellbeing measure to get quantative evalution. To get a fully-rounded view however, I believe we must also include a measure of the stressors or challenges a person is experiencing, AND a 360 measurement which expands our view to include vital input from others, rather than relying solely on self-report'.

Context matters

Dr Helen Street is an applied social psychologist and education consultant and an honorary research fellow in the Graduate School of Education at the University of Western Australia. She developed a contextual model of wellbeing to encourage schools to address context rather than focusing solely on the individual. She emphasises the need to pay attention to students as social beings and to examine the social systems and motivation and reward structures we create for students to live in. Helen is the founder and chair of the Positive Schools Initiative and author of four books, including Contextual Wellbeing: Creating Positive Schools from the Inside Out.

'All too often we try to help a child who is distressed at school by encouraging them to change or to develop as an individual. We want them to be more confident, more resilient, less anxious. What if the answer is not about trying to help that individual change – in whatever capacity – but, instead about creating a healthier environment for that individual, and then helping them to connect to that environment?

Wellbeing is not simply about individual expressions of thoughts, feelings and behaviours; it is not an isolated or solitary pursuit. It is just as much about the connections we form with others, the tasks we pursue, and our wider sense of the world. Wellbeing concerns our "being well" as social beings, not just human beings. It is about creating and reacting to a social context in a healthy and positive way. Ultimately, lasting wellbeing and happiness have far less to do with any aspect of our individual functioning than we might like to think, and far more to do with the spaces between us. This expanded definition of wellbeing suggests that, if we are truly to help young people to feel happy and live happily, we need to pay attention to the social systems in which we live and learn, as much as we need to support individual development.

Our attempts to understand young people cannot succeed if we do not consider the context in which they spend their school week, every Monday to Friday. Too often, if a student is unmotivated, disengaged and disruptive in the classroom, we ask "what is wrong with them?" Perhaps the answer is nothing. They may be demonstrating a perfectly "well" response to a non-nurturing, unhealthy or unhelpful context. They may be struggling with their academic learning, as many disruptive kids do. They may feel they have no autonomy – because they are always being told what to do, which is often seen as the only way to achieve order and compliance in the classroom. Alternatively, they may be struggling to belong in a social world from which they are largely excluded. Consider how many teachers choose to send a disruptive child out of the room, rather than bringing them in closer.

It is of little surprise many high school teachers come to think of teenagers as exhausting. By the time most young people get to high school they have come to the bleak realisation that school does not offer the choices, the engagement and the opportunity for success they'd been led to expect. If we expand our definition of wellbeing to include the context around us, then we are in a better position to create an environment conducive to educating our increasingly troubled children.

Anyone can be happy in the right context, if they have the necessary skills and opportunity to connect with that context. Equally, anyone will be unhappy in the wrong context, no matter how many skills and opportunities they may be presented with.

The majority of school-based wellbeing programmes have been built on psychological therapies designed for individuals and individual understandings of wellbeing. They have largely failed to overcome the difficulties of changing the behaviour of large groups, such as whole classes and whole school populations. The more successful attempts aim to embed wellbeing strategies within the whole school environment, but even these fail to pay significant attention to the context into which the strategies are embedded. For example, there is little point in teaching students the importance of mindfulness on Monday mornings, if the students are overscheduled and feeling rushed the rest of the time. Energy spent promoting a "growth mindset" in your "wellbeing class" is wasted if, for the rest of the week, you focus on forthcoming assessments. Equally, the value of trying to make learning "fun" is greatly diminished if you take away their intrinsic motivation by rewarding students for outcomes. Furthermore, effectiveness in teaching social and emotional skills is severely compromised when the teacher is so over-loaded, they have lost all signs of social and emotional competency themselves.

The implications here raise profound questions about improving wellbeing in schools. If we could create a truly equitable, stimulating and cohesive context for education, would we even need to explicitly teach wellbeing to children? Perhaps wellbeing programmes are really band aids for broken educational contexts?

Under the right circumstances (where programmes reflect the whole school context and address the problems caused by competitive, inequitable education systems) wellbeing programmes can offer valuable support to the pursuit of a flourishing life. Clearly, we need to ensure young people can see the relevancy of wellbeing teaching to their daily lives, that they feel autonomy in their learning, and they feel wellbeing is a real-world possibility. Only then can we attempt to teach them all our well-researched strategies and ideas for wellbeing. Our role as educators is not to tell someone how to be well, or to reward them for behaving well. We have to provide young people with a context in which they can flourish'.

Our final thoughts

Some of the most important lessons *we've* learned include:

- One size doesn't fit all – context is king;
- Good things take time;
- Don't go it alone but bring diverse voices with you – and listen to them;
- Consider the policies, practices and pedagogy of your school through a wellbeing lens;
- Learn from your mistakes but be kind to yourself and others making mistakes;
- Provide multiple and diverse opportunities (delivery time, format, content, depth and duration) for all stakeholders to increase their knowledge of and capacity for wellbeing;
- Be curious, not defensive, about the detractors and naysayers and listen to but don't be completely de-motivated by them; and
- Slow down; if working on wellbeing is making you miserable, you're going too fast.

The last point really does bear repeating. This work is about wellbeing. We are doing it because it matters – and your wellbeing matters too. We will not build whole-school wellbeing more quickly or effectively by whipping ourselves along at a sprint. Notice when the work is feeling onerous. Stop and have a cup of tea. Re-group, remember why you are doing this work, prioritise and start again on something small but useful.

Notes

1 Greenberg, M. T., Domitrovich, C. E., Weissberg, R. P., & Durlak, J. A. (2017). Social and emotional learning as a public health approach to education. *The Future of Children, 27*(1), 13–32.

2 Noble, T., & McGrath, H. (2018). Making it real and making it last! Sustainability of teacher implementation of a whole-school resilience program, Chapter 17. In M. Wosnitza, et al. (Eds.), *Resilience in education.* Springer International Publishing AG. https://doi.org/10.1007/978-3-319-76690-4_17

3 Duckworth, A. L., Peterson, C., Matthews, M. D., & Kelly, D. R. (2007). Grit: Perseverance and passion for long term goals. *Journal of Personality and Social Psychology, 92*(6), 1087–1101.

4 Brunzell, T., Stokes, H., & Waters, L. (2018). Why do you work with struggling students? Teacher perceptions of meaningful work in trauma-impacted classrooms. *Australian Journal of Teacher Education, 43*(2), 116–142. doi:10.14221/ajte.2018v43n2.7

5 Keyes, C. L. M. (2009). Towards a science of mental health. In S. J. Lopez & C. R. Snyder (Eds.), *Oxford handbook of positive psychology* (2nd ed., pp. 89–95). New York: Oxford University Press.

6 Brunzell, T., Stokes, H., & Waters, L. (2016). Trauma-informed positive education: Using positive psychology to strengthen vulnerable students. *Contemporary School Psychology, 20*, 63–83. doi:10.1007/s40688-015-0070-x

Index

Note: Page references in *italics* indicate figures, and those in **bold** indicate tables.

Printed in Australia
AUHW010218260422
362674AU00001B/1

9 780367 236052